LIMITED CHURCH:
UNLIMITED
KINGDOM

Uniting Church and Family
in the Great Commission

BY ROBRIENOW

randall house

114 Bush Rd I Nashville, TN 37217
randallhouse.com

Published by Randall House Publications

114 Bush Road
Nashville, TN 37217

ISBN 978-0-8926-5676-9

Printed in the United States of America

*Dedicated to my mother, Angie,
who taught me to love
and believe the Bible.*

ACKNOWLEDGMENTS

I am so thankful for God's grace and mercy in my life. He has continued to show me His forgiveness and the power of His Word to change my heart. This book comes out of many seasons of repentance.

God has used my wife, Amy, to encourage, motivate, and sharpen me throughout our marriage. Her love for the Lord and for His Word is a continual blessing in my life.

Thanks to Angie and Jack Herklotz, my mother and step-father, who provided many hours of editing, and great encouragement to me. It is a joy to share in this ministry with my family.

I am thankful for the pastors that I have served under during my first twenty years in ministry. God used Bob Johnson, Gary Dausey, and Rob Bugh to help my understanding of God's mission for the local church. Thanks also to the congregation at Gospel Fellowship church for joining me in the journey of church planting.

Thanks also to the great team at Randall House, pastor Michael Johnson, Dave Onufrock, and the many reviewers who blessed me with their encouragement and critique during the writing process.

May the Lord use these words to point every reader to His Word!

TABLE OF CONTENTS

SECTION 5: UNITING CHURCH AND FAMILY IN THE GREAT COMMISSION

INTRODUCTION

T he singular passion of this book is the advance of the Gospel of Jesus Christ to the ends of the earth. Before Jesus ascended to the Father, He gave His followers this mission,

> *"Go therefore and make disciples of all nations, baptizing them in the name of the Father and of the Son and of the Holy Spirit, teaching them to observe all that I have commanded you. And behold, I am with you always, to the end of the age."*—Matthew 28:19–20

Most likely, you are a part of a local church that speaks often of this Great Commission. Your church probably even has a mission statement that draws much of its focus from these words of Jesus.

With mission statement in hand, or at least in the desk drawer, we pack the calendar with innovative programs, stretch the budget, work overtime to recruit volunteers, neglect our families for days or weeks at a time, and then . . .

Can we honestly say that our jam-packed church calendar and our dynamic programs for every demographic group are making radical disciples for Jesus Christ?

When was the last time you looked at your church's results? Are the Christians in your church growing in faith, godliness, and character? Are the Christians in your church deepening in their love for, understanding of, and obedience to the Bible? Are the Christians in your church becoming better equipped and more dedicated to evangelism in their communities?

The reality is many Christian churches today are offering more and more programming, and making fewer and fewer true disciples. Just because the seats are full, doesn't mean disciples are being made.

In the last ten years, a number of research projects have revealed some ugly realities. Many churches are a mile wide and an inch deep. Fewer and fewer believers have a biblical worldview. Perhaps worst of all, we are losing the majority of our own children and grandchildren to the world.

George Barna's research from 2006 indicates that eighty percent of young adults in their twenties are disconnected from church. Three out of four of these young people were connected in church as teenagers but drifted away. Barna surveyed not only church connections for young adults, but also their faith convictions. He set out to discover what percentage of adults in their twenties and thirties expressed a strong commitment to faith in Christ and belief in the Bible. He wanted to determine specifically how many people:

- Have made a personal commitment to Jesus Christ;
- View their commitment to Christ as very important in their lives today;
- Believe when they die they will go to heaven because they have confessed their sins and have accepted Jesus Christ as their savior;
- Believe God wants them to share their faith;
- Believe eternal salvation is possible only through grace, not works;
- Believe Jesus Christ lived a sinless life on earth;
- Assert that the Bible is accurate in all it teaches;
- Describe God as the all-knowing, all-powerful Creator who is actively involved in all things.

Take a moment and reread the list above. Does that list describe you? Barna found these basic benchmarks of biblical Christianity in only 6 percent of young adults in their twenties and thirties.[1]

Researcher Thom Rainer, from Southern Baptist Theological Seminary, affirms this heartbreaking reality. He led a study to determine what percentage of Americans claimed to be Christians based upon having put their faith in Christ. In other words, what percentage of Americans identify themselves as Christians and understand that being a Christian means putting one's faith in Christ alone for salvation? Here's what he found. Among Americans born before 1946, 65 percent identified themselves as Christians and were able to articulate the basics of the gospel. For those born between 1946 and 1964, the number dropped to 35 percent. For those born between 1965 and 1976, it fell to a scant 15 percent. Finally, among Americans born between 1974 and 1994, only 4 percent of the population identified themselves as Christians and had trusted Christ alone for salvation.[2]

Evangelism and discipleship are in dire crisis, and it is a generational crisis.[3] We're losing more of our own children to the world than we are winning adult converts to faith in Christ. As a result, the percentage of Bible-believing Christians in the United States is in steady decline. The United States in fact, is following in the footsteps of Western Europe. The lands that birthed the Reformation are now overwhelmingly secular, with Bible-believing Christians making up just one percent of the population in some countries.[4]

How could this be happening? This is the age of mega-churches, mega-programming, mega-budgets, mega-conferences, and mega-leadership training. We have Christian books, DVDs, and curriculum for every age group on every subject. Our outreach events, service days, retreats, and short-term mission trips are never ending. We are doing more than ever before, but are we making disciples more than ever before?

During my twenty years in full-time ministry, eighteen as a pastor, and two as a missionary, I have lost track of the number of times I have heard words like these from church leaders:

- I feel overwhelmed every day. Why does everyone expect the church staff to do everything around here?
- What can we do to help these people move from just coming to church on Sunday morning to getting involved in the mission of the church?
- I am putting all my time, energy, and resources into our youth ministry. Why are the majority of young people leaving the church and their faith when they go to college?
- I spend all day helping everyone else grow spiritually, but I am losing the hearts of my family. I am loved at church, but I feel like a disappointment at home.
- I tell everyone else how important it is to pray and read the Bible. If they only knew that I rarely take the time to do those things myself.

If we are serious about the Great Commission, if we are serious about making disciples, it is time for our local churches to start doing less. You read correctly. Less!

Don't forget, the singular passion of this book is the advance of the Gospel of Jesus Christ to the ends of the earth. So how can that happen if the local church starts doing less? That is what this book is all about.

Perhaps this analogy will help get us started. You are likely familiar with the concept of "limited government." Christians have traditionally believed that God created the institution of government for a specific, limited number of purposes.

For example, according to Romans 13, God created earthly governments to protect its citizens and bring justice against wrongdoers. God did not create earthly governments to provide everyone with a job. God did not create earthly governments to replace parents. These roles are outside the divine purpose, or proper jurisdiction, of government.

Those who believe in limited government believe that when government exercises limited authority within its proper jurisdiction, the maximum number of people are free, safe, and have the opportunity to prosper. On the other hand, when government seeks to exercise authority, control, and direction outside its God-given jurisdiction and responsibilities, the citizens are increasingly dominated, in danger, and lose the ability to provide for themselves and their families.

A limited government, built on biblical principles, blesses the maximum number of people. An out-of-control government, which does what it wants when it wants, is a curse, and becomes an oppressor.

In the same way, God created the institution of the local church with a specific mission, and gave the local church specific practices to accomplish that mission. When a local church limits itself to its God-given mission, the maximum numbers of people are blessed. On the other hand, an out-of-control church, which does what it wants when it wants, actually hinders the mission and stunts the spiritual growth of the congregation.

What happens when the leaders of a local church chooses to narrow their focus on the specific mission and practices given by God in the Bible? More and more true disciples are made, and the Christians and Christian families within that local church powerfully engage in ministry at home, in their neighborhoods, and to the ends of the earth.

THE PATH AHEAD

We will have to wrestle with many difficult things in the pages ahead. I expect this will be one of those books that ends up with underlines, cross-outs, and many written notes in the margin. There will be five major sections, and the first two are by far the most important and treacherous.

SECTION 1: THE SUFFICIENCY OF SCRIPTURE

The great battle of the 20th century within the church was over the inerrancy of Scripture. Was the Bible true? Could it be trusted? Was it reliable? Within evangelicalism, the Bible was victorious! When I survey attendees at our Visionary Family Conferences, and ask them, "How many of you believe the Bible is true?" almost every hand goes up.

The next battle is upon us, and the war is now waging within the church over the doctrine of the *sufficiency* of Scripture. Sure, the Bible is true, but is it enough? Is the Bible enough for God's people when it comes to the nature and purpose of marriage and parenting? Is the Bible enough for God's people when it comes to the role of the pastor? Is the Bible enough for God's people when it comes to how we ought to do youth ministry, women's ministry, etc?

My writings will begin, proceed, and end with the conviction that God, in the Bible, has told us not only *what* He wants done, but also *how* He wants it done. God has given us both the ends, and the means of ministry . . . His mission and His methods. I am convinced that the doctrine of the sufficiency of Scripture is the lost key we need to accelerate the Great Commission!

SECTION 2: THE LOST DOCTRINE OF JURISDICTION

Building upon the biblical doctrine of sufficiency, we will explore a largely forgotten aspect of Christian theology—the principle of jurisdiction. Put simply, God created different institutions to accomplish different aspects of His will. He created the individual, the family, the church, and government.

Imagine with me that your neighbor is outside and sees your child misbehaving. Would it be OK if he told your child to go into his house and proceeded to discipline your child? Of course, not! Why? It is a violation of biblical jurisdiction. He is usurping your parental authority.

In the same way, if someone steals $100 from you, God would call you to forgive that person and turn the other cheek. However, what would happen if the government operated with the same principles? There would be chaos and injustice. The individual's jurisdiction is to turn the other cheek. It is the government's jurisdiction to prosecute the crime.

Tragically, today's world and today's church have confused, mixed, mingled, and lost the clear purposes and jurisdictions of the local church and the Christian family. As a result, neither our churches nor our homes are advancing the gospel as God intended.

These first two sections will be the most important, foundational, difficult, and controversial portions of this book. Please read them carefully, as what follows will stand or fall on the strength of these foundations.

SECTION 3: GOD'S MISSION FOR THE LOCAL CHURCH

God created the institution of the local church to advance His Gospel and build His kingdom. The church was God's idea, not man's. In the Bible, God details the specific ways He wants His people to worship Him, and the specific things the local church is to do in order to advance the gospel. We cannot claim that the ministries in our church are "biblical" if there is no command or pattern in the Bible for what we are doing.

SECTION 4: GOD'S MISSION FOR THE FAMILY

God created the institution of the family as the foundation for all of human life, in all places, and in all times. He created the family to advance His gospel to the ends of the earth. In His Word, through examples and commands, God calls the Christian family to accomplish specific aspects of His Kingdom mission.

SECTION 5: UNITING CHURCH AND FAMILY IN THE GREAT COMMISSION

God created the institutions of the family and the local church so that the earth might be filled with the worship, Word, glory, and love of God! Both have been given an essential role in advancing the gospel of Jesus Christ. In this final section, we will seek to apply the doctrine of the sufficiency of Scripture to ministry at church and at home.

I have prayed about many things during the preparation of this book. I have prayed that God's words, not mine, would take center stage. I have prayed, according to Psalm 138:2, that the Lord would "exalt above all things, His name and His Word." I continue to pray for myself, and everyone who reads this, that we might be like the Bereans in Acts 17:11 who examined the Scriptures daily to see if the preaching of the Apostles was true. If any of my words are not in line with God's Words, let them quickly fall away and be forgotten.

With God's Love,

Rob Rienow

ENDNOTES

[1]Barna Group, "Most Twentysomethings Put Christianity on the Shelf Following Spiritually Active Teen Years," September 11, 2006, www.barna.org.

[2]Polly House, "Survey Notes Heightened Challenge of Reaching Children for Christ," Baptist Press, October 20, 2000, www.bpnews.net.

[3]Rob Rienow, *When They Turn Away* (Kregel Publications: Grand Rapids, MI, 2010) 17–18.

[4]See Greater Europe Mission, www.gemission.org.

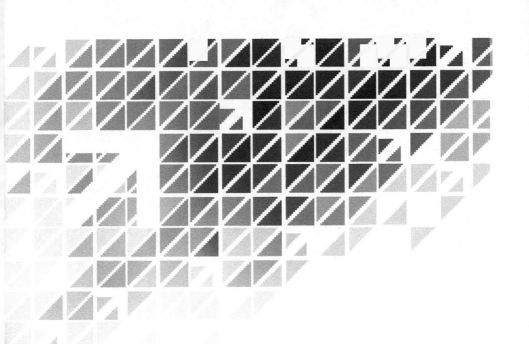

SECTION 1:

THE SUFFICIENCY
OF SCRIPTURE

CHAPTER 1:
THE BATTLE OF THE CENTURY

". . . For you have exalted above all things your name and your word."
—PSALM 138:2b

T he church service finished about fifteen minutes ago. You are talking with a group of Christian friends, when a visitor approaches you and says, "I have some questions. Can you talk to me?"

You and your friends are eager to help. "Sure, what's on your mind?"

"Well, for starters, I have been thinking a lot about Heaven. What will it be like there?"

What would you say? My guess is you would begin to talk about how God will one day create a brand new earth, and that those who have trusted Christ will live together with Him. In Heaven, there will be no more tears, or crying or pain! It will be a perfect place, free from all sin and evil, and it will last forever.

The visitor responds softly, "Heaven sure sounds like a wonderful place. I don't have much hope in this life . . . but I could hope for that. How do you know these things?"

"These aren't my ideas. In the Bible, God has given us the truth about Heaven, Hell, and His plan to save us from our sins. The things I am telling you are written down at the end of the book of Revelation."

Now imagine that one of your friends eagerly chimes into the conversation and said, "You are right, Heaven is going to be wonderful! Just last week, I was watching this amazing show on TV, and a man was being interviewed who actually had gone to Heaven. Then this person was brought back to life. He said after he died, the first thing that happened is he was invited to a banquet table where he had a meal with all of his relatives who had died. After that, he was teleported to the pearly gates where Moses and Noah were standing. They told him he had not been good enough in this life to enter Heaven, so he was being sent back to try to be a better person. It was very inspiring and made me want to be a better person too. He wrote a great book about his experience, you should really check it out."

The conversation has taken a new direction. How are you feeling right now? I hope you are about ready to jump out of your skin and are formulating a plan to interrupt your friend as quickly as possible!

But what's the problem? Why would you be concerned about this shift in the conversation? The answer is obvious. When someone asks us a question such as, "What is Heaven like?" we only need to refer to one book—the Bible.

The Bible is sufficient to answer this question. Only in the Bible do we have God's revealed truth about what Heaven will be like. To bring any other source of knowledge to the conversation is at best dangerous, and at worst heresy.

When it comes to questions such as,

- "Why did Jesus have to die?"
- "How can I be saved?"
- "Why should I be baptized?"
- "Who is the Holy Spirit?"
- "Where is God?"

Most Christians I know would use their Bible, and their Bible alone, to find the answers. They might need to make use of a reference book, but only so they might find the appropriate Scriptures. Christians believe that not only is the Bible true, it is enough. It is sufficient.

But what about these questions:

- "What should be our strategy in youth ministry?"
- "What should we teach this year in women's ministry?"
- "Should we have children in our worship services?"
- "How can we reach more singles?"
- "How can we do a better job caring for the poor?"

For many years in pastoral ministry, I rarely opened my Bible to seek answers to these questions. Think of your own first response to questions like these. If someone asked you, "What should be our strategy in youth ministry?" Would you begin your reply with, "Well, in the Bible, God speaks to this issue and He lays out for us His plan for how children are to be evangelized and discipled. Let me show you . . ."?

Or what about, "How can we reach more singles?" Would your first response be, "That is a great question! God has a lot to say about singleness in the Bible, and in the New Testament we find some very specific things that the early church did to minister to singles. Let me show you . . ."?

This next statement may shock you. In some seminaries today, pastors are not trained to use the Bible for ministry decisions. We are trained to use the Bible for "doctrinal" issues like the ones listed above, but when it comes to daily church decisions pragmatism, innovation, creativity, and human wisdom rule the day.

For the first decade of my pastoral ministry, I sought to get all my "doctrine" from the Bible, while I made ministry decisions myself and with my staff team. The Bible was enough for me when it came to my systematic theology, but not enough when it came to *how* God's institutions of the family and the local church should function.

THE BATTLE IS ON

The church faced a cataclysmic battle in the 20th century. A war was waged over the Bible. Was it true? Could it be trusted? Was it inspired and authoritative? Many churches and denominations were lost, as they abandoned their belief in the Bible as the inspired Word of God.[1]

However, God never abandons His church. In the lives of millions of Christians, thousands of churches, and many denominations, the Holy Spirit defeated the demonic attack of liberalism, and there was a renewed commitment to the authority and truth of the Bible. The so-called Search for the Historical Jesus was demonstrated to be fraught with inconsistencies and poor scholarship.[2] Significant archaeological finds dramatically increased in the 20th century, and to the shock and amazement of the world, continued to support the true history as recorded in the Bible.[3]

My guess is that if you were to ask your congregation, "How many of you believe the Bible is completely true and trustworthy?" almost every hand would go up! Praise God!

I can remember reading both the scholarly and popular writings defending God's Word against any and all comers. In high school, I devoured Josh McDowell's, *Evidence That Demands a Verdict*[4]*, and More Than a Carpenter.*[5] My son is now starting to read them. In college and graduate school, it was a privilege to be able to learn from the more rigorous and technical apologetic resources dealing with hermeneutics and canonical development.[6] You do not need to check your brain at the door to follow Christ and believe the Bible.[7]

At this point, I need to make a dangerous assumption about you. I am going to assume that you are completely convinced the Bible is the inspired, true, authoritative Word of God. Everything that follows in this book is based on that core conviction.

If you are not convinced and convicted about the inspiration and truth of the Bible, you may want to stop reading and look at some of the books I mentioned above. If you don't already believe the Bible is true, the rest of this book will make little sense.

THE BIBLE IS TRUE BUT IS IT ENOUGH?

The church faces a new battle in the 21st century. The battle in many Christian churches today is not "Is the Bible true?" but "Is the Bible enough?" The challenge in the 20th century was over inerrancy, the challenge in the 21st century is over sufficiency.

Do we believe the Bible, or *do we believe the Bible alone?* Do we allow the Bible to shape our thoughts and opinions on every subject? How we answer these questions radically shapes how we live out our faith, and seek to advance the Gospel of our supreme Lord and Savior, Jesus Christ.

In some ways, the issue at the heart of the Protestant Reformation has returned. During the 14th–16th centuries the church powerfully united, and powerfully divided around five "onlys." In Latin, we call them the five "*solas.*"

Only is a powerful word. It is extreme. It picks a fight. It draws a line in the sand.

> During the Reformation, believers in Jesus Christ staked their families, their fortunes, their reputations, and their very lives on five *solas* . . . five onlys. These are words many died for, and many are still[8] dying for.
>
> *Sola Scriptura*—Only Scripture—The Bible and the Bible alone is our authority in all matters of faith and life.[9]
>
> *Sola Gratia*—Only Grace—We don't deserve salvation and forgiveness. We are saved by the unearned loving grace of God.[10]

Sola Fide—Only Faith—We do not earn points with God through doing good things. We cannot earn His favor or salvation by being virtuous. We cannot lose salvation by being extra bad. We are forgiven and made right when we respond to God's grace with repentance and faith.[11]

Solus Christus—Only Christ—God has made one and only one way for sinful men and women to be forgiven and saved, and that is through Jesus' death, resurrection, and glorious ascension.[12]

Soli Deo Gloria—Only for the Glory of God—This is the purpose of life—the purpose of working, eating, marrying, coming to church, planting your garden, reading your Bible, and volunteering—it is all for the glory of God.[13]

It was on these five biblical doctrines that men like John Wycliffe, Jan Hus, William Tyndale, Martin Luther, and John Calvin sought to bring about a re-formation of the church. *Sola Scriptura* served as the foundation for the other four *solas*. What would you use to teach someone the doctrine of grace? How would you seek to persuade someone that Jesus was the Christ, the one and only Son of God? What would you use to explain to someone the nature of God, and what it means to worship Him? You would use the Bible, and the Bible alone, to teach and understand the doctrines of grace, faith, Christ, and worship. The protestant reformation was centered on, grounded in, and built upon the doctrine of the sufficiency of the Bible.

The history of Christianity in general, and the history of each Christian person specifically, is a constant journey of reforming and recalibrating. Satan and the world are constantly seeking to pull the church and individual believers away from the true worship of God. This has been so true in my life. I go through times when I give the enemy a foothold, allow a sin to grow in a dark corner, or I find myself thinking just like the world. God then brings the truth of the Bible to that situation, the Holy Spirit convicts my heart, I repent, confess, and by God's grace get back on track. God continually forms me, and re-forms me into the image of His Son. Most nights during family worship, as my children would tell you, I thank God for His grace, mercy, and patience with me, a sinner.

The same is true in the history of the church. Individual churches and entire denominations at times have fallen into disobedience, false teaching, and heresy.

There are numerous instructions in the New Testament that elders/pastors are to make absolutely sure they guard the doctrine taught in the church. Make sure everything comes from the Bible! Don't have any wiggle room for false teachers who want to bring in legalism, who want to bring in ideas from the godless culture around us, or who want to mix faith in Christ with other world religions.

Tragically, this is exactly what happens in personal lives, in churches, and entire global networks of churches. If you don't pull the weeds, they take over.

The Christian life is one of continually re-forming, always seeking to re-align our churches, our families, and ourselves with the true worship of God, as He has revealed it to us in the pages of Scripture.

BELIEVING THE BIBLE IS TRUE IS NOT ENOUGH

There are many places in God's Word where He teaches us that the Bible is not only true, but sufficient. One of these texts is found in 2 Timothy 3:14–17. Paul writes this to Timothy, who was a young pastor:

"But as for you, continue in what you have learned and have firmly believed, knowing from whom you learned it and how from childhood you have been acquainted with the sacred writings, which are able to make you wise for salvation through faith in Christ Jesus. All Scripture is breathed out by God and profitable for teaching, for reproof, for correction, and for training in righteousness, that the man of God may be complete, equipped for every good work."[14]

Paul's first challenge to Timothy is for him to continue in what he has learned and has firmly believed. The more a believer studies God's book, the more one becomes intellectually convinced of its supernatural origin. Paul reminds Timothy his mother and grandmother first taught him God's Word. I can relate to Timothy in this. My mother became a Christian three months after I was born. My father was a secularist, and I praise God for a mother who filled my heart and mind with prayer and Scripture. As a side note here, parents, it is never too early to be reading the Bible to your children! Timothy's mom and grandma were reading Scripture to him "from infancy." My wife, Amy, has done this with our little ones as well. She puts the baby on a blanket, sets down some toys, and reads the Bible out loud. She calls it the "Bible spa," as the room is filled with the Words of God, and the Holy Spirit is working on a little heart.

God then, through Paul, teaches us truth about His Word.

". . . the sacred writings, which are able to make you wise for salvation through faith in Christ Jesus."—2 Timothy 3:15

The Bible has supernatural power. It is able to make us wise for salvation. The Bible has the ability through the Holy Spirit to bring us to repentance, transform us, change us, and renew our minds. God teaches us this in many places in His Word:

"For the word of God is living and active, sharper than any two-edged sword, piercing to the division of soul and of spirit, of joints and of marrow, and discerning the thoughts and intentions of the heart."— Hebrews 4:12

The Bible is, in a spiritual sense, alive. The words of the Bible[15], because they are God's words, can penetrate the human heart, convict us of sin, and bring us face to face with the truth and love of God.

You have read from Hebrews 11:6 that, "without faith it is impossible to please [God]." But how do we get faith? If we need it to please Him, where does it come from?

"So faith comes from hearing, and hearing through the word of Christ."—Romans 10:17

God's words are powerful. These revealed words, in the hands of the Holy Spirit, are able to bring people to repentance and faith in Jesus! When a sermon is preached, it is not the wise or eloquent words of the preacher that have the power to transform lives, rather it is when he speaks the words God has already given us. As a parent, my words do not have the power to renew the minds of my children, but God's words do!

If you were Satan and the demons, what do you think one of your strategies might be to keep people from faith in Christ, and for those who have faith, to keep them from growing? You would keep them as far away from the Bible as you possibly could. His attack in the church is subtle. Maybe he can get us to read many Christian books, books about the Bible, but spend only a few minutes here and there in the real thing. In fact, the best use of your time right now might be to put this book down, and pick up His book. Most Christians I know, including myself, struggle to spend consistent time reading and studying the Bible. I believe it is because of this constant spiritual attack.

The sufficiency of Scripture was the center of the conflict during the protestant reformation. At that time within the Roman Catholic Church, the Bible was only available in Latin and was administered only through the priests. It was thought and taught that the common people could not possibly be expected to read or understand the Bible on their own. This was not as much an issue of literacy, as it was theology. The Roman Catholic Church[16] at that time taught explicitly that the "Word of God" was not the Bible alone, but rather the "Word of God" was the Bible along with the official interpretation of the church. This doctrine has continued to be taught and is expressed this way in the Catechism of the Catholic Church.[17]

> Both Scripture and Tradition must be accepted and honored with equal sentiments of devotion and reverence. (Catechism Part 1, 82)

> The task of giving an authentic interpretation of the Word of God has been entrusted to the living church alone. (Catechism Part 1, 85)

> The task of interpreting the Word of God authentically has been entrusted solely to the Pope and to the Bishops in communion with him . . . and this interpretation is irrevocably binding for the faith of Christian people. (Catechism Part 1, III, 94, and Part 1, III, 88)

The Roman Catholic Church believed 100% in the inerrancy, infallibility, and authority of the Bible. There was no debate in the church about whether or not the Bible was true, whether or not it was God's Word. The world-changing issue was whether or not the Bible was enough. Was the Bible sufficient?

The reformers were rightly convicted that the church of their day was teaching doctrines not found in Scripture. In addition, they saw the church instructing believers to worship God and practice their faith with means and methods also not found in Scripture.

Martin Luther risked his life for the doctrine of *Sola Scriptura*. He believed that the Bible, and the Bible alone was the Word of God, and that no human being had authority over it, or beside it. Some of his most famous words were uttered on April 16, 1521, at the Diet of Worms when he proclaimed,

> "Unless I am convinced by Scripture and plain reason—I do not accept the authority of popes and councils, for they have contradicted each other—my conscience is captive to the Word of God. I cannot

and I will not recant anything, and to go against conscience is neither right nor safe. God help me. Amen."

When Luther translated the Bible into German and Guttenberg's moveable type enabled the Bible to be mass-produced, spiritual reformation spread like wildfire.

TAKE YOUR STAND

The church today is desperate for leaders who will take this same courageous stand! Not only do we believe the Bible, but we believe the Bible alone for every matter of faith and life. I am convinced we can trace much of the passivity and ineffectiveness in the modern church to our slippage on this vital doctrine.

It is surely a coincidence that the acronym for "Sufficiency of Scripture" is S.O.S., but as we dig deeper into this doctrine and its practical applications in our journey ahead, I hope you will join me in calling out "S.O.S!" to your brothers and sisters in Christ. The urgent call is not "Save Our Ship" but "Save Our Church!" As you will see, this is a battle we cannot afford to lose.

Questions for Reflection and Discussion:

1. Before reading this chapter, what would you have said was the difference between the doctrines of inerrancy and sufficiency?

2. To what degree does your church use the Bible as a sufficient guide for making ministry and programming decisions? How often is the Bible referred to when discussing ministry strategy?

3. What role does the Bible play in your personal life and in your family?

4. In what ways have you experienced spiritual attack aimed at keeping you away from the Bible?

ENDNOTES

[1] John Gresham Machen, *Christianity and Liberalism* (Charleston, SC: Bibliolife, 2009)—originally printed in 1923.

[2] Lee Strobel, *The Case for Christ* (Grand Rapids, MI: Zondervan, 1998).

[3]Alfred Hoerth and John McRay, *Bible Archaeology* (Grand Rapids, MI: Baker Books, 2006).

[4]Revised and Updated Edition—Josh McDowell, *The New Evidence That Demands a Verdict* (Nashville, TN: Thomas Nelson, 1999).

[5]Josh McDowell, *More Than a Carpenter* (Carol Stream, IL: Tyndale House Publishers, 2009).

[6]D. A. Carson and John D. Woodbridge, *Hermeneutics, Authority, and Canon* (Eugene, OR: Wipf and Stock Publishers, 2005).

[7]A great example of this principle can be found in Luke 1:4. Luke tells his readers that the essential purpose for his labors in writing down a careful history of what Jesus did and taught was so that we might have "certainty concerning the things [we] have been taught."

[8]See www.persecution.org.

[9]2 Timothy 3:16–17.

[10]Ephesians 2:1–10.

[11]Ibid.

[12]John 14:6.

[13]1 Corinthians 10:31.

[14]Unless otherwise noted, Scripture references will be taken from the English Standard Version.

[15]I hold to the historical Christian doctrine that the Bible is inerrant and inspired in its original writing. This is not to say translations are of no value, but we should take great care to avoid preaching from translations which do not closely follow the original languages. God inspired the words (plenary inspiration) of the Bible, not just the ideas.

[16]In the early chapters of the book I will briefly summarize key biblical doctrines which stand in contrast to the historic teaching of the Roman Catholic Church. I have many close friends who are devout Catholics and we discuss these issues with respect, frankness, and love. All local churches and denominations are led by fallen and sinful men. No church or denomination is perfect. God only works through imperfect churches, because that is all there is. However, God used the men and the movement of the Reformation to bring millions, and now billions, back to the beliefs and practices of the early church, which are found in the Bible alone.

[17]*Catechism of the Catholic Church* (Mahwah, New Jersey: *Paulist Press*, 1994).

CHAPTER 2:
EVERYTHING IMPORTANT

"Now the serpent was more crafty than any other beast of the field that the LORD God had made. He said to the woman, 'Did God actually say...'"

—GENESIS 3:1a

A few years ago, I had the honor of having lunch with Pastor Don Cole, from Moody Bible Institute. I asked him how he would define the doctrine of the sufficiency of Scripture. I'll never forget his words. "In the Bible, God has given us everything important, about everything important. He has given us everything that matters about everything that matters."

If something is important, God has given us everything we need to know about that issue in the Bible. If it matters, God speaks to it in the Bible, with absolute truth to all people, in all places, and in all times.

I am not saying the Bible is sufficient to learn *everything about everything.* You may need to learn how to do a root canal because you have chosen to be a dentist. You may need to learn how to repair a sink because you have chosen to be a plumber. While God has not given us all truth about all things[1], He has given us everything we *need* to know in order to faithfully serve Him and build His Kingdom.

Let's dig deeper by returning to our text in 2 Timothy 3, a keynote passage on the doctrine of sufficiency.

> *"All Scripture is breathed out by God and profitable for teaching, for reproof, for correction, and for training in righteousness that the man of God may be complete, equipped for every good work."*—2 Timothy 3:16–17

Zero in with me on verse 16. "All Scripture is breathed out by God and profitable for teaching, for reproof, for correction, and for training in righteousness ..."

Look at these four powerful words:
- Teaching—how to think right
- Reproof—how not to think wrong
- Correction—how not to act wrong
- Training in righteousness—how to act right

We could dive into each of these, but don't miss the intentional comprehensiveness. The Word of God speaks to both our thoughts and our actions. In the Bible, God tells us how to think correctly and He confronts wrong thinking. In the Bible, God tells us how to act correctly and He confronts wrong action. Can you see what God is claiming here? He is declaring, in no uncertain terms, that His Word speaks to every important matter of thought and life. All of life falls under one of those two categories.

THE SLIPPERY SLOPE

Consider these four questions. I have asked these same questions to Christian groups many times. I ask people, if their answer to the question is "yes," to raise their hands. Here we go:

Question 1: Do you believe the Bible is God's Word? In the context of a church service, or a Christian conference, almost every hand quickly shoots up.

Question 2: Do you believe the Bible is true in all that it intends to say?[2] Once again, the room is filled with bold hands in the air.

Question 3: Are you willing to submit all your thoughts and opinions on every subject to what it says? Awkward pause. A few hands are held high. About half the hands are partially raised.

Question 4: Are you willing to do what the Bible says, even if you don't want to? After a longer pause, about a quarter of the hands go up.

Do we, as Christians, believe the Bible is God's Word? Absolutely! No question about it. We believe the Bible comes from God. Do we believe it is true? Of course!

Are we willing to submit our thoughts and opinions on every subject to what it says? Whoa! Slow down there. Let's not get carried away.

In regard to the last question, "Are you willing to do what the Bible says, even if you don't want to?"—I am not talking about willful disobedience. There are plenty of times, to my shame, that I know well what God says about something in His Word, but I don't do it God's way, I do it my way. I sin. Maybe you have some experience with this as well. If there is anything "good" about willful disobedience, at least we acknowledge that God's Word is true and that we are choosing to disobey it.

I believe we have an increasing number of Christians today who say, "I know the Bible says to save sex for marriage, but the Bible was written a long time ago and I am not sure those standards apply in today's world." This person has made the decision that the Bible is not a sufficient guide for every matter of faith and practice, and replaced the clear teaching of God's Word with the values of the world. On the surface, this person has rejected God's plan for sex, but at a deeper level, they have rejected the authority of His Word. Today we have a new kind of Christian, a person who says, "I love Jesus! But I don't believe every word of the Bible."

IN THE BEGINNING

Our response to the Word of God has been the central issue from the beginning of history. At the beginning of Genesis 3, God has already made Adam from the dust of the ground, and made Eve from Adam's rib. God's perfection is completely reflected in a perfect world. Then Satan, an angel who had rebelled against God and become a demon, comes to Eve. The first words out of his mouth set the stage for the same spiritual war that rages today.

> *"Now the serpent was more crafty than any other beast of the field that the Lord God had made. He said to the woman, 'Did God actually say, 'You shall not eat from any tree in the garden?'"*—Genesis 3:1

First words are important. They set the stage for what is to come. Satan leads with his primary strategy to lead people into sin, which is to make them doubt the words of God. Did God actually say? This is the first line of almost every demonic temptation. "Don't trust God's Word. God doesn't care about this. God hasn't spoken to this, and if He has, you don't need to listen to what He thinks. What do you think?" The central question facing the church today is whose authority, thoughts, words, and wisdom will we stand on?

How did Satan attack Jesus in the wilderness? He twisted and distorted the written Word that God had spoken through the prophets. How did Jesus defend Himself? He took up the sword of the Spirit, which is the Word of God. He would not allow the devil to twist and misuse even one word of the Bible. Jesus understood this was a battle for truth, who gets to define it, and whether or not he would live by it.

Jesus knew His Bible. Not only was He the divine author, but as a man He carefully studied it. The doctrine of the sufficiency of Scripture from 2 Timothy 3 is repeated through the Old Testament.

> *"And now, O Israel, listen to the statutes and the rules that I am teaching you, and do them, that you may live, and go in and take possession of the land that the Lord, the God of your fathers, is giving you. You shall not add to the word that I command you, nor take away from it, that you may keep the commandments of the Lord your God that I command you."*—Deuteronomy 4:1–2

> *"Everything that I command you, you shall be careful to do. You shall not add to it or take from it."*—Deuteronomy 12:32

> *"Every word of God proves true; he is a shield to those who take refuge in him. Do not add to his words, lest he rebuke you and you be found a liar."*—Proverbs 30:5–6

In these texts, God is proclaiming to us the doctrine of *sufficiency*. Not only is His Word true, it is enough. God gives us a strong warning not to take away from His words. We need all of them! Then on the other side, we have the divine warning not to add to His words. We don't need any more divine revelation than what we have. We must never be so arrogant as to mix our wisdom with God's. His Word is sufficient. He has declared it to be enough.[3]

Jesus Himself taught this doctrine. In the Sermon on the Mount, Jesus was speaking about the Scriptures God had given up to that point in history, the Old Testament.

> *"Do not think that I have come to abolish the Law or the Prophets; I have not come to abolish them but to fulfill them. For truly, I say to you, until heaven and earth pass away, not an iota, not a dot, will pass away from the Law until all is accomplished."*—Matthew 5:17–18

Jesus was preaching *sola Scriptura*! He wanted to make sure His hearers understood that to believe in Him meant believing all the Scriptures, and to believe in all the Scriptures, was to believe in Him.[4] There can be no separating believing in Jesus, and believing every word of His written revelation.

Some in the church today say we should focus our attention on the red letters. In many Bibles, the words of Jesus are written in red. Most of my life, I have used "red letter edition" Bibles. Despite the fact that this is a helpful way for us to find Jesus' teaching in the New Testament, we must remember this was not God's idea. When the Holy Spirit was inspiring John to write his Gospel, He did not say, "OK for this next paragraph, put down that black pen, and pick up the red one."

Jesus' words above stand diametrically opposed to a thought process that puts the red letters above all the others. If we really wanted to be consistent in writing all of Jesus' words in red, we would have to print the whole Bible in red. The Bible is the divine Word of our triune God. He is the Author of every word, and Jesus wanted to make it clear to us that we needed every one—no more, no less.

DEATH IN THE DITCHES

Perhaps you have heard the phrase, "There are two ways we can fall off on this." The doctrine of the sufficiency of Scripture is a narrow path that leads to pleasing God in all things, but there are deep ditches on both sides. These ditches are the detours to sin and death. On one side is the ditch of rebellion, on the other side the ditch of legalism.

I believe the ditch of rebellion is easier to see. Do you remember the warnings from Deuteronomy and from Jesus not to "take away" any words of the Bible? This is a warning against rebellion. God has said do A, but I am going to do B. God has said not to do C, but I am going to do C. We can rebel in both our thoughts and our actions. When we deliberately think or act contrary to God's revealed will in the Bible, that is rebellion. When we disregard any portion of Scripture, we have begun sliding down the steep slopes of rebellion.

One of the most surprising things I have learned as I have explored the doctrine of the sufficiency of Scripture is that there are more warnings in the Bible against adding to what God has said compared to the warnings against taking away. For whatever reason, the ditch of rebellion seemed like the big, scary one, with the sharp rocks and wolves waiting at the bottom. The other side, the ditch of legalism, was bad, sure, but certainly not as bad as rebellion . . . Right? Not according to God.

In the Scriptures we looked at above, we saw the repeated warning from God not to add to the words He has revealed to us in the Bible. This dire warning is repeated in the last chapter of the Bible as well.

> *"I warn everyone who hears the words of the prophecy of this book: if anyone adds to them, God will add to him the plagues described in this book."*—Revelation 22:18

When we take away from God's Word that is rebellion. When we add to God's Word that is legalism. This is going to be a major theme in our journey ahead. I am convinced that many churches today are filled with legalism, and they don't even know it!

Simply defined, legalism is creating human rules for righteous living, which are not in the Bible, and judging yourself and others by those human rules.[5] One of Satan's greatest victories in the modern church is his success in causing us to believe a false definition of legalism. Satan's definition of legalism is, "Taking the Bible seriously on every subject and trying to obey the Bible in every area."

Imagine meeting a Christian who says, "I am trying to obey God's Word in every area of my life. I want to rightly apply every moral principle and command I find to my life at home, my life at church, and my life at work . . . I want the Bible to direct my every thought and every action!"

Many Christians today would say that sounds "legalistic." The reality is there is not a single shred of legalism in the paragraph above. Legalism *is not* seeking to follow the Bible in every area of thought and life. Legalism is adding human rules and regulations on top of the Bible.[6]

The other great "success" Satan has had in this battle is causing the word "legalist" to become one of the worst insults in the Christian church. To be called a "legalist" is to be dismissed, demeaned, and discarded. So look at how crafty the devil is! First, he redefines "legalist" to mean "anyone who takes the Bible seriously," and then he causes the word to become a powerful insult.

Forgive me as I reiterate this point, because we can't move forward without reclaiming this word from the devil's deception. A legalist is not someone who seeks to rightly obey and apply every word of the Bible to his or her life. A legalist is someone who disobeys the Bible by adding to the Bible human rules and regulations for thought, life, and morality, and proceeds to judge themselves and others by these rules. A legalist is not someone who places divine law above all else. A legalist is someone who places human law above all else.[7]

The early church continually had to beat back the subtle deceptions of legalism. A spirit of legalism attacked the church in the area of doctrine, worship practices, church structure, and ministry methodology. When the early church did things *their* way, when they did what was right in their own eyes, churches were filled with conflict and ministry was hindered. However, when they did things God's way, by following the commands and patterns for ministry He had given to them in His Word, that ministry flourished and the Gospel message accelerated.

This was at the heart of Paul's warning to the church at Corinth.

> *"I have applied all these things to myself and Apollos for your benefit, brothers, that you may learn by us not to go beyond what is written, that none of you may be puffed up in favor of one against another. For who sees anything different in you? What do you have that you did not receive? If then you received it, why do you boast as if you did not receive it?"*—1 Corinthians 4:6–7

Paul is pleading with them to give their full and undivided attention to God's revelation[8] as a final and sufficient guide for every area of Christian life, at church, at home, and in the marketplace. When legalism infects a church, the results are predictable. Leaders become prideful and divisions grow. This is the inevitable result when church decisions are made based on human wisdom, human creativity, and human innovation rather than the revealed Word of God.

LEGALISM AND THE REFORMATION

In the previous chapter, we identified the sufficiency of Scripture as the root issue of the Protestant Reformation during the 14th–16th centuries. Which way had the Roman Catholic Church fallen, into the ditch of rebellion or legalism? Had the church taken away from what God had said, or had they added human wisdom and human regulations on top of the Bible? The answer is the latter. The greater issue was that the church was teaching that there were additional requirements, beyond what was written in the Bible, which were needed for salvation and for pleasing God. These new humanistic regulations included attendance at certain masses, repeatedly praying specific prayers, and enduring purgatory. Indulgences could be purchased to shorten the length of your suffering there as well as speed your loved ones on to Heaven. Prayers were to be offered to and for the dead. Mary was elevated to sinless status, and was deserving of worship along with Christ. These things, which are not found anywhere in Scripture, were added by the church to what it meant to live a faithful Christian life.

Because of their love for God's church, men like Luther and Calvin risked their lives to call the church back to *sola Scriptura*. Their intent was not to break away but to reform the church using the Bible alone. The reformation and the reformers were far from perfect. As Francis Schaeffer puts it, "The reformation was no golden age; and our eyes should not turn back to it as if it were to be our perfect model."[9] They had sin in their personal lives just as we do. The churches they eventually established had problems, just like our churches do. Nevertheless, they were striving to return to the practices of the early church, as described by God in the Bible.

If God has given instruction or direction to us in Scripture, church leaders are morally bound to encourage and call the congregation to obedience. If God has not given an instruction to us in Scripture, it is therefore not *necessary* for faithful Christian living. If God has not commanded it, the church must not require it.

THE GUARD RAIL

I am so thankful God has chosen to reveal Himself, His will, and the true history of our world through the written revelation of the Bible. We would literally be lost without it.

How do we stay on the narrow path of following God's will in every sphere of life? How do we maintain sure footing and not fall into the temptation of rebellion on one side, or the temptation of legalism on the other?

God has not sent us out across a tightrope! Yes, the path is narrow, but on both sides of the path is a solid handrail, driven down deep into the rock. What has God given to us that we might not rebel against Him? He has given us His sufficient Word. What has God given us that we might not become legalists and elevate our words above His? He has given us His sufficient Word.

The handrail is the sufficiency of Scripture. Walking the path of the Christian life, without holding on to this railing is the height of foolishness. I have a lot of personal experience with this foolishness, as I will share in the pages ahead, and I don't ever want to go back. The mission God has entrusted to us is too important!

Questions for Discussion:

1. Do you agree we have a new kind of Christian in the world today who says, "I love Jesus, but I don't completely believe the Bible."? Why or why not?

2. In your life, are you more frequently tempted by the sin of rebellion (ignoring what God has said) or legalism (adding your own rules on top of what God has said)?

3. Do you see more rebellion or legalism in your local church? In your family? Why do you think this is?

4. Can you see any invasions of legalism in your church? Are there human programs or practices so "strongly encouraged" that people might feel guilty if they don't do them?

ENDNOTES

[1] Deuteronomy 29:29.

[2] This question is worded in such a way as to adhere to the doctrine of "intentional" inerrancy. Each text of Scripture means what God, through the human author, intended it to mean. For instance, in Psalm 91:4 we read, "He will cover you with his pinions, and under his wings you will find refuge." Based on our study of this passage, do we conclude that it is the intention of the author to declare that God has literal feathers and wings? No, we would make the interpretive choice that God, through the human author, is using a metaphor that describes God's caring protection of His children.

[3] God provided each era of the Church with all the revelation it needed at that time. The Torah was completely sufficient for the Israelites in the wilderness. God then added to His revelation through the prophets, forming the entire Old Testament, which was sufficient for God's people until the time of Christ. With the work of Christ, new Scripture was given, completing the New Testament. What a blessed age we live in to have so many words from God! We can eagerly look forward to the expansion of divine revelation when Christ returns!

[4] As we will discuss later, we must seek to rightly interpret and apply what God has said. For instance, in the Old Testament God commands that animals be sacrificed. We do not "obey" that commandment today because God tells us in the New Testament that the sacrificial system has been superseded by Christ and is no longer necessary.

[5] The term legalism is also sometimes used to refer to the doctrine of "works righteousness" or the belief that we can earn or merit our salvation through good deeds.

[6] There are two fundamental definitions of the word legalism. The first has to do with "works

righteousness" or seeking to merit salvation with our good deeds. The second is the focus of our discussion; the adding of human rules and regulations to the Bible, and judging oneself and others by those additional human rules.

[7]Jesus did not confront the Pharisees for seeking to be obedient to the Bible, but rather for adding human rules and regulations (legalism) on top of what God had said in His Word.

[8]At this point the church in Corinth had the Old Testament, and most likely some of the early writings of the New Testament. Clearly, they had the apostolic instruction from Paul contained in his letter.

[9]Francis Schaeffer, *How Should We Then Live* (Crossway, Wheaton, IL: 1976), 105.

CHAPTER 3:
EVERY GOOD WORK

"Your word is a lamp to my feet, and a light to my path."
—PSALM 119:105

N ow let's take the first of many treacherous steps toward bringing together the sufficiency of Scripture with the mission God has given us to reach the world with the Gospel.

Think about this question for a moment. What is an example of a good work? See if you can quickly come up with five "good works." Consider jotting them down on a piece of paper or in the margin.

Now think about putting those good works into action. How would you (or someone else) go about doing the good works you came up with? How could those things not just be done, but also be done in a way that honors God? Let's return to God's words from 2 Timothy 3.

> *"All Scripture is breathed out by God and profitable for teaching, for reproof, for correction, and for training in righteousness, that the man of God may be complete, equipped for every good work."*—2 Timothy 3:16–17

In verse 16, God uses clear and comprehensive language so we would understand we need all the words of His written revelation, no more, and no less, and that these words speak to every essential sphere of thought and action.

In verse 17, God applies His doctrine of the sufficiency of His Word to our ministry and mission in the world. We are called to advance His Gospel, build His Kingdom, and bring Him glory. We have myriad opportunities every day to do these things in our roles as children, spouses, employees, neighbors, parents, volunteers, and church leaders.

God makes a dramatic claim about the Bible at the end of verse 17. God claims that His written Word is able to make you complete, and to equip you for every good work. Do you want to be a complete parent? God's Word can thoroughly equip you. Do you want to be a complete servant in your church? God's Word can thoroughly equip you.

If something is true, right, noble, pure, lovely, excellent, admirable, or praiseworthy, God says that the Bible will equip us for success. In the Bible, the Lord not only tells us what His will is, but how He wants His will carried out. He gives us His ends, and His means.

The NIV translation emphasizes this point.

> *"All Scripture is God-breathed and is useful for teaching, rebuking, correcting and training in righteousness, so that the servant of God may be thoroughly equipped for every good work."*—2 Timothy 3:16–17 (NIV)

Look back at your list of "good works." Do you believe the Bible can thoroughly equip you for every one of them? This presses us on whether or not we really believe in the doctrine of the sufficiency of Scripture. Is the Bible enough for us when it comes to what it means to be a husband, a mother, a women's ministry leader, or a preacher? Do we believe that in the Bible we have all we need to please God and grow His Kingdom?

THE FOUR LEVELS OF SCRIPTURE

God has given us four levels of truth in His Word. For much of my Christian life, I only saw the first two!

Level 1—God's Truth (Doctrine)

God has given us all the truth we need about who He is, who we are, life, death, Heaven, hell, and salvation. The list of essential truth could go on. I don't need to belabor this point, because you already agree! The Bible is sufficient for all matters of doctrine.

Level 2—God's Will (Righteousness)

Not only has God given us His truth in the Bible, He has given us His will. Every thought and action He requires, and every thought and action He forbids, is given to us in His Word.

Level 3—God's Ways (Methodology)

In the Scriptures, God not only tells us *what* to do, but *how* to do it. As I hope to demonstrate in the pages ahead, the Lord not only gives us His ways, but His means as well.

Level 4—God's Call (Jurisdiction)

Particular aspects of God's will are assigned to specific jurisdictions. God gives particular instructions to pastors, government leaders, children, parents, etc. Therefore, God not only reveals *what* He wants done, *how* it is to be done, but also *who* should do it.

PROPER DEVOTION

Consider the following illustration. Imagine a new believer comes to you seeking spiritual advice. He says, "I know God is a personal God, and He wants me to draw near to Him in worship." Your friend has just demonstrated a correct understand of God's revelation in regards to level one and level two—doctrine and righteousness. "God is a personal God," is a statement of biblical doctrine. "God wants me to draw near to Him in worship," is a true statement that reflects God's righteous will. So far, so good.

Your friend continues, "So in order to draw near to God, I am going to go up to the top of the mountain each morning, scrape myself with sharp rocks and jump in the fire. These are things that help me to worship God and feel close to Him."

How would you counsel your friend? I expect that you would affirm him for his desire to worship God, but would lovingly confront him on his proposed plan for worship. His doctrine was right. His understanding of God's will was correct. But when it came to *how* to do God's will, in this case *how* to worship Him, he departed from Scripture and chose his own path.

If God is a personal God, and wants us to draw near to Him in worship, *how* should we do that? Scripture is sufficient to answer the question of *methodology*. God calls us to pray, meditate on His Word, fast, worship Him with our families, worship Him with our church, etc. The believer is not simply called to believe the truth and seek to do God's will, but to do God's will, God's way.

A tragic shift took place in some parts of 20th century Christianity, and many believers I know, including myself, were taken in by it. This was explained to me in the extraordinary book by Francis Schaeffer, *How Should We Then Live?*[1] If you have not read the book, or watched the DVD series, I encourage you to do so. It is one of the best resources for Christians who want to relate to and minister to our broken world with grace and truth. The book traces the history of religion, philosophy, art, and culture, from the Roman Empire to the present day.

The shift, as Schaeffer explains it, had to do with how Christians during the 20th century changed the way they related to, understood, and applied the Bible. Look at the pictures below. In the center of the Bible, we have "religion." Here we find issues such as the nature of God, the nature of man, original sin, the person and work of Christ, the afterlife, etc. Then on the outer edges, you find "real" stuff like money, work, science, education, and church. It is here where we find the issues, roles, disciplines, and institutions we interact with on a daily basis.

The cataclysmic shift in the 20th century in many of our churches, hearts, and homes was removing the authority and sufficiency of the Bible from the outer circle, and restricting the authority of God's Word only to matters of "religion." So if a group of Christians today are discussing the question, "Who was Jesus?" They will use the Bible and the Bible alone. "How can we be saved?" Let's open the Bible and find out. "What is the role of the Holy Spirit?" God has answered this question for us in many different places in the Bible. When it comes to these "religious" questions, most Christians rely on Scripture, and Scripture alone, in their search for answers. However, the issues we face in daily life are effectively pushed beyond the authority of the Bible. The result of this shift in our culture, churches, and families has been devastating.

THE BIBLE IS SUFFICIENT FOR HISTORY

History is important to God. It has become a bit cliché but is still true: History = His-Story. Therefore, we can have confidence that everything we need to know about the history of the world is in the Bible.[2]

The Bible is not a *comprehensive* book of history. Many real events have taken place that are not recorded in the Old and New Testaments. Nevertheless, God has given us the true historical events, which He wants us to know and understand. He wants us to know about the true history of how our first parents brought sin into the world. He wants us to know the true history of God's judgment against sin through a global flood. He wants us to know the true history of the fragmentation of language at the Tower of Babel. He wants us to know the true history of how He led His people out of Egypt. You get the point. God made the choice that certain events in the history of His universe needed to be revealed and preserved for all people. The Bible is a sufficient guide to human history in that it contains everything God says we need to know in order to know Him, love Him, and follow Him faithfully.

If we want to understand history rightly, we must first understand and believe the God of the Bible is sovereign over all things, and He is working all things together for His glory. We must also understand and believe that the pinnacle of history this side of eternity centers on Christ's death and resurrection from the dead. Apart from these truths, which are revealed to us by God in the Bible, we cannot rightly understand history.

This is the point where Christians start squirming. Perhaps you have been reading up to this point, thinking, "Yeah, yeah, yeah, the Bible is true, the Bible is sufficient." But now we are talking about the Bible as a true and sufficient book for history? Wait a minute! Is the Bible really meant to be used that way? This is the question we must answer.

THE BIBLE IS SUFFICIENT FOR SCIENCE

God created and ordered the physical universe. He gave us rational and inquisitive minds, and He commanded us to take dominion over the earth. He wants us to study it, figure it out, and be a good steward of it. Science was God's idea, and He tells us everything we need to know about it in the Bible.

OK, Rob. Now you have gone off the deep end. First, you tell me that the Bible contains everything we need to know about history. Now you think we should use it as a textbook in science class.

Stay with me! In the chapters ahead, we are going to apply this ministry-transforming, Gospel-accelerating doctrine to family life and church life, and I need to use as many examples as I can to lay a solid foundation.

Just as the Bible is not a comprehensive record of human history, the Bible is not exhaustive on matters of science. You won't find microbiology in the Bible. You won't find details about quantum physics. What you will find is everything God says we *need* to know about the world He created, and everything we need to know about how to study it.

For starters, if you want to explore God's created discipline of science properly, you need to know that He created the world. The universe is not here by chance. Life did not evolve from non-life. There was no accidental "big bang."

If you want to engage in true science, and come to true conclusions, you need to understand that people are not animals, but we are in a separate category of creation. It is true that humans have biological similarities to mammals, but we are not animals. We are special, unique, and set apart. Why can we say such a thing? We can say this because we believe God wrote down the true history of how He created the world.

God also went out of His way to inspire Moses to write down the scientific and historical fact that animals and plants do not change from one kind to another. God tells us, no fewer than five times in the first chapter of Genesis, that His creatures reproduce "according to their kinds."[3] Christianity and Darwinian evolution are totally incompatible with one another.

Again, the Bible only contains a small fraction of all available scientific knowledge. However, God has given us true, authoritative, divinely-revealed facts about His creation. God has given us what we *need* to know about His universe. The question is whether or not we will believe what He has revealed. The temptation of rebellion is calling! Just cut out some of God's words about how He created the world. No problem. It's not a big deal. The temptation to replace God's truth with man's truth is calling! You can believe the Bible and mix in some atheistic Darwinian evolution. No problem.

Look how confused our thinking has become. Atheistic science declares the resurrection to be impossible. Christians completely reject "science" on this point and declare the resurrection a historical fact. Atheistic science declares the virgin birth to be impossible. Again, Christians completely reject "science" and stand firm on the historical reality that the Holy Spirit alone was responsible for the conception of Jesus in Mary's womb. Why are Christians so unbending on these points of history? Because the Bible declares these things to be true! So why is it when atheistic science declares the creation timeline in Genesis to be impossible, do we become confused and weak-kneed about standing with faith and reason upon what God has said?

It is uncomfortable for Christians today to talk like this. We have been brainwashed into thinking the Bible has nothing to do with the outer circle (from the previous diagram). This was not the case for the reformation Christians. In fact, modern science was born and developed out of a biblical and distinctively Christian worldview. Men like Newton believed first and foremost the God of the Bible had created the world, and because this God was a God of order, His creation could be studied. They believed that scientific inquiry would yield results simply because a perfect God had made the world.

Few Christians will say it, but many act and think as if God's Word has nothing to do with real life. Sure, the Bible is a great book for religious stuff, but it can't help us out there in the world in which we live.

At this point, many will disagree with me and say it is not right to use the Bible like this. Did God mean to give us historical facts in the Bible? Did He mean to give us scientific facts in the Bible? Those are the million-dollar questions. You know what I think. What do you think? Where do you stand?

THE BIBLE IS SUFFICIENT FOR THE FAMILY

The family was the first Gospel-advancing, Kingdom-building institution God created. The family is the foundation for all of human life, in all places, and in all times. Every person comes into the world through a father and a mother. It might be a broken family, adopted family, foster family, Christian family, or atheist family, but it is a family never the less.

God has created many roles within the family, and each of these roles is important in the eyes of God. Being a son or daughter is a divine calling, and it is a "good work." Being a sibling is a divine calling, and it is a "good work." God calls many into the role of husband or wife. Ministering to and with one's spouse is a "good work." God has blessed many of us with sons and daughters of our own, and we have therefore become fathers and mothers. Parenting and grand parenting are Great Commission callings, and therefore are "good works" of Christian ministry.

If something is important, as we would all agree family is, then we can be sure God's Word can thoroughly equip us for success and faithfulness.

God gives clear roles and responsibilities to husbands and to wives. He gives a clear mission to parents. He gives clear commands to sons, daughters, and siblings. Is the Bible a comprehensive guide on family life? No. It would be nice if there was a chapter on how best to do laundry and meal preparation for eight people. You may never be on top of the laundry, and the meals may never be gourmet, but your family can still be used by God to make disciples and grow His Kingdom. God has promised us in 2 Timothy 3:17 that His Word will thoroughly equip us for every good work, and this promise applies to the ministry God has called us to within our families.

THE PURPOSE OF FAMILY

Consider this question. What is the purpose of family? Write down your answer in the margin or on a note pad.

I have posed this question to many Christians and church leaders. More often than not, there is an awkward pause following the question as their minds scramble for a spiritual-sounding answer.

Few churches have a theology of family, and as a result, their evangelism and discipleship ministries are largely ineffective. God created two institutions to build His Kingdom and advance His Gospel, the local church and the family. In many communities, the Great Commission is going full-tilt in the church building, and is barely on the radar screen for individuals and families in their neighborhoods.

Trying to reach a community for Christ without embracing God's plan for the local church and the local family to *both* engage in the Great Commission is like pedaling a bike with only one pedal. It is awkward, tiring, and very slow.

In the fourth section of the book, we will carefully walk through the Bible to build a theology of family, and discover God's marvelous plan for the Christian family to advance the Gospel and expand His Kingdom.

REPENTANCE

This part of the discussion is deeply personal for me. For many years, I did not follow the simple instructions God gives to fathers. There are many Scriptures that speak to dads, but perhaps the clearest is Ephesians 6:4.

> *"Fathers, do not provoke your children to anger, but bring them up in the discipline and instruction of the Lord."*

The summer of 2004 was a dark summer. My wife, Amy, and I had been blessed with four children at that time. (We now have six!) I had been serving as a youth minister for over a decade. If you had asked me at that time what my priorities in life were as a Christian man, I would have responded quickly and with conviction, "My first priority in life is my personal relationship with God, followed by my love relationship with my wife. My kids come next, and my fourth priority is my ministry in the church." God, spouse, kids, others.

Not only did I preach about this prioritized Christian life, I lived it. If the phone rang and my boss was on the other line with a crisis, and at the same time the other phone rang and Amy was on the line with a crisis, where would I go? How would I respond? I would go home. In a crisis, I would not put my work ahead of my wife.

Over the course of that summer, the Holy Spirit began to press me with a difficult question. "What are your priorities if there is no crisis?" During a normal week, where did I give the best of my heart, passion, energy, leadership, and vision? When I considered my life in light of that question, I did not like what I saw. I preached the Christian life priorities of God, spouse, kids, and others, but in my everyday life, the order was completely backwards: others, kids, Amy, God. It sounds horrible to say it this way, but my heart was at my job. When I was at work, I was thinking about work. When I was at home, I was thinking about work. This was followed by my relationship with my children. I was not an absent father, physically or emotionally. I tried to spend time with them and connect with them personally. However, I had no plan, whatsoever, to pass my faith on to my children. As a youth pastor, I had tremendous strategic plans to pass my faith on to everyone else's children! But with the immortal souls that God had entrusted to my care . . . I was just showing up. I gave them my spiritual leftovers after I poured myself out at work.

My next priority was my marriage to Amy. After I gave my best at work and gave the leftovers to the kids, Amy got what few scraps were left. This is not to say that I did not try to spend time with her and do what I could to help around the house, but my heart was not with her first and foremost. I was seen as a strong spiritual leader at my church, while I was providing virtually no spiritual encouragement for my wife.

Because my life was upside down and backwards, I was also far from God . . . and I did not even know it. It was a dark summer because I had to admit that the life I thought I was living was a mirage. I was not a man who put my ministry to my wife and children first. God brought me to a place of brokenness and repentance. I confessed and acknowledged the broken state of my life to God and repented to my wife and children. Then God began graciously to rebuild my family on the sufficiency of His Word and His grand purpose for our lives. Now, eight years after the rebuilding began, our family continues to learn, grow, repent, and seek God together.[4]

THE BIBLE IS SUFFICIENT FOR THE LOCAL CHURCH

God created the local church.[5] The local church was not a human invention. The disciples did not sit around after Christ's ascension and brainstorm the local church into existence. God instituted the church, with Christ as its head. The Holy

Spirit inspired the apostles and the writers of the New Testament to build His church on specific structures and practices. Leading and serving our local church is a "good work" and God promises the Bible can thoroughly equip us for success.

God cares deeply about your church. He has created the Church in general and your local church in particular to advance His Gospel to the ends of the earth. Thankfully, He has not asked us to build our church on human wisdom, creativity, and innovation. In the Bible, God has given us everything we need to know about how His church is to function. As we will discover, God has entrusted the institution of the local church with a *limited* set of responsibilities and purposes. The local church is most effective, and brings God the greatest glory, when it fulfills the specific purposes God has given to it in the Bible—no less, and no more.

PASTORAL REPENTANCE

For the first decade of my pastoral life, I had little to no understanding about the sufficiency of Scripture as it related to my leadership in the church. During those years, I was a youth pastor, and one of my favorite principles was, "I have an unchanging message in a constantly changing package." In other words, the message of the Gospel is unchanging, but my ministry methods will be constantly changing to meet the changing needs of youth culture. I was quite proud of how missiological this sounded! I felt I could and should do anything to evangelize and disciple the teens in my community.

But there was a terrible problem with this philosophy. When it comes to ministry in the local church, God is not silent on the method. The Bible doesn't say, "Here is the Gospel, get it to children however you want to." Instead, God's Word is filled with His ends *and* His means. He tells us what He wants *and* how He wants it done.

Remember that God has spoken to us on four levels in the Bible. I only saw the first two levels of "God's truth" and "God's will." I believed and embraced that the Bible taught God's love and heart for children (God's truth). I believed and embraced that in the Bible God expresses His will that children are to be evangelized and discipled (God's will). But, that was as far as I went. I completely missed His methods and His jurisdictions. I embraced God's ends, but not God's means. I did not understand that He had given the local church responsibility and authority to nurture, bless, and equip the Christian family for spiritual success.

In the Bible God not only tells us His heart to reach children for Christ, but He tells us how He wants it done. If you locked yourself in a room with the Bible and you asked the question, "God, how do you want young people to be evangelized and discipled?" what do you think the answer would be? What method has God given us to raise the next generation for the glory of God?

If you used the Bible and the Bible alone, the answer would be overwhelmingly clear. God created parents and grandparents to be the primary spiritual trainers of their children at home. God created parents and grandparents to shepherd and disciple their children. This is the divine strategy for next generation ministry.

Despite the fact God has spoken so clearly about this in the Bible, I created a youth ministry where parents could drop their kids off with me and the other "professionals" so we could teach them the Bible, equip them for ministry, pray with them, and keep them accountable.

In the same way I had to repent of my lack of following the Bible in my life at home, I had to repent in my professional life at church. When it came to ministry decisions, I was doing things my way, in my wisdom, with my innovations, and through my creativity. I had to repent of the fact I was leading an unbiblical ministry. This is not to say everything I was doing was sinful, but when it came to my youth ministry, I was not allowing the Bible to determine my methods.

I believe that ministering to children and youth is a "good work!" Therefore, I believe in the Bible God has given us everything we need to be successful. Not only is the Bible sufficient for youth ministry, but for every "good work of the church." When we believe this—it changes everything.

• Do you believe the Bible is sufficient for women's ministry in your church?

• Do you believe the Bible is sufficient to direct your church in how you care for the poor?

• Do you believe the Bible is all you need to develop a strategy to minister to singles?

• Do you believe the Bible is sufficient to teach us how we are to worship God?

The easy answer is, "yes!" But how often is the Bible open in your ministry planning sessions? Are your leadership decisions based on what you think will work best, what seems most creative, or what God has specifically said in His Word? Do you seek to make every ministry decision in light of the commands and patterns for the New Testament church? God has spoken clearly and directly about every necessary ministry in His church, but are we listening? More importantly, are we seeking to be obedient to what He has said?

RIGHT IN OUR OWN EYES

The book of Judges is one of the saddest books in the Bible. There is a refrain that runs through the chapters, "Everyone did what was right in his own eyes."[6] For many of my years as a pastor, this phrase described how I made ministry decisions. I did what I thought was best. My team and I made decisions about what we thought would be most effective. Pragmatism, not God's Word, far too often was the driving principle.

A few years ago, I spoke at a Christian high school weekend retreat. They asked me to preach on John 15, the passage where Jesus teaches about the vine and the branches. Jesus' primary call to His disciples in that passage is that they "abide in me." Jesus begins to explain what this means in verse 7 when He says, "If you abide in me and my words abide in you . . ." Then in verse 10 He makes it plain, "If you obey my commands, you will abide in my love." We spent the weekend talking about the importance of giving our best to obeying God's Word—the Bible.

At the end of the retreat, we had a question-and-answer session. A young man asked me a great question: "Can you be a Christian and not go to church? I don't like going to church." A group of students around this young man seemed to share his sentiments. I began my answer this way: "I appreciate your honesty, and I can understand your feeling disconnected in your church. I don't want to be offensive, but I do want to answer your question in a straight-forward way. If a person claims to be a follower of Jesus, and is not faithfully involved in the local church, then he or she is a disobedient Christian. I can't comment on anyone's salvation, but in Hebrews 10:25, God says we should 'not give up meeting together, as some are in the habit of doing.'"

The young man responded, "I get that, but we don't like our church. Here's what we want to do. We're going to meet at our friend's house every Friday night, sing some songs, pray, and talk about Jesus. Our youth pastor told us that church was all about encouraging each other spiritually, so that's what we want to do. What do you think about that?"

I replied, "Wow! I love what you're talking about. You're committing to meet every Friday night with your friends to focus on spiritual growth together? That's terrific and I admire that. I do have a couple questions for you. First, will there be preaching of the Bible when you meet?"

"No."

"Will you have baptisms?"

"No."

"Will you have communion?"

"No."

"Will you have multiple, biblically-qualified elders there?"

"No."

"Again, I don't have anything negative to say about your meeting every week like you described. It sounds wonderful. But . . . it's not a church. Church is not man's idea. We didn't think it up. Church is God's idea. He's the one who instituted it, and He is the one who gave us, in the Scriptures, the specific patterns and practices He wants for it."

"Well, Pastor Rob, where does it say in the Bible that you have to have elders?"

At this point, I confess . . . I got lucky. I likely wouldn't have known the answer to that question off the top of my head. But God knew that this question would come my way this weekend, and so a few days earlier I "just happened" to be reading in the book of Titus. So I replied, "In Titus 1:5, Paul instructs the church that the first thing they were to do is appoint elders in every town."

At that moment, the young man responded with a question I'll never forget. He said, "How about another one?" In other words, do you have *another* Bible passage that supports what you're saying? My heart fell inside of me, and I quietly said, "I didn't know I needed more than one."[7]

This was a retreat with students who professed faith in Christ. I realized in that moment this young man and I were not having a disagreement about the nature of church—but rather a disagreement about the nature of the Bible. This young man, like many of his Christian peers, did not view the Bible as a sufficient guide for every matter of faith and life—in this case, the particular nature and function of the church.

He'd asked me a question. I answered his question with a plain Scripture. To my dismay, it wasn't enough to change his mind, nor the minds of many around him. The Bible alone was not enough for him in regards to how the local church should function.

This is one of the great crises facing the church today. We have a generation of young people who, while they may have been taught the doctrine of inerrancy, and would say they believe "the Bible is true," have never been taught the doctrine of sufficiency. In my opinion, this has contributed to many young people abandoning their faith when they become adults.

Now is the time to return to the Bible alone for every matter of faith and practice!

Questions for Discussion:

1. Why do you think there is often tension and conflict when someone brings the Bible into "the outer circle," i.e. into conversations about history, government, marriage, etc.?

2. Can you think of examples in the Bible where God tells us what He wants and how He wants it done?

3. In your experience in the local church, is there a greater emphasis on pragmatism (what will be most effective?) or God's Word (what has God said about this particular ministry in His Word?)?

4. What part of this chapter did you most agree with? What part did you most struggle with?

ENDNOTES

[1]Francis Schaeffer, *How Should We Then Live* (Wheaton, IL: Crossway, 1983).

[2]Our family has developed an iphone/ipad game to teach children the chronology of the Bible and ancient history. You can find the app in the app store under "Bible History Game."

[3]Genesis 1:11, 12, 21, 24, and 25.

[4]Rob Rienow, *Visionary Parenting* (Nashville, TN: Randall House, 2009).

[5]When I speak of "the church" in this book, I am referring specifically to "the local church." There is, of course, the "church universal" which includes all believers on earth at a given period of time, as well as those believers who are already home with the Lord. When I talk about "the mission of the church" and "God's will for His church" I am focusing on God's specific will for His institution of the local church.

[6]Judges 17:6.

[7]Rob Rienow, *When They Turn Away* (Grand Rapids, MI: Kregel, 2010).

CHAPTER 4:
A DANGEROUS DOCTRINE

"So the word of the Lord continued to increase and prevail mightily."
—Acts 19:20

M ake no mistake! The doctrine of the sufficiency of Scripture is a dangerous doctrine. While God's Word will perfectly guide you toward pleasing Him and living out the Great Commission, it will also lead you into great difficulty, challenge . . . even suffering and persecution.

DANGER TO OUR PRIDE

The doctrine of the sufficiency of Scripture requires me to say, "I am not smart enough to know the difference between right and wrong. I am not wise enough to figure out how to please God. My reason is fallen and inadequate. The only chance I have of thinking rightly and understanding truth is through God's revelation to me in His written Word."

If we chose to believe in the truth and sufficiency of the Bible, God will lovingly and ruthlessly deal with the pride in our hearts. This is part of His perfect plan to mold us into the image of His Son.

DANGER TO OUR STANDING IN THE WORLD

Choosing to believe in the truth and sufficiency of the Bible is not the path to popularity. It is quite the opposite.

> *"For the word of the cross is folly to those who are perishing, but to us who are being saved it is the power of God."*—1 Corinthians 1:18

Christianity is built on a pre-modern worldview. Even writing that feels embarrassing. Much has been said about our current age of post-modernism. In a post-modern worldview, the ultimate authority for what is true, right, noble, and good is me, my feelings, and my experience. I am the ultimate arbiter of truth. Therefore, I can have my truth; you can have yours, etc. If it feels good to me, then it is good for me.

You don't have to look far to find Christians decrying the evils of post-modernism and its destructive effects on the souls of this generation. However, some of these critiques seem to imply, "If only we could return to the modern view of the world, which was supportive and compatible with biblical Christianity."

But what is the ultimate authority for what is true, right, noble, and good in the modern worldview? Human reason is the arbiter of truth for the modern mind. If it can be studied, examined, repeated, and made to submit to logic, then we can believe it.

The Christian rejects the worldview of this age (post-modernism) and the worldview of the previous age (modernism). We do not believe our feelings and personal experience determine truth for ourselves or for anyone else. We also don't believe our human reason is the ultimate measure of all things.[1] Instead, we believe our experience, feelings, reason, and logic are all fallen and thus potentially dangerous.

So where does that leave us? As followers of Christ, we embrace a pre-modern path to ultimate truth. My feelings will not lead me to the truth. My experience will not lead me to the truth. My reason will not lead me to the truth. I need supernatural revelation from God. God has graciously revealed His truth, for all people, in all places, and in all times, in the Bible.

God calls His children to stand up and declare, "Our experience is unreliable. Our feelings are unreliable. Our reason is unreliable. We must rely on the Word of God alone." To utter such things is a sure path to ridicule and rejection from the world.

DANGER TO OUR STANDING IN THE CHURCH

Most Christians understand that following Christ means swimming upstream, against the flow of the godless culture around us. The early Christians were encouraged to take joy in their rejection, because it was a validation and confirmation of their obedience to Christ.[2]

While God calls us to take encouragement from persecution, it can be deeply hurtful, especially when we experience rejection and ridicule from members of our own family who are not believers.

It is one thing to experience rejection from the world because of our commitment to the Bible, but as awful as it sounds, we may experience rejection in our churches as well.

How can this be? Our local church is supposed to be a gathering of people who share our faith, beliefs, convictions, and worldview. This was Paul's prayer and encouragement for the church in Rome.

> *"For whatever was written in the former days was written for our instruction, that through endurance and through the encouragement of the Scriptures we might have hope. May the God of endurance and encouragement grant you to live in such harmony with one another, in accord with Christ Jesus, that together you may with one voice glorify the God and Father of our Lord Jesus Christ."*—Romans 15:4–6

How could these believers be unified in spirit and mission? They could be unified because they had the Bible. They had the instruction and encouragement of the Scriptures to ground them in God's truth and direct them to God's will in all things.

It was this same unity that the leaders of the Reformation wanted to see in the churches of their day. Here is how Francis Schaeffer described them:

> The Reformers turned not to man as beginning only from himself, but to the original Christianity of the Bible and the early church. Gradually they came to see that the church founded by Christ had since been marred with distortions. However, in contrast to the Renaissance humanists, they refused to accept the autonomy of human reason, which acts as though the human mind is infinite, with all knowledge within its realm. Rather, they took seriously the Bible's own claim for itself—that it is the only final authority.[3]

POST-MODERNISM IN THE CHURCH

So how is it possible for a Christian to face resistance and even ridicule in his or her own church for holding to the doctrine of the sufficiency of Scripture? The reason is because the humanist philosophies of post-modernism and modernism have subtly and successfully infiltrated many of our churches.

What are the signs of this infiltration? If post-modernist philosophy has crept into a church, there will be increasing elevation of personal experience as the benchmark of spiritual life. It is the Christian version of, "if it feels good, it is good." This manifests itself in many different ways.

Church members begin to measure their walk with God based on how close they feel to Him, rather than on their trust in Christ and obedience to the Bible. People then begin to question the assurance of their salvation because of their on-again off-again *feeling* of closeness to God. When this takes root in a church, there is a constant search and emphasis on creating programs, events, and environments designed to elicit this emotional response. Emotional responses to programs become the benchmark by which ministry is judged.

There is an increasing divide between a person's church life and "real life." I have vivid memories of youth group worship events with the room packed with hundreds of students, hands raised, passionately singing praise to God. Then ten minutes after the event was over, these same students would jump in their cars, spin their tires in the parking lot, and recklessly speed away down the street. Students would later say that the worship event was "awesome" and "I felt so close to God."

To the degree post-modernism infects a church, moral decisions are increasingly made on personal feeling rather than the Bible alone. I have lost track of the number of times I have heard a man or woman tell me they had decided to divorce their spouse. As a pastor, I would share my deep sorrow for their pain, try to understand how they reached that decision, and see if there was a path to reconciliation. In many of these sad conversations, I discovered there was no abandonment, physical abuse, or adultery. So how could this faithful, long-time member of the church be choosing divorce? This is what I heard, time and time again, "Pastor Rob, I have prayed long and hard about this. I know God wants me to be happy. I have felt a sense of release from the Holy Spirit that this is the right thing for me to do. I can't really explain it, other than to say that I know God is OK with this." I don't want in any way to minimize the pain and suffering my friend was going through. My father was divorced four times, and my mother twice. My concern is that replacing Scripture with our feelings is an even greater crisis than the rising divorce rate!

MODERNISM IN THE CHURCH

Just as post-modern philosophy can corrupt a local church, so can the worldview and values of modernism. As noted above, the final arbiter and guide for truth in the modern worldview is human reason. The action principle that emerges from this foundation is pragmatism.

On a personal level, when modernism rules a believer's life a spirit of Pharisaism is usually not far behind. It is possible for a person's head to be filled with knowledge of the Bible, but they do not believe it or act upon it.

> *"Woe to you, scribes and Pharisees, hypocrites! For you are like whitewashed tombs, which outwardly appear beautiful, but within are full of dead people's bones and all uncleanness. So you also outwardly appear righteous to others, but within you are full of hypocrisy and lawlessness."*—Matthew 23:27–28

So a man in the church can ace a "doctrine test," but he is not reading the Bible with his children at home. A teenager has all the answers in her small group Bible study, but she is sexually promiscuous. A woman can explain the four spiritual laws, but she is neglecting her aging parents.

Jesus told a parable of four soils, four different kinds of people responding to the Word of God. What made the good soil good? Why did the good soil produce a crop?

> *"But those that were sown on the good soil are the ones who hear the word and accept it and bear fruit, thirtyfold and sixtyfold and a hundredfold."*—Mark 4:20

According to Jesus, two fundamental things are required for us to bear fruit for Him. First, we must hear the Word. Second, we must accept the Word. Hearing the Bible in church each week and reading it at home during personal devotions and family worship is not enough. We must believe that the words we are hearing and reading are the very words of God, and therefore seek to apply them to every area of our lives.

> *"But be doers of the word, and not hearers only, deceiving yourselves. For if anyone is a hearer of the word and not a doer, he is like a man who looks intently at his natural face in a mirror. For he looks at himself and goes away and at once forgets what he was like. But the one who looks into the perfect law, the law of liberty, and perseveres, being no hearer who forgets but a doer who acts, he will be blessed in his doing."*—James 1:22–25

On a church level, when the spirit of modernism is allowed access, staff meetings are increasingly filled with the question, "What will work best?" The base principles sound like, "We can and should do anything we possibly can to reach people for Christ. We need to be more creative. We need to be more innovative."

Imagine your pastoral team is discussing the previously mentioned question, "What should we do with children in regard to the weekly worship service?" Where would that conversation lead?

With post-modern values many of the comments will begin with, "In my experience," or "When I was growing up," and "For my family we have found . . ." When modernism drives the conversation sentences begin with, "I think it will be most effective if," or "It works better when," and "It makes the most sense to . . ."

My purpose here is not to bash experience or reason. God gives us both, and there is a proper use for them. But if we believe in the truth and sufficiency of the Bible, we do not base our personal, family, or church decisions on our experience or pragmatism. Instead, we diligently search the Bible, to discover what God has already said about the issues at hand.

So the question is on the table, "Do kids belong in church?" God would have the first response begin with, "Let's open our Bibles, and see what God has said about this in His Word."

DOUBLE TROUBLE

For most of us as individual Christians, and in our local churches, we are far more infected by post-modernism and modernism than we realize. We become twisted and governed by a bizarre mix of feelings, personal experience, human wisdom, and pragmatism, rather than the Scriptures.

There is a great risk for a church leader in standing on Scripture alone. It is one thing for the world to call us "Bible-bangers" and an entirely other thing for that accusation to come from our brothers and sisters in Christ.

If you seek to embrace and apply the sufficiency of Scripture in the life of your church, one response you can count on is being called a legalist. But as we explored earlier, this is a warped application of the word. A legalist is someone who does not believe the Bible is sufficient, and so they add additional human rules and regulations for morality and church life on top of what God has said. Legalism is an archenemy of the doctrine of the sufficiency of Scripture! Sadly, this is the word that is often used to dismiss and minimize those who want to try and humbly apply God's revelation to every area of life.

THE PATH AHEAD

We must do three things if we want to have the Word of God be a lamp to our feet and a light to our path.[6]

1. We Commit to Using the Bible Rightly

Seeking to apply the doctrine of the sufficiency of Scripture requires that we do all we can to properly interpret the Bible. This is not a comprehensive book on principles of Bible interpretation, but I hope they come through on every page.

I believe the Bible is its own interpreter. When we find a difficult passage on a particular subject, the first thing to do is to look for other passages on the same subject, which can bring clarity.

In the pages ahead we will tackle a wide variety of Great Commission issues including preaching, being a dad, women's ministry, honoring parents, youth evangelism, and many more. When discussing these issues, we will use primary texts where God speaks directly to the issue at hand.

Great abuse takes place in the church when we use secondary texts, at the expense of primary texts, in determining doctrine and making practical decisions. This kind of misuse of God's Word is rampant.

Here are some examples, which I hope will clarify this point. Let's consider the question, "Is homosexual behavior right or wrong?"[7] Many primary texts in the Bible directly answer this question. One would be:

> *"For this reason God gave them up to dishonorable passions. For their women exchanged natural relations for those that are contrary to nature; and the men likewise gave up natural relations with women and were consumed with passion for one another, men committing shameless acts with men and receiving in themselves the due penalty for their error."*—Romans 1:26–27

However, during the past 20 years in particular, another Scripture has been suggested as a more helpful response to this question:

"There is neither Jew nor Greek, there is neither slave nor free, there is no male and female, for you are all one in Christ Jesus."—Galatians 3:28

This verse has been used to declare that God sanctions and approves of homosexual behavior. This is a gross violation of the primary text/secondary text principle. The many primary texts, the ones that speak directly and clearly to the issue of homosexual behavior, are ignored, while a secondary text, which in this case has nothing to do with sexual behavior at all, is used to validate and support the person's opinion.

- When we are talking about youth ministry, we need to look at the specific Scriptures in which God speaks to the evangelism and discipleship of children and youth.

- When we are discussing the ministry of marriage, we turn to the specific instructions God has given to husbands and wives.

- When we are discussing our worship services, we need to look at the specific Scriptures where God instructs us how He wants us to worship Him.

- When we are wrestling with our strategy for women's ministry, we need to look at the specific Scriptures where God gives us His direction for how women are to minister to one another.

We will explore these issues in the final section of the book.

2. We Commit to Following the Example of the Bereans

In the book of Acts, the Gospel first spread among the Jews. In Acts 17, Paul and Silas travel to the town of Berea. Shortly after they arrived, they went to the synagogue and began to preach from the Old Testament that Jesus was the promised Messiah. How did the Bereans respond?

"Now these Jews were more noble than those in Thessalonica; they received the word with all eagerness, examining the Scriptures daily to see if these things were so. Many of them therefore believed, with not a few Greek women of high standing as well as men."—Acts 17:11–12

Paul was speaking radical words to the Bereans. He was making outrageous claims. How could the Bereans test Paul's words? How could they discern if Paul was speaking from his own human wisdom or speaking the truth of God? Simple, they examined the Scriptures[8] to see if Paul's claims were indeed true. They knew they could completely trust God's written revelation in the Bible. If Paul's words matched up with God's then they would accept Paul's words. If not, they would reject them.

We should follow the example of the Bereans. How can you determine if what your pastor preaches is really true? Simple, examine the Scriptures to see if your pastor's words match up with God's. What measure can you use to judge and evaluate the words I have written in this book? Evaluate them against the Bible, and the Bible alone.

Where will we find wisdom and guidance for the practical decisions that must be made in our homes and churches? Let us stand with the prophet Isaiah and answer, "To the teaching and to the testimony!"[9]

Perhaps you have heard that it is rude to answer a question with a question. But this is exactly what followers of Jesus Christ must do each and every day. When we face difficult questions, we must quickly ask, "What has God said about this in His Word?"

It is possible for two whole-hearted followers of Jesus Christ to seek direction from the Bible and arrive at two different interpretations. God will most certainly straighten out all of my wrong beliefs, interpretations, and doctrines when I enter eternity. While I have deep convictions about what the Bible teaches, I don't claim that my interpretation is inspired. Brothers and sisters in Christ will have honest disagreements about God's intended meaning in particular passages of Scripture. But let these disagreements never arise from a lack of humble and diligent study.

We need to be prepared and accept the reality that one believer may say, "I have become convinced these particular passages of Scripture instruct us to organize the church this way," and another says, "I have become convinced these particular passages of Scripture instruct us to organize the church that way." The beauty here is that both are seeking to humbly and honestly apply God's Word to the situation at hand.

3. We Prepare to Stand Alone

If you choose to follow the path of the sufficiency of Scripture for every matter of faith and practice, it may become a lonely journey. You will be choosing a path that is in radical opposition to the secular culture around you, as well as in opposition to any post-modern or modern philosophies in your church. You will be following the path of the Apostle Paul who said,

> *"For am I now seeking the approval of man, or of God? Or am I trying to please man? If I were still trying to please man, I would not be a servant of Christ."*—Galatians 1:10

Faithfulness is worth it. Obedience is worth it. Doing what God wants, and doing it His way is worth it. God has spoken in His Word to every important matter of faith and life. He has given us in the pages of Scripture everything we need to worship Him, please Him, and fulfill the Great Commission He has entrusted to us.

> If I profess with the loudest voice and clearest exposition every portion of the truth of God except precisely that point which the world and the devil are at that moment attacking, I am not confessing Christ, however boldly I may be professing him. Where the battle rages, there the loyalty of the soldier is proved, and to be steady on all the battlefield besides is mere flight and disgrace if he flinches at that point.[10]—Martin Luther

Questions for Discussion:

1. Which of the "sola" doctrines has God recently used in your life to deal with your pride?

2. Have you ever experienced rejection or ridicule from non-believers because of your belief in the Bible?

3. Have you ever experienced rejection or ridicule from believers because of your belief in the Bible?

4. Do you see any signs of post-modern or modern philosophies infecting your church?

5. What examples have you experienced of Christians misusing the Bible, and as a result, abusing people?

ENDNOTES

[1]Thomas Aquinas (1225–1274) contributed to a tragic shift in the church during the late middle-ages. Aquinas, borrowing heavily from Aristotelian philosophy, redefined the biblical doctrine of original sin by suggesting that mankind fell morally, but not intellectually. He believed human reason had not been damaged by sin. This accelerated the influence of humanism in the church. This increasing humanism in the church was the primary driving force behind the reformers and their quest to see the church return to the doctrine of "Scripture alone." Francis Schaeffer's *How Should We Then Live*, as noted below, provides a solid historical overview for this critical period in world history.

[2]1 Peter 1:6–7, James 1:2–4.

[3]Francis Schaeffer, *How Should We Then Live* (Wheaton, IL: Crossway, 1983), 81.

[4]http://www.childrensministry.com/articles/where-should-children-worship.

[5]Debbie Rowley made reference to Psalm 46:10 and Matthew 21, but neither of these passages are in any way related to the issue of children being a part of the corporate worship service of the church.

[6]Psalm 119:105.

[7]This is not the same question as, "How should Christians respond to friends and family struggling with homosexuality?" but rather a straightforward question regarding the morality of the behavior in the eyes of God.

[8]The Bereans would have only had the Old Testament at this point.

[9]Isaiah 8:20a.

[10]Luther's Works. Weimar Edition. Briefwechsel [Correspondence], vol. 3, p. 8.

SECTION 2:

THE LOST DOCTRINE OF JURISDICTION

"Oh that my ways may be steadfast
in keeping your statutes!
Then I shall not be put to shame,
having my eyes fixed on all your commandments."

—PSALM 119:5–6

T he singular passion of this book is the advance of the Gospel of Jesus Christ to the ends of the earth. We want Jesus to receive all the worship and glory due Him! God has called us to this mission. God clearly communicated His mission in the pages of the Bible, but also He has given us His methods. God has told us what He wants done, and *how* He wants it done. If soldiers want to win a war they must each do what the general says. If each soldier does what he wants, or does what he thinks is best at the time, rather than following orders, the war is lost.

But God gives us even more than what He wants done and how He wants it done. He tells us *whom* He wants to do it. God has established distinct institutions and distinct roles within nations, churches, and families. God has created each of these institutions and roles for His glory and the advancement of His gospel. Sons and daughters are called by God to glorify Him in a special way[1] by honoring their parents.[2] Pastors are called by God to glorify Him in a special way by preaching the Bible in the local church.[3] Governments are called by God to glorify Him in a special way by punishing wrongdoers and thereby protecting the citizenry.[4]

This is the biblical doctrine of jurisdiction, which in my judgment has been largely lost in today's church. We see the Great Commission, and we accept it. Then we carelessly ignore the clear messages God has given us about how the mission is to be carried out and who is responsible for its different facets. If we want to radically commit ourselves to the Great Commission, we must reclaim the biblical doctrine of jurisdiction.

COPS AND ROBBERS

I am sure you have seen an old cops and robbers movie where the bank robbers jump in their getaway car and the police follow on a wild, high-speed chase. The bad guys are heading for the Canadian border! They know if they cross the line before the officers catch them they might be able to escape. Why? Well, at least on the movie screen, the police don't have the jurisdiction to continue their pursuit into the other country. It is beyond their authority to make an arrest in another jurisdiction. The fugitives deserve to be arrested, but the officers have only been given authority to act within certain boundaries.

God has established four foundational realms of authority, areas of jurisdiction, in society. These four jurisdictions[5] are:

- The individual
- The family
- The local church
- The government

These institutions have all been created and instituted by God, for His purposes and for His glory. Adam and Eve did not take a walk one day and come up with the out-of-the-blue idea of marriage. Rather, God created the family, with its specific roles and responsibilities, so that the earth might be filled with people who love Him. In the same way, the local church was not man's idea. God established the church and in the Bible God gave us the church's mission, structure, and practices. God also has given the institution of human government unique authority to carry out His will.

CRIME AND PUNISHMENT

Let's walk through a series of examples to see how the biblical doctrine of jurisdiction is connected to God's will and purposes in the world.

Imagine there is a terrorist attack and one of my relatives is killed. I am furious and want justice to be done, so I go buy a gun, hunt down the perpetrators, and personally deliver the punishment they deserve.

As an individual follower of Christ, have my actions pleased God, or have I sinned? My desire for justice to be served was right, but what I did was wrong. Why? Because in the Bible, God speaks to me, as an individual Christian, in regards to what my responsibility is in responding to such a tragedy.

"But I say to you who hear, Love your enemies, do good to those who hate you, bless those who curse you, pray for those who abuse you."— Luke 6:27–28

What action does God want me to take in response to the terrorists? Most importantly, God wants me to forgive them.[6]

So then, who is responsible to bring them to justice? To which institution has God given the authority to hunt them down and punish them for their crimes? God has granted this authority to the institution of government.

*"Let every person be subject to the governing authorities. For there is no authority except from God, and those that exist have been instituted by God. Therefore whoever resists the authorities resists what God has appointed, and those who resist will incur judgment. For rulers are not a terror to good conduct, but to bad. Would you have no fear of the one who is in authority? Then do what is good, and you will receive his approval, for he is God's servant for your good. But if you do wrong, be afraid, for he does not bear the sword in vain. For he is the servant of God, an avenger who carries out God's wrath on the wrongdoer. Therefore one must be in subjection, not only to avoid God's wrath but also for the sake of conscience."—*Romans 13:1–5

God established the institution of government and provided it with specific jurisdictional authority and responsibilities.[7] The terrorists have killed my relative. I am responsible before God to forgive. The government is responsible before God to bring them to justice. God has declared that it is morally right for human governments to "bear the sword" and "carry out God's wrath on the wrongdoer." God created the government as a primary institution for combating crime and keeping people safe.

God takes jurisdictional violations seriously. When institutions act outside their God-given authority, (1) the crisis will not be solved and (2) the institution that is responsible for responding properly to the crisis will be robbed of motivation, time, and resources, making it more difficult for that institution to respond in the future.

If the lines of jurisdiction are not kept clear, sin is added upon sin, and suffering added upon suffering. If I violate my biblical individual jurisdiction and execute vigilante justice, I have sinned against God, and now the government has two criminals to deal with. Imagine if everyone took the law into their own hands! The government would be overwhelmed by the chaos, and would be robbed of time and resources to go after the "real criminals." If the right thing is done by the wrong jurisdiction, it's wrong!

On the other hand, if the government violates its biblical governmental jurisdiction, and does not pursue the bad guys and bring them to justice, the government has sinned against God, and the terrorists are emboldened to increase their violence.

Our failure to think carefully and biblically about jurisdiction can lead to many bizarre and confusing conversations. I have had Christian friends say to me, "9/11 was a terrible event, but as a Christian nation, should we not respond to violence with peace? Should we not as a nation turn the other cheek? How will responding to violence with violence ever solve anything?"

While I fully share my friend's hatred of suffering and love for peace, this line of reasoning is not biblical because it is mixing jurisdictional responsibilities. To whom is Jesus speaking in Luke 6:29 when he says, "To one who strikes you on the cheek, offer the other also . . ."? Is he speaking to individuals or to governments? Clearly, Jesus is speaking to the moral responsibility of individuals, and God wants this command obeyed. Governments, however, as God has explained in Romans 13 above, must not turn the other cheek. If a government permits violence against its citizens, it is in violation of its God-given responsibilities and jurisdiction.

SUNDAY SCHOOL CHAOS!

Just as the doctrine of the sufficiency of Scripture is dangerous, so is the doctrine of jurisdiction. Examples of jurisdictional violations often make us feel uncomfortable. Here is another situation. During the past few weeks, the Sunday school classes in your church have been out of control. Kids are bouncing off the walls, defying their teachers, and defacing church property. Before your pastor begins his sermon, he addresses this urgent issue with the congregation.

"Some of you may have heard about the issues we are facing in our Sunday school classes. I must tell you the behavior we are seeing is unacceptable and we have developed a new action plan to deal with it. It's really simple. When your kids misbehave in class, we are going to spank 'em! Each classroom will be equipped with a rod and teachers will be trained and prepared to lovingly administer it.

Our plan is to begin this new policy next week, and I welcome any thoughts or suggestions you may have."

How would the congregation react to such an announcement? Lord willing, there would be an overwhelming negative response. "There is no way you are going to spank my kid!" "My kid just spent his last week in Sunday school!"

Why would the congregation be so upset about this? Is it because they do not care about the behavior of children in church? Is it because they do not care about what the teachers are dealing with? Is it because they do not care about the lack of safety in the classroom? No, they care about all these things. Their strong negative reaction would come from a simple conviction, "You don't have the right to spank my child."

That is proper jurisdictional thinking.[8] While the congregation may not use the term, that is what this conversation is about. Why doesn't the church have the right to spank kids when they get out of line? The answer is because, in the Bible, God does not give the local church the jurisdiction and with it the responsibility to discipline children with the rod. Has God given anyone the authority to discipline children with the rod? Yes, He has given that jurisdiction to parents within the institution of the family.[9]

While it makes many uncomfortable, God says that the loving use of the rod is a righteous method of discipleship. However, if a Sunday school teacher uses the rod, it is a violation of the will of God. If a right thing is done by the wrong jurisdiction, it's wrong.

SEXUAL EDUCATION

On May 13, 2007, the Chicago Sun Times ran a story from an Illinois middle school where students, as part of a Health Class, were made to watch the R-rated movie about homosexuality.[10]

Not only is this movie extremely graphic in regards to homosexual behavior, but a major theme of the film is the validation and approval of same-sex relationships. According to some of the students in the class, the context and purpose for which the film was shown was to teach these students to understand and celebrate this alternative lifestyle. The teacher said to the students, "What happens in Ms. Buford's class stays in Ms. Buford's class."

Thankfully, there was outrage from some parents. How dare you show my child this graphic, R-rated, pro-homosexual film in school? As you might imagine, there were many heated conversations between parents, teachers, and school board members in the days following this incident.

On the surface, this appears to be a controversy about sexuality, culture, and what is appropriate material for twelve-year-olds. But those are only symptoms.

The broad issue here is the moral education of children. The public school teacher was attempting to persuade the students toward a particular moral conviction, in this case an immoral conviction.

We would all agree that it is important for young people to learn morality. The question is, to whom has God given the responsibility to accomplish this?

Consider God's four fundamental institutions (jurisdictions): the individual, the family, the church, and the government. Which of these four institutions has God given the jurisdiction and responsibility to teach children right from wrong?

God has given this jurisdictional authority to two institutions, first to the family, and second to the local church.

> "Fathers, do not provoke your children to anger, but bring them up in the discipline and instruction of the Lord."—Ephesians 6:4

> "Hear, O sons, a father's instruction, and be attentive, that you may gain insight, for I give you good precepts; do not forsake my teaching."—Proverbs 4:1–2

Throughout God's Word, we find the call to parents, particularly fathers, to take the lead in impressing the hearts of their children and grandchildren with a love for God.

In addition to the family, the community of faith in the Old Testament and the local church in the New Testament is ordained by God to make disciples of children. The local church is essential, not optional, in God's plan to pass faith to the next generation. Children were included in the corporate worship gatherings of God's people, alongside their parents, so they would be spiritually formed through the worship of God and preaching of the Bible. We have examples in the Scriptures of godly men and women, in addition to parents, providing spiritual encouragement to children.

The responsibility for the moral training of children rests first with the family and secondly with the local church. You will not find anywhere in the Bible where God gives the state the responsibility to provide moral training for children.

So while many of these parents were crying out against the specific content of this movie, the controversy and issues at hand were deeper and far more significant. A massive jurisdictional violation had taken place! The secular government was usurping the divine jurisdiction of the family and the local church.

What happens when institutions act outside their God-given authority? First, the crisis will not be solved. For decades our government schools have sought to teach morality to our children. Are our children becoming more or less moral? Can you think of any successful state-based morality initiatives? Have our government schools solved the drug problem? Bullying? Cheating? Not only is it impossible for the government to teach "character" apart from a Christian worldview, it is jurisdictional violation for a secular government to attempt it at all. I do not dispute that the motives of many public school teachers are noble, and that many of the children in our public schools do not come from healthy families. But the principles of jurisdiction don't change. Good motives + jurisdictional violation = tragic results.

Second, whenever there is a jurisdictional violation, the institution that is responsible for responding properly to the crisis will be robbed of motivation, time, and resources, making it more difficult for that institution to respond in the future.

During my youth ministry years I talked with parents who told me, "I know I should talk with my kids about drug use, but at least they hear about it in school." When the school crossed over into the parental jurisdiction, it reduced the motivation to fulfill their role as parents. They could relax. The professionals would take care of it.

A vicious cycle then begins. The more the government takes responsibility for the moral education of children, the more parents and churches are robbed of time, resources, and motivation to do the job. The more parents and churches abdicate their role, the more the power and influence the government demands.

God has decided to accomplish different aspects of His will through individuals, families, churches, and governments. In our next chapter, we will continue to explore the doctrine of jurisdiction, so that we might become increasingly faithful and effective in making disciples and filling the earth with the worship of God.

Questions for Discussion:

1. What other examples can you think of in which the government over-extends its influence? What is the result of that over extension?

2. Can you think of situations in which a local church inadvertently takes over the responsibilities that God has given to Christian individuals or Christian families?

3. What is your church's method in caring for the poor? Does your church's approach line up with the jurisdictional principles in the Bible?

ENDNOTES

[1] The following are examples of the many ways in which God calls children, pastors, and governments to glorify Him.

[2] Exodus 20:12.

[3] 2 Timothy 4:1–2.

[4] Romans 13:2–4.

[5] Some suggest there are five jurisdictions with the fifth being that of the "employer" or "the work place." While I do not disagree that God speaks to moral and ethical considerations in the workplace, I have chosen to limit the scope of our discussion to the four primary jurisdictions of self, family, church, and government.

[6] Note that this is an entirely different issue than that of the use of violence in self-defense. God has spoken in the Bible that it is a righteous and acceptable thing for His children to use force to protect their families and prevent violence against the innocent. See Exodus 22:2–3, Nehemiah 4:17–18, Luke 11:21, and Luke 22:36.

[7] God's jurisdictional spheres only have the authority which God gives them. For instance, a government does not have the authority to command parents to limit the number of children they have. Such a law is "unlawful" because it violates the higher law of God, and in such situations Christians are obligated to obey God rather than man.

[8] This jurisdictional violation existed in public and private schools for many years.

[9] Proverbs 22:15, 23:13, and 29:15.

[10] http://articles.chicagotribune.com/2007-05-13/news/0705120631_1_substitute-teacher-movie-brokeback-mountain.

CHAPTER 6:
WHEN MORE IS LESS

"The sum of your word is truth, and every one of your righteous rules endures forever."
—Psalm 119:160

J ust as God cares about the choices made by individuals, He cares about the choices made by families, local churches, and governments. Individuals make choices that are either in line with the revealed will of God or against it. The same is true for institutions. Families, churches, and governments make important choices that are righteous or unrighteous.

A WORLD OF SPHERES

The doctrine of jurisdiction has often been referred to "sphere sovereignty."[1] The individual, family, church, and government are distinct spheres of society that God has ordained to accomplish different aspects of His divine will. Sin has infected every aspect of God's creation. Individuals, even those who have been born again, suffer with and struggle against sin and temptation. Because of sin, as Paul says in Romans 3:23, we have all "fallen short" of our created purpose, which is to glorify God in all things.

Our sinfulness infects every sphere of our lives. Families are made up of sinful people, therefore all families sin. Local churches are made up of sinful people, therefore all churches sin. The same is true of human governments. Sinful people necessarily create sinful institutions.

When institutions go against the will of God, the effects of sin can be dramatically compounded. Consider the wicked decisions of a dictator leading to murder of millions of people, or the cult leader who deceives his congregation resulting in mass suicide. When "spheres" sin, the destructive effects of sin are multiplied.

LIMITED AUTHORITY

While a Christian individual is subject to the jurisdictions of family, church, and government, he or she is not commanded to obey and submit to these institutions blindly. For instance, God has placed children under the authority of their parents. However, a parent does not have the jurisdictional authority to tell their child to sin.

> *"Children, obey your parents in the Lord, for this is right."*—Ephesians 6:1

What does "in the Lord" mean? It means that if a parent instructs their child to break into the neighbor's house and steal their TV, that child should disobey. To obey would be to sin against God who stands in authority over all institutions. Parents, church leaders, and government leaders do not have the right to lead people into sin.

You have likely heard the phrase, "Power tends to corrupt. Absolute power corrupts absolutely."[2] History has shown us the constant temptation the larger spheres fall prey to, namely the temptation to usurp the roles and responsibilities of the spheres beneath them.

We probably all know a family that has "over-provided" for one of their children. A thirty-year-old son, who has all the skills and capability of working and providing for himself, is still living at home.[3] The son is working part-time, paying $100 in rent, and excelling at video games and fantasy football. In such a situation, the parents are likely to be loving and well meaning. Is it their intent to hurt their son or stunt his growth as a man? Surely not, but this is the end result of the sphere of family doing too much. It has gone beyond its jurisdiction and damaged the smaller jurisdiction, in this case the individual.

> *"For we hear that some among you walk in idleness, not busy at work, but busybodies. Now such persons we command and encourage in the Lord Jesus Christ to do their work quietly and to earn their own living."*—2 Thessalonians 3:11–12

In a case like this, the son is walking in idleness, and while he could be working, he is not. He is living in disobedience to God who commands him "to do [his] work quietly and earn [his] own living."

The larger[4] the institution the greater temptation it faces to usurp the responsibilities of the jurisdictions beneath it. Whenever this happens, a vicious cycle begins.

LARGER INSTITUTION USURPS RESPONSIBILITY

LESSER INSTITUTION ABDICATES RESPONSIBILITY

In the illustration above, the institution of the family went beyond its proper jurisdiction and over-provided for an adult son who was fully capable of working. Despite the loving intentions of the parents, a cycle of suffering is initiated. The more the parents provide, the more the son is tempted and given freedom to abdicate his personal responsibility to work. The more the parents act, the more the son becomes passive.

There is a second pattern common in jurisdictional sin.

LARGER INSTITUTION ACTS RIGHTEOUSLY

LESSER INSTITUTION UNRIGHTEOUSLY REBELS

Here is a sad situation I encountered many times in pastoral ministry. A woman would come to me for counseling regarding her marriage. Things were difficult at home. Her husband was not attentive, and was not functioning as the loving spiritual leader of their home. He was passive, distant, and uninvolved. The children could sense the tension and lack of love in the relationship. This had been going on for many years. She was "done" and didn't feel she had any more to give. She had made an appointment with an attorney and was preparing to proceed with a divorce. She wanted the church's help and guidance for the difficult months ahead.

It is heartbreaking to hear stories like this, and my hope is that when you encounter people in situations like these your heart is filled with compassion.

After listening and seeking to understand the details of her situation, it became clear she had no biblical grounds for divorce. There was no adultery, abandonment, or pattern of physical abuse. While the pastors were ready to love and support her through this difficult time, and reach out to her husband as well, we could not support her proceeding with a divorce. Church leaders are bound by the Bible, not by our emotions.

In some situations like these, the Holy Spirit does a marvelous work in a person's heart. They are convicted by the plain words of Scripture and repent from the actions they had planned. However, many people, when rightly confronted by their church elders, choose to rebel. They refuse to submit to the proper authority of the church acting rightly within its biblical jurisdiction.

This cycle is repeated millions of times over in homes when parents set appropriate rules for their children, yet children choose to rebel. Governments establish just laws for the safety of all the people, yet some hate those laws, and choose to do what is right in their own eyes.

LIMITED CHURCH?

It feels sacrilegious to use this phrase, "limited church." I don't want anyone or anything to put down, set aside, or to minimize the universal Church or the local church, which God has instituted. However, it is necessary for us to understand God has created the local church with specific roles and purposes for the advance of His Kingdom. Just as the institution of government can overstep its proper jurisdiction, which inevitably leads to increased suffering and chaos, so too the institution of the local church can go beyond what God has called it to do. The intentions are usually good, but when the church oversteps its biblical bounds, the Great Commission is hindered.

The doctrine of jurisdiction and "limited church" was a key component of the Protestant Reformation. A major impetus for men like Hus, Tyndale, Wycliffe, Luther, and Calvin was that the Roman Catholic Church of that day had set itself up as sovereign over every sphere of society. The government was subject to the authority of the church.[5] Even non-believers were considered subject to the authority of the priests and Pope. The Christians of the Reformation confronted the Roman Catholic Church for going beyond their biblical jurisdiction and seeking to exercise control over the state, as well as legalistic control over families and individuals.

Remember the proper definition of legalism. Legalism is adding human rules and regulations to the Bible, and judging others based on these new humanistic rules. Legalism is not taking the Bible seriously on every point. That is Christianity. The more the Roman Catholic Church added new rules and regulations to the Bible (becoming more legalistic) the more authoritarian and unhealthy it became. The church does not have the jurisdiction or the authority to command families and individuals to do things not instructed of them in the Bible.[6]

Consider how Calvin spoke to this issue in his comments regarding the trial of Peter and John before the Sanhedrin:

> But if it happens that [church leaders] abuse their office, the Spirit makes plain there as in a mirror that whatever they order and decree ought to be regarded as void. The authority of pastors in particular has fixed bounds which they are not to overstep. If they venture to do so, we may lawfully refuse to obey them; for to obey them would then be the height of wickedness ... We must obey princes and others who are in authority, but only in so far as they do not deny to God and his rightful authority as the supreme King, Father, and Lord. If such limits are to be observed in civil government, they ought to be of still greater importance in the spiritual government of the church.[7]

Part of being a protestant Christian is holding fast to the belief in a limited local church. Do you want your church leaders leading criminal trials? Do you want your pastors forbidden from marriage? Do you want your congregation instructed to avoid certain foods on certain days? If you would answer "no" to these questions, as the men and women of the reformation did, then you believe the scope and authority of the local church is to be limited. When the church was "more," it was really "less."

As we will explore in the pages ahead, the local church is limited by the instructions given to us in the Bible. When the local church "limits" its focus and activities within its God-given jurisdiction, God blesses the church's ministry, and the Kingdom of God advances for His ever-increasing glory!

Calvin's words are far better than mine in this regard: "Ecclesiastical power, therefore, is not to be mischievously adorned, but it is to be confined within certain limits, so as not to be drawn hither and thither at the caprice of men."[8]

The local church is not our creative playground. It is not our institution to do with what we please. Man is not authorized by God to ignore any of God's instructions for the local church in the Bible, nor is man authorized by God to add our own rules, regulations, or purposes to His church.

Calvin continues, "For this reason it will be of especial benefit to observe how it is described by the prophets and apostles. For if we simply grant to men such power as they are disposed to take, it is plain to all how abrupt is the fall into tyranny, which ought to be far from Christ's church."[9]

RIGHTEOUS REBELLION

There is a third cycle of jurisdictional sin. In this cycle, the larger institution once again usurps responsibility from a lesser institution. In these circumstances, instead of the lesser institution abdicating responsibility, they righteously resist, and do all in their power to obey faithfully what God has called them to do.

It has often been in these cases when God has gained the greatest glory, and His Kingdom taken the most ground. Once again, we need look no further than the period of the reformation when God's people sought to return to *sola Scriptura*.

LARGER INSTITUTION USURPS RESPONSIBILITY

LESSER INSTITUTION RIGHTEOUSLY REBELS

The existence of the United States of America is the result of this jurisdictional cycle. In the late 1500s and early 1600s the church of England was increasingly falling into the same legalistic traps of the Roman Catholic Church. Worship services began to incorporate invented ceremonies, extra-biblical teachings, and books of prayer, which began to rival the place of the Bible itself. Between the years of 1608–1620, a small local church made the brave decision to righteously rebel against this increasingly "unlimited" church.

William Bradford, who ultimately led the "church-plant" from Holland to the New World, described Satan's strategy this way:

> He began to sow errors, heresies, and discord among the clergy themselves, working upon their pride and ambition ... woeful effects followed ... and Satan took advantage of them to foist in a number of vile ceremonies, with many vain canons and decrees, which have been snares to many poor and peaceable souls to this day.[10]

Bradford described Satan's diabolical strategy of persecuting true believers from within the church itself. The three issues at the heart of the matter were (1) the sufficiency of the Bible, (2) the correct worship of God in accordance with the Bible, and (3) the proper jurisdictional lines between the church and the home.

> One party of reformers endeavored to establish the right worship of God and the discipline of Christ in the Church according to the simplicity of the gospel and without the mixture of men's inventions, and to be ruled by the laws of God's word dispensed by such officers as Pastors, Teachers, Elders, etc., according to the Scriptures.[11]

Nevertheless, they bore it all for several years in patience, until by the increase of their troubles they began to see further into things by the light of the word of God. They realized not only that these base ceremonies were unlawful, but also that the tyrannous power of the prelates ought not be submitted to, since it was contrary to the freedom of the gospel and would burden men's consciences and thus profane the worship of God.[12]

This local church first fled to Holland, in hopes they would be free to worship God according to the Bible and that their local church and families could function within God's will. They lived in Holland for almost twelve years, but they decided to "church-plant" in the New World. There were many reasons that led them to this decision. The economy in Holland was terrible, and their older members and children were suffering. Not only were their children suffering physically, but spiritually as well as they began to adopt the rebellious attitude of the culture around them. These parents and grandparents were passionate about doing all in their power to impress the hearts of their children with a love for God and His Word.

Last and not least, they cherished a great hope and inward zeal of laying good foundations, or at least making some way towards it, for the propagation and advance of the gospel of the kingdom of Christ to the remote parts of the world, even though they should be but stepping stones to others in the performance of so great a work.[13]

The rest, as they say, is history. One hundred and fifty-six years after they sailed across the Atlantic on the Mayflower, one of the greatest nations in the history of the world came to be. It all started with the jurisdictional violation of the church, doing more than it was authorized by God to do, and a righteous remnant that refused to bow their knees to man above God.

OVERWHELMED, BURNED-OUT, AND DISCOURAGED

These three words describe many pastors I know. Their days are spent counseling, setting up chairs, answering email, attending strategic planning meetings, preparing to preach, reading about current events and culture, fixing the sound system, visiting the sick, interviewing for a new youth pastor . . . and that is just the list for Monday.

These pastors frequently tell me about how overwhelmed they are, and at the same time how frustrating it is for them that their congregation is not as "engaged in the mission" as they should be. Sure, there are 20% of the people doing 80% of the work. Thank God for those 20%, but what about those other 80%? How can we get them engaged? How can we get them to volunteer more?

What are pastors to do with all these passive people? We need to work harder. We need to lead better. We need to cast more vision. We need to offer more equipping and training. The pastors need to do more.

But what if the passive congregation is not the result of the church leaders not doing enough, but doing too much?

Remember our basic jurisdictional principle? When larger jurisdictions overstep their bounds, lesser jurisdictions suffer a loss of resources, time, and motivation to do what God created them to do. The lesser jurisdictions usually become less effective in their God-given role of advancing the Gospel and building His Kingdom.

Here is the ugly truth. Many Christians in our churches today are passive because they can be. They don't need to engage in the mission, because whether they engage or not, the church leaders will make it happen. I can just show up, sit, and soak, and all these wonderful programs happen anyway! Not only that, I can take pride in being a part of a church that offers such wonderful programs, even though I have no part in making them happen, other than an occasional donation.

The root of the problem is often not that Christians in the church are doing too little, but the leaders in the church are doing too much!

Could it be that our great youth and children's ministries have had the unintended effect of separating parents from their children and decreased the ability of parents to disciple their children at home? It is possible with all our great intentions of "reaching the youth" and "leading kids to Jesus" we have usurped the responsibility of parents to be the primary spiritual trainers of their children in the home? We didn't mean for this to happen, but in many cases we have robbed parents and families of the motivation, time, and resources they needed for their family to function as God intended.

Could it be that our dynamic and "non-threatening" evangelistic events at church have had the unintended consequence of Christian families and Christian individuals not being evangelistic in their own homes and neighborhoods? The evangelistic call to the Christian has changed from "Invite your neighbors into your home. Share your life with them. Pray for God to give you an opportunity to share the Gospel" to "We have an incredible outreach event here at church next month. Pray about who you can invite to church so they can hear the gospel from our special speaker." Is it possible that the more pastors and church leaders focus on running outreach events at church, the less Christians share their faith in their neighborhoods and workplaces?

IT'S NOT JUST PASTORS

Church leaders are not the only ones who are overwhelmed. Remember the 20% of the congregation doing 80% of the work? We usually focus our concern on how to get the 80% motivated and on-board. We need to pay equal attention to the probability that those 20% are just as overwhelmed, burned-out, and discouraged as the pastors are.

These are the ones who "answered the call!" They "stepped-up" to volunteer! They are the ones who are serious about living missional, externally-focused, gospel-driven lives . . . right? Maybe. Volunteering has become the gold standard for "serious" Christians.

But I have lost track of the number of people who have come to me for counseling because they were giving it all at church, volunteering in a wide range of ministries, yet their marriages were crumbling, and their children were walking away from God. All the wonderful programs of the church, and the pressure to be involved in them, can be a factor in robbing people of the time they need for their most important ministry, their ministry to their own family members.

I'll never forget one particular morning of ministry. At 9:00 a.m., I had an appointment with two young men. One was in his late teens, the other in his early twenties. I had known the family for some time, and the young men wanted to meet with me to talk about their struggles in their relationship with their father. To put it bluntly, they were struggling with feelings of hatred for him, and they wanted guidance with how to handle those feelings and develop a better relationship with their dad. It was not an easy meeting, but I admired their willingness to meet with me.

At 10:00 a.m., we had a pastoral leadership meeting. A special guest was invited to join us, the father of the young men I had just met with. He had done a great job volunteering in summer outreach ministry and one of the pastors had invited him in to celebrate his good work. I was the only one in the room with the knowledge of what was going on with his sons. Those two hours, back to back, broke my heart. Here was a group of pastors celebrating his impact in the lives of other children in the community, while his own children were struggling in a broken relationship with him. More had become less. I must commend my friend at this point. When he learned about this series of events, he deepened his commitment to reach out to his sons and restore his relationship with them.

When the leaders in a local church do too much, when the church goes beyond its biblical jurisdiction, the church becomes quickly filled with a mix of passive and exhausted Christian families and Christian individuals. When this cycle takes hold churches suffer, families suffer, individuals suffer, and the Gospel is hindered.

THE PATH AHEAD

"In the next major section, we will turn our attention to the mission of the local church. God created the local church to advance His Kingdom. In the Bible, He gives the local church its mission and specific jurisdictions so that it might bring Him glory!

Questions for Discussion:

1. Can you think of a time when someone wrongly rebelled against the righteous action of a local church?

2. Why do you think so many Christians are passive or "disengaged" in the local church?

3. To what degree do you agree or disagree with the two proposed foundations of "the sufficiency of Scripture" and "jurisdictions"?

4. Are there some areas where you think church leaders should do less, and the congregation should do more?

ENDNOTES

1. David E. Holwerda, ed., *Exploring the Heritage of John Calvin* (Grand Rapids, MI: Baker, 1976).

2. John Acton, *Letter to Bishop Mandell Creighton*, 1887.

3. I am in complete support of parents doing all they can to help their children launch successfully into the adult world. In these economic times, the transition from home to being self-sufficient is increasingly difficult. It is more important than ever for families to develop a multi-generational view of money, provision, and generosity. In this example, I am speaking specifically of a situation in which a young adult is not doing all in their power to pursue employment and establish their own family.

4. "Lesser institution" refers to size rather than importance.

5. This is not to say that human governments should not act "Christianly." God would have His people, who love Him and love His Word, lead their governments according to the biblical principles for nations and laws. God desires earthly government to be led by Christians acting Christianly. The point here is that the Bible does not support the notion of a New Testament elder having jurisdictional authority over a civic magistrate. This reformation theology is well expressed in the Belgic Confession (Acts of Synod (CRC), 1910, 104–105), "This phrase concerning the office of civil government in relationship to the church arises out of the idea of a state-church, implemented first by Constantine and later in many Protestant countries. History argues, however, not in favor of the principle of state domination over the church, but rather for a certain separation of church and state. [A state-church] is also in conflict with the New Testament . . . to grant to the state the right to reform the church according to its will and to deny the church the right to take its stand as an independent sphere alongside the state. The New Testament does not place the Christian church under the authority of civil magistrates to be controlled and extended by the power of the state, but places it solely under the Lord and King as an independent sphere alongside of and wholly free from the state, to be ruled and built up only by its own spiritual powers. Therefore, nearly all Reformed churches have already rejected the idea of a state-church as contrary to the New Testament and have come to defend the autonomy of the churches and personal freedom of conscience in the service of God. [We do not support] the office of civil government to entail the exercise of governmental power in the sphere of religion by introducing a state-church and maintaining and promoting it as the only true church, nor [should the government] resist, eradicate, or destroy by the power of the sword all other churches as false religions. Rather we firmly believe that within its own worldly sphere civil government has a divine calling to fulfill with respect to both the first and second tables of the divine law. We hold moreover that both state and church mutually, as institutions of God and Christ, have received rights and duties from above and are thus bound to fulfill a very holy calling in relationship to each other through the Holy Spirit who proceeds from the Father and the Son."

6. Committed Christians may disagree regarding the Bible's instructions. One church may instruct memembers not to drink any alcohol, based upon their interpretation of the principles of Scripture, while another church may only forbid drunkenness. In this case, these two

churches share a common commitment to the authority of the Bible, but share a genuine difference regarding its interpretation.

[7]John Calvin, Commentary on Acts 4:13–24.

[8]John Calvin, Institutes, IV, viii, 1. As translated at http://www.ccel.org/ccel/calvin/institutes.vi.ix.html.

[9]Ibid.

[10]William Bradford, *Of Plymouth Plantation* (San Antonio, TX: Vision Forum, 1999), 2.

[11]Ibid, 3–4.

[12]Ibid, 7.

[13]Ibid, 21.

SECTION 3:

GOD'S MISSION FOR THE LOCAL CHURCH

CHAPTER 7:
THE WORSHIP OF GOD

"So then, brothers, stand firm and hold to the traditions that you were taught by us, either by our spoken word or by our letter."

—2 Thessalonians 2:15

T he passion of this book is the advance of the Gospel of Jesus Christ to the ends of the earth! In the first two sections, we examined the doctrines of the sufficiency of Scripture and jurisdiction.

Here in the third section, we turn our attention to the local church. God established this institution after Christ ascended to Heaven to take His place at the right hand of the Father. When we speak of the church it is important to distinguish between "big C" Church and "little c" church. The "big C" Church is the body of all true believers, from all Christian denominations, in the world. One can also use this term to refer to a group of believers in a particular area, i.e. "the Church in Europe," "the Church in Tokyo," or "the Church in America." However, "little c" church refers to a specific local congregation. First Christian Church of Smithville is a "little c" church. It is a unique, specific, local body, with particular spiritual responsibilities and authority regarding its members.

The focus of this section, and the hope of this book, is to encourage local church leaders to re-examine their ministry in light of the pattern and commands for the local church given in the New Testament.

Like the family, the local church is a temporary institution. The local church of which you are a part will not exist in Heaven. There will be no "First Christian Church of Smithville" in eternity. God ordained the establishment of temporary local churches to build His everlasting Church.

The local church was God's idea. The local church is His, and He alone determines its purposes and the rules by which it is to be governed.

THE BIBLE ALONE

But, do we really believe the Bible is an all-sufficient guide for what the local church should do and how it should be governed? For the first decade of my pastoral ministry, I did not think in these terms. Because I didn't understand the doctrine of sufficiency, I led my church ministries with a bizarre mix of loose biblical principles and human innovation.

One of the exciting movements of the Holy Spirit in the 21st century is the increased passion and focus on returning to the model of the early church. Wonderful conversations are taking place about our need to recover and reclaim the authentic, Gospel-driven lives of the early Christians.

What would our local churches look like if we used the Bible, and the Bible alone, to determine what we do? What if God's commands and the revealed practices of the local church in the New Testament were our *only* guide for our church programming? What if we *limited* ourselves to only doing what God has told us to do, and sought to do it according to His revealed methods?

The final section of the book is dedicated to addressing these questions. I have not attempted to speak to all the important issues facing the church today. These chapters are not comprehensive studies of *all* God has said in the Bible about how His local church is to function. Many of these issues have been debated for centuries, and I don't have a corner on the truth. But God does! The Bible does!

My prayer is that I would present myself to God as one approved, a worker who has no need to be ashamed, rightly handling the word of truth (2 Timothy 2:15). Perhaps you will disagree about my interpretation of particular Scriptures. I expect it, welcome it, and would love to learn from you. When Christians debate and disagree, the basis of argument should be simple. One person should say, "Based on these texts, I believe God's Word calls us to do this, and to do it this way." The other person is then free to respond, "I disagree, I believe God instructs us through those texts to do that, and to do it that way." In a conversation like this, both parties are seeking to follow the Bible and the Bible alone.[1] But, when it comes to church decisions, do we turn to the Bible alone? Is the Bible open during our church leadership meetings? Are we continually turning to God's Word for direction about what we are to do, not to do, and how we are to do it?

The local church is of the utmost importance to God. He did not leave it to be governed by human creativity. He did not leave its tasks to be determined by human reason and experience. The work of the local church is a *good work* and God has given us the Bible to thoroughly equip us for success.

THE MISSION OF THE LOCAL CHURCH

What is the local church called by God to do in order to fulfill its role in building the Church? There are many ways to organize the particular tasks God has given to the local church. I have chosen to use these four categories:

- Worship God

- Preach the Bible

- Care for believers

- Equip believers for works of ministry

In the pages ahead, we will examine the Scriptures to see what God has said about each of these responsibilities. In the final section of the book, we will seek to apply the sufficiency of Scripture to the vital issues of church leadership, evangelism, youth ministry, men's ministry, caring for the poor, and much more.

WORSHIPING GOD—HIS WAY

The centerpiece of God's local church is the gathering together for corporate worship. It is a gathering of the entire faith community for the worship of God under the authority of His Word. God calls all believers to faithfully participate in the corporate worship service of their local church.[2] All other functions of the local church flow through and from the weekly worship gathering.

But, when we gather for church what should we do? How should we spend that time? To answer these questions we must turn to Scripture.

You are likely familiar with the 20th century martyr and missionary Jim Elliot. His passion for the Gospel led him and his friends to Ecuador where they were killed in the jungle by the Auca Indians. Jim's passion was not only to see the Aucas converted and saved, but he wanted God to be worshiped *properly* in that corner of the world. He wanted whole households of Aucas to come to Christ and then to establish local churches which would function according to the Bible and the Bible alone. Consider these words from Elliot's journal:

> The pivot point hangs on whether or not God has revealed a universal pattern for the church in the New Testament. If He has not, then anything will do so long as it works. But I am convinced that nothing so dear to the heart of Christ as His Bride should be left without explicit instructions as to her corporate conduct. I am further convinced that the 20th century has in no way simulated this pattern in its method of 'churching' a community, so that almost nothing is really 'working' to the glory and pleasure of God. Further, it matters not at all to me what men have done with the church over there or in America, it is incumbent upon me, if God has a pattern for the church, to find and establish that pattern, at all costs.[3]

Was Jim Elliot right or wrong? Has God revealed a universal pattern for the church in the New Testament? Has God left His Bride without explicit instructions as to her corporate conduct? I am convinced God does have a pattern for His church, and it is incumbent upon us, to find and establish that pattern at *all costs*.

Jim Elliot echoed the convictions of the Christian Pilgrims three centuries earlier. We praise the Pilgrims for their bravery and dedication to God. They loved the Lord, their children, and the Great Commission so much they were willing to risk their lives to move to the other side of the world. For many years, this was about all I could tell you about the Pilgrims and why they came to America. I didn't understand that the driving force behind these amazing acts of Christian courage was the conviction God wanted to be worshiped in a *particular* way.

The truth is the Pilgrims were free to worship God in England. They were free to worship God in Holland. Churches were open and ready to receive them. So what was the problem? They believed the Bible was a sufficient guide for the worship of God and how the local church should function. So, they were *free* to worship God according to the traditions of men, but not according to the pattern in the Word of God. Their love for God, His Word, and His local church compelled them to cross the ocean; and in the words of Jim Elliot, "establish that pattern at all costs."

GOD REGULATES HIS WORSHIP IN THE OLD TESTAMENT

While the focus of our discussion here is the proper worship of God in the New Testament local church, it is important to establish the theological foundation in the Old Testament. He created us to worship Him.[4] From the beginning, God has taken His worship seriously. As God, He determines what is acceptable worship and what is not.

The first recorded sin takes place in the context of the marriage relationship. The second takes place in the context of the sibling relationship and the correct worship of God.

> *"In the course of time Cain brought to the* Lord *an offering of the fruit of the ground, and Abel also brought of the firstborn of his flock and of their fat portions. And the* Lord *had regard for Abel and his offering, but for Cain and his offering he had no regard. So Cain was very angry, and his face fell. The* Lord *said to Cain, 'Why are you angry, and why has your face fallen? If you do well, will you not be accepted? And if you do not do well, sin is crouching at the door. Its desire is for you, but you must rule over it.'"*—Genesis 4:3–7

What was God's message to Cain? You did not worship me *properly.* The *manner* in which you sought to show me your devotion was unacceptable. Now, try again and if you worship me properly, I will accept it. God tells us in Hebrews 12 that unlike his brother Abel, Cain did not making his offering with *faith.* In 1 John 3:12 God says Cain's incorrect worship was *evil.* God takes His worship seriously.

"BORING STUFF"

Have you ever tried to read through the Old Testament? I know this is a wrong way of thinking, but some sections are more engaging than others. Genealogies, lists of tribes, and chronologies seem to pale in comparison to the events, dramas, and battles. Consider Exodus 25–40. Sixteen long chapters. With the exception of the golden calf in chapter 32 and the covenant renewal in chapter 34, these sixteen chapters are entirely focused on God's instructions for worship. The tabernacle was to be built with exact dimensions and specific materials. Worship services were to be conducted at specific times and performed in particular ways.

From Deuteronomy 12–26, fifteen straight chapters, God once again gives the people of Israel detailed commands related to *how* they were to worship Him.

Many of these specific Old Testament worship commands, particularly those related to the sacrificial system, have been fulfilled in Christ. Christians are no longer commanded to sacrifice animals. To do so would be to disregard the finished work of Christ on the cross! But, notice how much care, attention, and specific instruction God gives us in regards to *how* He wants to be worshiped! God's glory, and therefore the manner of how we worship Him, has always been His highest priority.[5]

UNAUTHORIZED FIRE

In Leviticus 8, God tells us of the ordination of Aaron and his sons to serve as priests for Israel. God gave specific instructions for their preparation, and those instructions were followed. In Leviticus 9, Aaron and his sons follow God's specific instructions as they worshiped the Lord through sacrifice. This was a special time of joy and worship for the Israelites. However, things quickly change in the next chapter:

> "Now Nadab and Abihu, the sons of Aaron, each took his censer and put fire in it and laid incense on it and offered unauthorized fire before the LORD, which he had not commanded them. And fire came out from before the LORD and consumed them, and they died before the LORD. Then Moses said to Aaron, "This is what the LORD has said: 'Among those who are near me I will be sanctified, and before all the people I will be glorified.'" And Aaron held his peace."—Leviticus 10:1-3

Nadab and Abihu had just been consecrated as priests of the Lord! This was their first act of leading the people of Israel in corporate worship and before the service ended, they were dead. Why? Did they disobey a command of God? The text is specific about this. It says they "offered unauthorized fire before the LORD, which he had not commanded them."

While we don't know exactly what they did, we do know God had not told them to do it. They went beyond what God told them to do. They were not killed for disobeying something God told them to do regarding His worship. They were killed for doing something *beyond* what God told them to do regarding His worship. Their motives may have been good. Their enthusiasm for worship may have been correct. But, they added to God's words regarding His worship, and they paid the ultimate price.

REVIVAL

One of the great revivals in the Old Testament took place when the servants of King Josiah found the lost Book of the Law (The portions of the Bible that had been given up to that point in history). It is presumed Josiah's wicked grandfather Manasseh had hidden the Word of God so it might be as far away from him and the people as possible.[6]

> "When the king [Josiah] heard the words of the Book of the Law, he tore his clothes. And the king commanded Hilkiah the priest, and Ahikam the son of Shaphan, and Achbor the son of Micaiah, and Shaphan the secretary, and Asaiah the king's servant, saying, 'Go, inquire of the LORD for me, and for the people, and for all Judah, concerning the words of this book that has been found. For great is the wrath of the LORD that is kindled against us, because our fathers have not obeyed the words of this book, to do according to all that is written concerning us.'"—2 Kings 22:11–13

Josiah knew God expected His people "to do according to all that is written." Josiah committed himself to this task. First, he read all of God's words to all the men, women, boys, and girls of Jerusalem (2 Kings 23:2). Then he systematically went through the entire land of Israel, tearing down the high places and removing any method of worship not commanded in the Book (2 Kings 23:4–20). The priests who had worshiped using methods contrary to the Book were executed (2 Kings 23:20). Josiah then called all the people to worship God correctly.

> "And the king commanded all the people, "Keep the Passover to the LORD your God, as it is written in this Book of the Covenant." For no such Passover had been kept since the days of the judges who judged Israel, or during all the days of the kings of Israel or of the kings of Judah. But in the eighteenth year of King Josiah this Passover was kept to the LORD in Jerusalem."—2 Kings 23:21–22

When I first read this, I didn't believe it. The year is approximately 620 B.C. The period of the Judges was 1350–1100 B.C. The people of Israel had not worshiped God through the Passover celebration for over 500 years! God had *commanded* the people of Israel to worship Him through this particular celebration.[7]

Because Josiah made the *proper* worship of God his top priority, God says that he stands apart from all kings before him and all kings after him.

> "Moreover, Josiah put away the mediums and the necromancers and the household gods and the idols and all the abominations that were seen in the land of Judah and in Jerusalem, that he might establish the words of the law that were written in the book *that Hilkiah the priest found in the house of the LORD. Before him there was no king like him, who turned to the LORD with all his heart and with all his soul and with all his might,* according to all the Law of Moses, *nor did any like him arise after him.*"[8]—2 Kings 23:24–25

God takes His worship seriously.[9] He tells us in the pages of Scripture the manner and methods we are to use to worship Him rightly.

GOD REGULATES HIS WORSHIP IN THE NEW TESTAMENT

In John 4, Jesus has an amazing conversation with a Samaritan woman. The last portion of their conversation focused on the proper worship of God.

> "The woman said to him, "Sir, I perceive that you are a prophet. Our fathers worshiped on this mountain, but you say that in Jerusalem is the place where people ought to worship." Jesus said to her, "Woman, believe me, the hour is coming when neither on this mountain nor in Jerusalem will you worship the Father. You worship what you do not know; we worship what we know, for salvation is from the Jews. But the hour is coming, and is now here, when the true worshipers will worship the Father in spirit and truth, for the Father is seeking such people to worship him. God is spirit, and those who worship him must worship in spirit and truth."—John 4:19–24

Here, Jesus affirms the words He had spoken throughout the Old Testament.[10] God sets the terms for His worship. He doesn't just say, "Worship me!" He says, "Worship me like this!" First, Jesus says God requires His people worship Him *in spirit*. This is directly connected with the next sentence, *God is spirit.* Jesus' words echo the second commandment from Exodus 20.

"You shall not make for yourself a carved image, or any likeness of anything that is in heaven above, or that is in the earth beneath, or that is in the water under the earth."—Exodus 20:4

The first commandment speaks to the *object* of our worship (God alone). The second commandment speaks to the *method* of our worship. Because God is spirit, He forbids the creation of any physical thing that represents Him. We are forbidden to worship any created thing or to represent God, His Son, or His Spirit with any physical, human creation.[11]

While we make use of the bodies God has given us in worshiping Him (singing, raising hands, etc.), true worship comes out of our spirits for the purpose of praising God who is spirit.

Second, Jesus says God requires His people worship Him *in truth.* True worship cannot be separated from the *truth* about God. Where is such truth found? In the Bible alone.

"And take not the word of truth utterly out of my mouth, for my hope is in your rules."—Psalm 119:43

"The sum of your word is truth, and every one of your righteous rules endures forever."—Psalm 119:160

Later in the book of John, Jesus affirms the synonymous relationship between *truth* and the *Word of God.* Praying for His disciples, Jesus said:

"Sanctify them in the truth; your word is truth."—John 17:17

Jesus' teaching on worship here in John 4 focuses on *methodology.* Jesus is affirming the rest of His words in the Bible that God not only desires to be worshiped, but desires to be worshiped in particular ways and with particular practices.

In some of the conversations I have had with friends about this issue, I sometimes hear the response, "This sounds so legalistic." We need to remember the proper definition of legalism in this context.[12] Legalism is *adding human rules, traditions, and regulations* to the Word of God and judging ourselves and others based on those human rules. Legalism is *not* seeking to rightly obey all the words of Scripture. A central message of this book is a call to wage war *against* legalism in your local church! When it comes to the worship of God, let us do only what God has said; no more, and no less.

WORSHIP IN THE LOCAL CHURCH

The early Christians sought to worship God in spirit and in truth. Through the revelation of the New Testament, God tells us what His people are to do when they gather together for corporate worship.[13] This is not to say the early Christians did not struggle with the ancient sin of doing things their own way. Paul confronts the church in Thessalonica with these words:

> *"So then, brothers, stand firm and hold to the traditions that you were taught by us, either by our spoken word or by our letter."*—2 Thessalonians 2:15

He challenges the Corinthian church with the same message:

> *"I have applied all these things to myself and Apollos for your benefit, brothers, that you may learn by us not to go beyond what is written, that none of you may be puffed up in favor of one against another."*—1 Corinthians 4:6

ELEMENTS OF CORPORATE WORSHIP

The heart of the mission and purpose of the local church is the gathering together of believers to worship God in spirit and in truth. Every Lord's Day, the entire church family—every man, every woman, every boy, and every girl—is called together by God to worship Him in the splendor of His holiness and under the authority and power of His Word. We should have a hard time going to sleep the night before church in anticipation of what awaits us!

When we gather for the corporate worship service, what should we do?[14] What could we possibly do that God would enjoy and receive as worship and praise? There is a great pressure in some churches today to plan worship services so the congregation can "feel close" to God or to "experience" His presence. Again, consider the words of missionary martyr Jim Elliot, responding to this exact issue:

> What in all eternity has [your feelings in worship] got to do with it? Have personal likes and dislikes any right to dictate method in the holy church of God? It is this attitude that has brought hopeless confusion into our present order . . "Let God be true and every man a liar!" . . . Is this His way? Then let my personal likes be filed in the waste-can. Let me follow by afforded grace. It is neither [your] job

or mine to commend or condemn any system of gathering. It is the responsibility of both of us to search the Scriptural principles, [and] find the all-important "Thus saith the Lord."[15]

Building on the commands and patterns of authorized worship in the Old Testament, in the New Testament God reveals the following elements for worship in His local church.

God is worshiped when we preach the Bible

Paul instructs the young Pastor Timothy with these words:

> *"I charge you in the presence of God and of Christ Jesus, who is to judge the living and the dead, and by his appearing and his kingdom: preach the word; be ready in season and out of season; reprove, rebuke, and exhort, with complete patience and teaching."*—2 Timothy 4:1–2

The centerpiece of corporate worship is the unashamed proclamation of God's Word. The next chapter will be devoted to this issue.

God is worshiped when we read the Bible.

Not only does God want the Bible preached, He wants it to be read. Again, Paul instructs Pastor Timothy, and all pastors today, to publicly read the Bible as a part of the corporate worship service.

> *"Until I come, devote yourself to the public reading of Scripture, to exhortation, to teaching."*—1 Timothy 4:13

Unless the Bible is read systematically, week after week, in our corporate worship services, it is likely there will be portions of God's Word the congregation never hears. God wants *all His Words* to be given to *all His people.*[16]

God is worshiped when we pray.

God calls individual Christians and Christian families to pray "at all times in the Spirit, with all prayer and supplication" (Ephesians 6:18). But, prayer is not only meant for personal use, or private use in Christian homes, but for corporate use in the local church.[17]

"And they devoted themselves to the apostles' teaching and the fellowship, to the breaking of bread and the prayers."—Acts 2:42

"First of all, then, I urge that supplications, prayers, intercessions, and thanksgivings be made for all people, for kings and all who are in high positions, that we may lead a peaceful and quiet life, godly and dignified in every way. This is good, and it is pleasing in the sight of God our Savior, who desires all people to be saved and to come to the knowledge of the truth."—1 Timothy 2:1–4

God is worshiped when we give our money.

Our worship of God is connected with the money He has entrusted to us. Money is directly connected to all of God's jurisdictions: the individual, the family, the local church, and the government.

The early Christians brought their tithes and offerings, as a part of the Sunday worship service, to the elders[18] of their local church.

"Now concerning the collection for the saints: as I directed the churches of Galatia, so you also are to do. On the first day of every week, each of you is to put something aside and store it up, as he may prosper, so that there will be no collecting when I come."—1 Corinthians 16:1–2

For giving to be pleasing to God, for it to be an acceptable act of worship, it must not be forced by human demand. God does not just want us to give He wants us to give *rightly.*

"The point is this: whoever sows sparingly will also reap sparingly, and whoever sows bountifully will also reap bountifully. Each one must give as he has decided in his heart, not reluctantly or under compulsion, for God loves a cheerful giver."—2 Corinthians 9:6–7

The elders in the early church used the donations for financial support of elders[19] and missionaries[20], to support poor believers[21] in the church, and provide for widows who did not have family to care for them.[22]

God is worshiped through song and music.

God, as the creator of song and music, loves it when His children sing His praise!

"Make a joyful noise to the LORD, all the earth! Serve the LORD with gladness! Come into his presence with singing!"—Psalm 100:1–2

"Let the word of Christ dwell in you richly, teaching and admonishing one another in all wisdom, singing psalms and hymns and spiritual songs, with thankfulness in your hearts to God."—Colossians 3:16

God also provides us with examples in the Bible when singing is accompanied with clapping, dancing[23], and with the raising of hands. It can be argued that since these are only recorded in the Old Testament[24] that the New Testament church did not practice them. From my perspective, however, the only Old Testament forms of worship, which are no longer applicable for the New Testament church, are those that have to do with the ceremonial law and sacrificial system. It is only those portions of the Old Testament that have been superseded by Christ.[25] God says, "Clap your hands, all peoples! Shout to God with loud songs of joy!" (Psalm 47:1). I cannot see any Christological reason to say that something God enjoyed prior to Christ (His children clapping their hands while they sing to Him), is now forbidden.

God is worshiped through communion and baptism.

The early church celebrated communion each Sunday.[26] Jesus authorized this new manner of worshiping Him in Matthew 26. But, as we see throughout Scripture, fallen humans continually depart from worshiping God according to His instructions. As a result, Paul had to call the Corinthian church back to the *proper way* to worship God through taking communion.

"When you come together, it is not the Lord's supper that you eat. For in eating, each one goes ahead with his own meal. One goes hungry, another gets drunk. What! Do you not have houses to eat and drink in? Or do you despise the church of God and humiliate those who have nothing? What shall I say to you? Shall I commend you in this? No, I will not.

For I received from the Lord what I also delivered to you, that the Lord Jesus on the night when he was betrayed took bread, and when he had given thanks, he broke it, and said, "This is my body which is for you. Do this in remembrance of me." In the same way also he took the cup, after supper, saying, "This cup is the new covenant in my blood. Do this, as often as you drink it, in remembrance of me." For as often as you eat this bread and drink the cup, you proclaim the Lord's death until he comes."—1 Corinthians 11:20–26

In the preceding verses, God speaks powerfully through Paul if communion is not done in the manner God has authorized; it will not be received as worship, and will result in strict judgment. God takes His worship seriously!

In fact, some of the Corinthians had been struck with illness, and God had even killed some, because they were not following His explicit instructions for communion.

"That is why many of you are weak and ill, and some have died."—1 Corinthians 11:30

In addition to the new worship practice of communion, God invites believers to worship Him through the ordinance of baptism. In the New Testament, baptism was normally performed immediately after conversion. Baptisms can take place in the context of the corporate worship service, but we find examples of the New Testament of baptisms taking place in public squares[27], in rivers[28], and even on the side of a road![29]

DOES YOUR CHURCH WORSHIP GOD RIGHTLY?

In reviewing the above elements of corporate worship, we find many of these things God has ordained being practiced every week in our churches.[30] Have you ever wondered why you sing *every week* in your church service? Where did that idea come from? It came from God's Word alone.

Have you seen a baptism where the pastor says, "I baptize you now in the name of the Father, and of the Son, and of the Holy Spirit."? Why does he say that? He says that because Jesus told us to baptize people in that *manner.*[31] It is doing baptism according to the instructions and ordained patterns in the Bible.

Try suggesting to your pastor the church have no preaching for the next month, and only worship through singing. What would his reaction be? I hope he would have nothing to do with such an idea. Lord willing, it would not be for his personal need to be in the pulpit each week, but rather that God has spoken in the Bible when His church gathers, His Word is to be preached!

However, are there some practices God has commanded that are being neglected in your church? Do you neglect the public reading of the Bible? Do the elders publicly discipline church members who are in unrepentant sin?

In the same way, have you *added* elements to your corporate worship service that God has not ordained in His Word?

God has intentionally given us every word in Scripture. Not one word is unnecessary, and not one more word is needed. All Scripture is breathed out by God . . . that the man of God may be *complete, equipped for every good work.*[32] Let us continually return, and return again, to worship God in spirit and in truth.

Questions for Discussion:

1. In what ways does your local church practice the biblical commands and principles for corporate worship?

2. Does your local church go beyond the Bible by including additional elements in the corporate worship service not commanded or patterned in Scripture?

3. Are there any worship practices of the early church absent in your local church?

4. The Pilgrims risked their lives to worship God according to the Bible. What are you willing to risk to do the same?

ENDNOTES

[1]The early church had its fair share of theological disagreements about the correct way to understand the revelation of God in the Old Testament, and the revelation currently being written (what we now call the New Testament.)

[2]Hebrews 10:25.

[3]Elisabeth Elliot, *Shadow of the Almighty: The Life and Testament of Jim Elliot* (Peabody, MA: Hendrickson, 2008), 191–192.

[4]Psalm 29:2.

[5]See also Numbers 15 as an example of the detailed instructions God gave to the people regarding the manner of their worship.

[6]Manasseh illustrates both great wickedness in the history of Israel along with the grace and mercy of God as Manasseh was brought to repentance six years before his death.

[7]Commanded in Exodus 13. The Passover celebration foreshadows the Messiah, which is why it is no longer required for the proper worship of God today.

[8]Italics mine.

[9]The religions of the world differentiate themselves, in part, based on how they believe their particular deity is to be worshiped. For instance, Muslims believe that Allah demands particular acts of worship, such as praying five times a day. For a Muslim, if Allah is not worshipped in this way, it is sin and an affront to Allah. A serious Muslim desires to see all people worship Allah in the particular way that they believe Allah has ordained.

[10]As discussed earlier, all the words of Scripture can rightly be called the words of Christ. The whole Bible is "red letters."

[11]Romans 1:18–23.

[12]Refer to section 1 of this book for a review of the different definitions of legalism.

[13]In the New Testament we have both descriptions and prescriptions for the local church. I will address this important tension later in the book.

[14]Our focus here is limited to how God calls us to worship Him in the corporate worship gathering of the local church. For instance, God has ordained fasting as a means of worshipping Him (Matthew 6:16–17), but that means of worship is to be done privately.

[15]Elliot, 192.

[16]God is also worshipped when His people respond to His Word with "Amen!" See Nehemiah 8:6, 1 Chronicles 16:36, and Psalm 106:48.

[17]While prayer is a spiritual activity, our bodies can engage in prayer as well. Bowing, kneeling, and prostrating are bodily positions used in making humble prayers to the Lord. God gives us examples in Scripture of these physical acts of prayer being done in private as well as in the company of other believers (Psalm 95:6, Deuteronomy 9:25, and Acts 20:36).

[17]See also Acts 11:30.

[19]1 Timothy 5:17–18.

[20]2 Corinthians 8:1–5.

[21]Acts 11:29.

[22]1 Timothy 5:3–16.

[23]Psalm 149:3.

[24]On the issue of dancing, an exception may be noted in the parable of the Prodigal Son where Jesus speaks of dancing as a part of the family celebration when the lost son returns. See also Matthew 11:17.

[25]Matthew 5:17.

[26]Acts 20:7.

[27]Acts 2:38–41.

[28]Acts 16:15.

[29] Acts 8:36.

[30] I appreciate Mark Dever and Paul Alexander's summary of the elements of corporate worship being "Read the Word, preach the Word, pray the Word, sing the Word, and see the Word (in the ordinances)." *The Deliberate Church*, (Wheaton, IL: Crossway, 2005), 81.

[31] Matthew 28:19.

[32] 2 Timothy 3:17, italics mine.

CHAPTER 8:
PREACHING THE BIBLE

"Man shall not live by bread alone, but by every
word that comes from the mouth of God."

—Matthew 4:4

N othing is more important in the local church than the preaching of the Bible. Hearts are turned, minds are transformed, and lives are changed when the Holy Spirit works through the proclamation of His Word.

When Wheaton Bible Church[1] built a new church building in 2008, the pulpit was placed in the center of the entire architectural plan. This decision was made because the leadership of the church wanted the physical structure of the church to reflect the theological reality, the most important thing that happens in a local church is the preaching and teaching of the Bible.

The supernatural, revealed words of God in the Bible are "living and active," able to "judge the thoughts and attitudes of the heart,"[2] and "able to make you wise for salvation through faith in Christ Jesus."[3]

> *"How then will they call on him in whom they have not believed? And how are they to believe in him of whom they have never heard? And how are they to hear without someone preaching? And how are they to preach unless they are sent? As it is written, "How beautiful are the feet of those who preach the good news!" But they have not all obeyed the gospel. For Isaiah says, "Lord, who has believed what he has heard from us?" So faith comes from hearing, and hearing through the word of Christ."[4]—Romans 10:14–17*

The elders[5] in the local church are instructed to preach and teach the Bible. It is a jurisdictional responsibility of the local church.[6] Preaching is a "good work,"[7] and therefore we can have complete confidence God's Word can thoroughly train and equip us to preach in a way that pleases God.

IF SCRIPTURE IS SUFFICIENT, WHY DO WE NEED PREACHING?

This is an important question. If the Bible is "all we need," then why don't elders just read the Bible and not add any additional "preaching" on top of it? The answer is simple. Church leaders preach, teach, and expound upon the Bible, because *in the Bible* God tells them to do it.

Why would God entrust *us* with the responsibility of proclaiming and explaining *His* words to others? It sounds like a foolish plan. Indeed it is.

> *"Where is the one who is wise? Where is the scribe? Where is the debater of this age? Has not God made foolish the wisdom of the world? For since, in the wisdom of God, the world did not know God through wisdom, it pleased God through the folly of what we preach to save those who believe."*—1 Corinthians 1:20–21

Preaching the Bible is among the most serious of Christian responsibilities. Is God really asking me to stand up in front of my local church and tell them what God, the King of the Universe, has said and what He demands of them? Yes.

Consider this powerful example from the Old Testament where the public reading of the Bible was brought together with proper preaching and teaching.

> *And Ezra opened the book in the sight of all the people, for he was above all the people, and as he opened it all the people stood. And Ezra blessed the* Lord, *the great God, and all the people answered, "Amen, Amen," lifting up their hands. And they bowed their heads and worshiped the* Lord *with their faces to the ground. Also Jeshua, Bani, Sherebiah, Jamin, Akkub, Shabbethai, Hodiah, Maaseiah, Kelita, Azariah, Jozabad, Hanan, Pelaiah, the Levites, helped the people to understand the Law, while the people remained in their places. They read from the book, from the Law of God, clearly, and they gave the sense, so that the people understood the reading."*—Nehemiah 8:5–8

God calls us to preach the text, in its proper context, in the tone of the text. I have been guilty many times of using *God's* words as a springboard to get to *my* words. The purpose for my words in preaching is to point to His words, His truth, His message, and His commands.

PREACHING THE BIBLE IS THE PRIMARY TASK OF THE PASTOR

Only someone who has served as a pastor truly knows how overwhelming it is.

There is never a day where the pastor leaves the church with the sense that all that needed to be done that day was completed.

Most churches expect their pastors/elders to do far more than the Bible expects of them, and the end result is often that time is taken away from their most important responsibility, the preaching and teaching of the Bible. This was the experience of the pastors in the early church as well. The local church was growing and the administrative demands of their ministry to widows were increasing.

> *"And the twelve summoned the full number of the disciples and said, "It is not right that we should give up preaching the word of God to serve tables. Therefore, brothers, pick out from among you seven men of good repute, full of the Spirit and of wisdom, whom we will appoint to this duty. But we will devote ourselves to prayer and to the ministry of the word."*—Acts 6:2–4

It was not that the elders felt serving the widows was beneath them, but rather nothing should be allowed to prevent them from giving their best time to prayer and preaching the Bible.

Throughout this book, we have returned to 2 Timothy 3:16–17 where God proclaims the power, centrality, and sufficiency of the Bible for every area of life.

> *"All Scripture is breathed out by God and profitable for teaching, for reproof, for correction, and for training in righteousness, that the man of God may be complete, equipped for every good work."*—2 Timothy 3:16–17

If every word of the Bible comes from God, what should pastors do? If the whole of Scripture is sufficient for every matter of faith and practice, what should pastors do?

Immediately following these words, Paul instructs Timothy, and all pastors/elders with this admonition:

> *"I charge you in the presence of God and of Christ Jesus, who is to judge the living and the dead, and by his appearing and his kingdom: preach the word; be ready in season and out of season; reprove, rebuke, and exhort, with complete patience and teaching."*—2 Timothy 4:1–2

Could these words be any stronger? I charge you in the presence of God! I charge you in the presence of Christ Jesus! Judgment is coming! Christ is coming again to reign forever! In light of these things, *Preach the word!*

Preach when things are going well. Preach when they are not. Preach when you see lots of fruit. Preach when you do not. Challenge. Confront. Be completely patient. Let nothing distract you from this, your primary responsibility.

Pastor, do you want to disciple people toward becoming complete in Christ? Preach the Bible.

Do you want to equip everyone in the church for good works? Preach the Bible. Do you want people to come to Christ and grow in faith? Preach the Bible.

I see a growing tendency today to minimize the transformational power of preaching. People say to me things such as, "We can't expect people to grow just by sitting and listening to some sermon." If by that we mean, "we can't expect people to grow who refuse to listen to the sermon and respond to God's word in obedience," I completely agree.

We live in a dangerous and precarious time where many people who claim to follow Christ no longer believe the proclamation of His Word has the power to bring people to repentance and transform their lives. For many years of my pastoral ministry, I fell into this trap as well.

I can remember many times when I have preached, beginning with an illustration, and then inviting the congregation to open their Bibles to the text for the day. Then when it was time to read the passage of Scripture, I would quickly read through it. Why would I quickly read the Scripture? Because I needed to get back to the good stuff, which was *me*, and *my* word, expounding on what God had said.

I had to repent of this. I preached as if *my words* were living and active, and sharper than any double-edged sword. When I preach today, in the moments when I am reading the words of God, my heart slows down, my words slow down, and in spirit I am aware if God is going to supernaturally work in someone's life that day, it is going to be through what *He* has said.

Have you ever heard a preacher say, "Now if you only remember one thing I say today, I want you to remember this."? I have used that phrase many times. It is a public speaking device designed to ask for a few seconds of full attention from your audience. What comes next? For me, the next words out of my mouth were always something pithy, profound, and memorable. I tried to summarize a deep truth or powerful application from the message, which I wanted people to remember.

I had to repent of this as well. Do I really believe a clever, pithy phrase has the power to bring people to repentance, transform their heart, or renew their mind? God's words are living and active, not mine. So I made a decision if I were to ever use that device again, and I have, the next words out of my mouth would be Scripture, the supernatural words of God. The preacher must be completely convinced it is God's words, not his, which have the power to transform souls.

THE WHOLE COUNSEL OF GOD

If the primary responsibility of pastors is the preaching and teaching of the Bible, how do pastors choose what to teach? This is a critical question, and God answers it for us. Preaching is a good work, therefore, the Bible is completely sufficient to equip us with essential principles for *how* to do it rightly.

First, pastors must commit themselves to preaching the entire Bible. This will require many years of systematically preaching through the entire Bible, but it must be done. Consider the example of the Apostle Paul, who discipled the local church in Ephesus through three years of daily Bible teaching.

> *"Therefore I testify to you this day that I am innocent of the blood of all, for* I did not shrink from declaring to you the whole counsel of God.[8] *Pay careful attention to yourselves and to all the flock, in which the Holy Spirit has made you overseers, to care for the church of God, which he obtained with his own blood."*—Acts 20:26–28

Paul then warned them of the spiritual battles that lay ahead of them. The battles would be against other so-called believers in the church who would teach false doctrine.

> *"I know that after my departure fierce wolves will come in among you, not sparing the flock; and from among your own selves will arise men speaking twisted things, to draw away the disciples after them. Therefore be alert, remembering that for three years I did not cease night or day to admonish every one with tears. And now I commend you to God and to the word of his grace, which is able to build you up and to give you the inheritance among all those who are sanctified."*— Acts 20:29–32

For many years of my preaching and teaching ministry, because I did not understand this doctrine, I decided which words needed to be preached, and which words did not. For instance, I would do a four-week series in the book of Ephesians. I would choose the four "key" texts in Ephesians and skip over the rest. I look back on that now and ask myself, "What right did I have to choose some words of God to preach, and choose others to skip over?" Not only did I not preach all of the words God had spoken in that particular book, I didn't even publicly read them all. I understand those who say, "We should major on the majors, and minor on the minors." But we should be careful. Who gets to choose what is major and what is minor? Too often that principle leads to "majoring" on the majors, and "zeroing" on the minors.

Jesus stressed the need for his followers to believe and obey all of God's words, and to teach others to do the same.

> *"Do not think that I have come to abolish the Law or the Prophets[9]; I have not come to abolish them but to fulfill them. For truly, I say to you, until heaven and earth pass away, not an iota, not a dot, will pass from the Law until all is accomplished. Therefore whoever relaxes one of the least of these commandments and teaches others to do the same will be called least in the kingdom of heaven, but whoever does them and teaches them will be called great in the kingdom of heaven."*—Matthew 5:17–19

Our need for *all* of God's words was repeated by Jesus in the Great Commission.

> *"Go therefore and make disciples of all nations, baptizing them in the name of the Father and of the Son and of the Holy Spirit,* teaching them to observe all that I have commanded you." [10]—Matthew 28:19–20

We cannot "make disciples" without teaching people to rightly[11] observe (obey) all of God's Word. When Jesus speaks of "all that I have commanded you," He is not only speaking of His words as recorded in the Gospels, but all of His words, which make up the entire Bible. In Romans 10:17 and Colossians 3:16, God refers to the Scriptures as "the word of Christ."

I appreciate the approach Pastor Jeramie Rinne has taken at South Shore Baptist Church in Hingham, MA. When they begin preaching through a book of Scripture, they take as long as it takes to preach every portion of it. Sometimes the preacher is able to exposit an entire chapter; other times only half a verse.

In our interview, Pastor Rinne said, "Why would we choose to skip any of God's words when preaching through one of His inspired books?"[12] Generally, they alternate preaching through books of the Old and New Testaments. In addition to preaching, they read a chapter from the Old Testament and a chapter from the New Testament as part of each worship service. If it takes seventy-five weeks to preach through Ephesians, the congregation has also been blessed and transformed by 150 other chapters from God's Word.

Our preaching plan should reflect the truth that all God's people need to hear and believe all of God's words.

PREACHING THE GOSPEL

In addition to the biblical requirement to preach the entire Bible, special emphasis is made on preaching the gospel. God is doing a marvelous thing here in the early part of the 21st century in calling His people back to the centrality of the gospel message for everything.

In the New Testament, "the gospel" is used in at least two major ways. One of these usages is often overlooked, if not completely ignored. God says the gospel = the Bible.

> *"In him you also, when you heard the word of truth, the gospel of your salvation, and believed in him, were sealed with the promised Holy Spirit."*—Ephesians 1:13

> *". . . because of the hope laid up for you in heaven. Of this you have heard before in the word of the truth, the gospel."*—Colossians 1:5

"The word of truth" refers to God's written revelation. God speaks through Paul in these verses and equates this "word of truth," God's written revelation, with "the gospel." What is the gospel? The complete answer is that "the gospel" is the sum total of all God has revealed to us in the Bible. Removing any portion of Scripture would be to remove a portion of "the gospel." This is another reason why, if a church desires to preach "the gospel," they must have a plan to preach the entire Bible.

The second usage of "the gospel" is more commonly understood. It can be rightly said the gospel is the message of God's plan of salvation through Christ alone, through faith alone, by grace alone. While the New Testament church sought to preach all of God's words, the centerpiece of biblical preaching is the death and resurrection of Jesus Christ.

". . . but we preach Christ crucified, a stumbling block to Jews and folly to Gentiles."—1 Corinthians 1:23

"Now I would remind you, brothers, of the gospel I preached to you, which you received, in which you stand, and by which you are being saved, if you hold fast to the word I preached to you—unless you believed in vain. For I delivered to you as of first importance what I also received: that Christ died for our sins in accordance with the Scriptures, that he was buried, that he was raised on the third day in accordance with the Scriptures, and that he appeared to Cephas, then to the twelve."—1 Corinthians 15:1–5

What must be of first importance in our preaching? That Christ died for our sins according to the Scriptures, was buried, and was raised on the third day.

From his passion to elevate Christ in everything, the 19th Century pastor J. C. Ryle said, "Read the Bible with Christ constantly in view. The whole book is about Him. Look for Him on every page. He is there. If you fail to see Him there, you need to read that page again."[198]

Why must we continue to preach Christ crucified? Haven't we heard that message enough? After we become Christians, don't we get to graduate to more important things?

We need the message of the Gospel every day. We need to face the truth about sin every day. We need the message of grace every day. We need the power of the resurrection every day. We begin the Christian life when, in response to God's grace, we repent and believe. We continue the Christian life when, in response to God's grace, we continue to repent and continue to believe.

If the gospel that is proclaimed in your church is simply, "Jesus loves you and wants to be in Heaven with you forever." That is not the gospel. Some people may raise their hands and say, "Sure! I'd like to go to heaven." While "the gospel" is good news, it begins with bad news. The true gospel begins with the reality that our sin has brought death into the world and because of our sin we are spiritually dead, and are rightly doomed to hell. Is this preached in your church? If not, you are not preaching the gospel. It is only after this "bad news" that the "good news" of God's great love for us, expressed through His Son Jesus Christ, means anything at all.[14]

If we are not sinners doomed to hell, what good is the offer of forgiveness? If we are not enemies of God, what good is the truth that Jesus propitiated God's wrath for us? If we are not spiritually dead, why do we need to be born again?

Not only do believers never "graduate" from our need for the gospel message, but unbelievers may also be present. As much as we don't like to admit it, some of those who are not converted may have been attending for a long time, and some may even have become members.[15]

The message of the gospel itself has sufficient power to regenerate souls. You don't need to do anything to dress it up or make it more dramatic. Just proclaim it boldly, simply, and biblically. The Holy Spirit will then do what the Holy Spirit desires to do.

> *"For I am not ashamed of the gospel, for it is the power of God for salvation to everyone who believes, to the Jew first and also to the Greek."*—Romans 1:16

If we are to preach the biblical gospel, we must use biblical language. There are no examples in Scripture where the following words are preached to unbelievers:

- "Invite Jesus into your heart."[16]

- "Give your heart to Christ."

- "Pray to receive Christ."

If we are going to share the gospel we have received through the Bible alone, we must use the words God has given us. What are those words? They are encapsulated in Jesus' first sermon, and repeated through the early church.

We find Jesus' first sermon in Mark 1:15, "The time is fulfilled, and the kingdom of God is at hand, repent and believe the gospel." Later in Luke 13:3 Jesus says, "No, I tell you; but unless you repent, you will all likewise perish."

When we preach the gospel, the call to respond must be simple and clear. "Repent! Believe"![17]

This was the message of the disciples when Jesus sent them out. "So they went out and proclaimed that people should repent" (Mark 6:12).

The disciples used these words when they preached in the book of Acts.

> *"And Peter said to them, "Repent and be baptized every one of you in the name of Jesus Christ for the forgiveness of your sins, and you will receive the gift of the Holy Spirit."*—Acts 2:38

"Repent therefore, and turn back, that your sins may be blotted out . . . "—
Acts 3:19

"Repent, therefore, of this wickedness of yours, and pray to the Lord that, if possible, the intent of your heart may be forgiven you."—Acts 8:22

"Then he brought them out and said, "Sirs, what must I do to be saved?" And they said, "Believe in the Lord Jesus, and you will be saved, you and your household."—Acts 16:30

The evangelistic sermons of the New Testament are bold on judgment, bold on sin, bold on grace, bold on mercy, and above all, they lift up the death and resurrection of Jesus Christ as the only means of salvation.

PREACH TO EVERYONE

I am going to end this chapter with a controversial issue. In the early church, children were included in the corporate worship service. A more detailed biblical discussion of this issue can be found in chapter twenty. The question, "do children belong in church?" is a doctrinal, theological question. Do we believe the Bible is sufficient to give us the answer?

Pastor Dustin Guidry (Ridgewood Church, Port Arthur, TX) tells the story[18] of how he and his fellow elders became convinced the early church was age-integrated. Families worshiped together. The church service was not an adult-education hour, but a gathering of the whole church into the presence of God, under the authority of His word.

Because of this theological commitment, children are intentionally welcomed and included in the church service. The bulletin for the worship service is designed for families to take home and use as a worship, discipleship, and prayer guide during the week. They believe the whole church, children included, should be taught the whole word of God and the Holy Spirit uses His Word in the lives of everyone, whether they are two or eighty-two. Pastor Guidry is also the blessed father of a special-needs daughter. She may never function at an adult level intellectually. If the church service is only for adults, when should Pastor Guidry's daughter be welcomed in the service? In their church, all children and all adults, regardless of age or mental capacity are welcome.

In an interview with Pastor Guidry[19], he told me what the response was from the older members of the congregation when they brought the children into the worship service. "I was surprised and blessed by their reaction. While they may not have understood all the theological and biblical reasons for the decision, they said, "Here is what we know for sure. We grew up going to church with our parents, and we are still here. Many of our children, however, grew up separated from us in the church building, and now many of them are no longer following the Lord."

Consider these few paragraphs to be my "pulling the pin and throwing the grenade" on this critical issue. We will pick up the live grenade a few chapters ahead.

PREACHING AGAINST ERROR

Another essential ingredient of biblical preaching is the confrontation of error and false teaching. It is not enough to proclaim the truth. Biblical preachers name and publicly lead the battle against lies.

The early church preached against deceptions in the world. Many Christians are impotent when they are confronted by godless philosophies because they have not been equipped from the pulpit with a graceful and truthful biblical response.

> *"For the weapons of our warfare are not of the flesh but have divine power to destroy strongholds. We destroy arguments and every lofty opinion raised against the knowledge of God, and take every thought captive to obey Christ."*—2 Corinthians 10:4–5

> *"See to it that no one takes you captive by philosophy and empty deceit, according to human tradition, according to the elemental spirits of the world, and not according to Christ."*—Colossians 2:8

If only heresy and false teaching were just "out there" in the world, and our local churches were safe and secure. A great responsibility in New Testament preaching and teaching was refuting and confronting those *within the church* who were bringing worldly, unbiblical thinking into the family of God.

> *"I appeal to you, brothers, to watch out for those who cause divisions and create obstacles contrary to the doctrine that you have been taught; avoid them. For such persons do not serve our Lord Christ, but their own appetites, and by smooth talk and flattery they deceive the hearts of the naive."*—Romans 16:17–18

"I am astonished that you are so quickly deserting him who called you in the grace of Christ and are turning to a different gospel—not that there is another one, but there are some who trouble you and want to distort the gospel of Christ. But even if we or an angel from heaven should preach to you a gospel contrary to the one we preached to you, let him be accursed. As we have said before, so now I say again: If anyone is preaching to you a gospel contrary to the one you received, let him be accursed."—Galatians 1:6–9

"For there are many who are insubordinate, empty talkers and deceivers, especially those of the circumcision party. They must be silenced, since they are upsetting whole families by teaching for shameful gain what they ought not to teach."—Titus 1:10–11

"Preach the word; be ready in season and out of season; reprove, rebuke, and exhort, with complete patience and teaching. For the time is coming when people will not endure sound teaching, but having itching ears they will accumulate for themselves teachers to suit their own passions, and will turn away from listening to the truth and wander off into myths. As for you, always be sober-minded, endure suffering, do the work of an evangelist, fulfill your ministry."—2 Timothy 4:2–5

Do the elders at your church ever speak like this? Are the elders at your church aware of what is being taught in all the discipleship environments in your church? The elders are charged by God to teach pure biblical doctrine, to protect that doctrine, and to confront anyone in the church who intentionally or unintentionally perverts it.

"Praise the Lord! Blessed is the man who fears the Lord, who greatly delights in his commandments!"—Psalm 112:1

Questions for Discussion:

1. If you grew up in church, what style of preaching did you experience?

2. Which elements of biblical preaching are regularly practiced in your church? Are there some elements often missing?

3. How would our preaching change if we were completely convinced God's words had the power to change lives rather than our words?

ENDNOTES

[1] Wheaton Bible Church is now located in West Chicago, IL. http://www.wheatonbible.org.

[2] Hebrews 4:12, NIV.

[3] 2 Timothy 3:15, NIV.

[4] Italics mine.

[5] The New Testament terms for elder, pastor, shepherd, and overseer are interchangeable—all referring to the same role.

[6] Preaching and teaching the Bible is not limited to the local church. Throughout the book of Acts we see individual believers preaching and teaching the Bible apart from the corporate worship gathering. The Bible is also to be preached and taught by heads of households in the Christian family. However, the preaching by the elders in the local church trains and equips believers for rightly teaching the Bible to others.

[7] 2 Timothy 3:16.

[8] Italics mine.

[9] Referring to God's written revelation of the Old Testament.

[10] Italics mine.

[11] As noted earlier, some commandments in the Bible, such as those related to the Old Testament sacrificial system, have been superseded by Christ's finished work on the cross and are no longer binding for Christians today.

[12] Phone interview conducted October 2, 2011. Pastor Rinne noted he will sometimes preach a group of representative texts as a single unit. For instance, if there are four sections in Deuteronomy which speak to the same issue using the same language, one of those sections will be preached, giving reference to the parallel texts as needed.

[13] J. C. Ryle, *Practical Religion*, (Carlisle, PA: Banner of Truth, 1998), 131.

[14] I encourage you to read the article, *Sufficiency and Exposition* by Pastor Jeramie Rinne, http://www.reformation21.org/articles/exposition-and-sufficiency.php.

[15] Matthew 7:21, 2 Peter 2:1, and Jude 1:4.

[16] In Revelation 3:30, Jesus says "Behold, I stand at the door and knock. If anyone hears my voice and opens the door, I will come in to him and eat with him, and he with me." These words of Christ are offered to believers who are a part of the church of Laodicea.

[17] The Greek word *pistis/pisteo* is translated in various places as "belief/believe," "trust/to trust," and "faith/to have faith."

[18] Dustin Guidry, *Turning the Ship*, (Maitland, FL: Xulon Press, 2009).

[19] Phone interview on 10/13/2011.

CHAPTER 9:
EQUIPPING AND CARING IN THE CHURCH

"... But God has so composed the body, giving greater honor to the part that
lacked it, that there may be no division in the body, but that the members
may have the same care for one another. If one member suffers, all
suffer together; if one member is honored, all rejoice together."

—1 CORINTHIANS 12:24–26

G od established the institution of the local church with specific roles and
responsibilities. As we have already seen, the local church gathers together
believers for the worship of God. The local church is also given the responsibility to
preach and teach the Bible. In this chapter, we will consider a third jurisdictional
mission of the local church, the equipping of and caring for believers.

EQUIPPING BELIEVERS FOR MINISTRY

One of the most radical and revolutionary doctrines in the New Testament church
was the priesthood of all believers. In the Old Testament, there was a distinct
priestly class apart from all the "regular people." The Holy Spirit did not indwell
all the people of Israel instead, the Holy Spirit temporarily "fell upon" particular
individuals to supernaturally empower them for the mission God had given them.[1]

There is no longer a priestly class in contrast to the "regular people." All believers
have full access to God through His Son. All believers are now priests and are given
the mantle of serving in ministry.

> *"But you are a chosen race, a royal priesthood, a holy nation, a people*
> *for his own possession, that you may proclaim the excellencies of him*
> *who called you out of darkness into his marvelous light."*—1 Peter 2:9

According to the Bible, all believers are priests and ministers of the Gospel. All believers are called to serve and obey Him as individuals, as members of families, and as members of churches. However, God gives different gifts, abilities, and callings to each believer; and therefore *ministry* looks different from one believer to the next.

In addition to preaching the Bible, a primary role of elders/pastors is the equipping of believers for works of ministry.

> *"And he gave the apostles, the prophets, the evangelists, the shepherds and teachers, to equip the saints[2] for the work of ministry, for building up the body of Christ, until we all attain to the unity of the faith and of the knowledge of the Son of God, to mature manhood, to the measure of the stature of the fullness of Christ, so that we may no longer be children, tossed to and fro by the waves and carried about by every wind of doctrine, by human cunning, by craftiness in deceitful schemes."*—Ephesians 4:11–14

THE INTERNALLY FOCUSED PASTOR

God's word is sufficient to define the role and work of the pastor[3]. That role and work is limited. As we have already discussed, pastors lead *believers* in the proper worship of God. Pastors disciple *believers* through the proper teaching of the Bible.[208] In the above text from Ephesians, God gives another jurisdictional responsibility to pastors, which is the equipping of *believers* for the work of ministry.

Look at the basic outline of God's mission for pastors in this text:

Equip the saints

For the work of ministry

For building up the body of Christ

Until we all attain to the unity of the faith

[until we all attain to the unity] of the knowledge of the Son of God

[until we all attain] to mature manhood

[until we all attain] to the measure and stature of fullness of Christ

So that we may no longer be children.

Here God focuses the responsibility of the pastor on his ministry to the believers in the local church. The pastoral role is fundamentally "internally focused." Don't let this term "internally focused" throw you. There is an intense pressure in some churches today for everything to be "externally focused." This can result in the term "internally focused" being immediately rejected as selfish and contrary to the Great Commission.

Remember, the passion of this book is the advance of the gospel to the ends of the earth! What will it take for Christians to embrace that mission and lay down their lives for it? If we want to see more externally focused Christians, we need more internally focused local churches. God created the institution of the local church to be radically "inward" (focused on the teaching, equipping, and care of believers) so that Christian individuals and Christian families would be radically "outward."

WORKS OF MINISTRY

What are the "works of ministry" for which pastors are to equip the members of the local church? Works of ministry are as varied as the gifts, passions, and callings of the Christians in the church. However, when the pastors view discipleship in a biblically ordered way the responsibility to equip the saints becomes clearer.

Consider this simple diagram of the rightly ordered Christian heart and life:

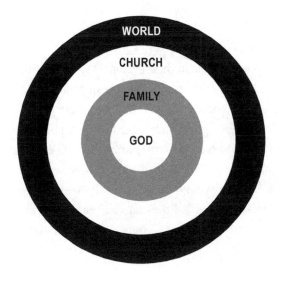

God desires that minds, hearts, and lives be rightly ordered. Our "loves" are to be in a particular order. Our first love is to be the Lord. God then calls us throughout the Bible to love, prioritize, and minister to our families. A child is to honor parents above all others. Spouses are to be devoted without compromise to one another. Parents are to disciple their children as their top Great Commission priority. Christians are to care for the poor, beginning with those in their own families.

Our relationships with our brothers and sisters in Christ come in the next sphere of Christian priority. Jesus taught that being in right relationships with our brothers and sisters in Christ was a prerequisite for effective ministry and evangelism in the community. He taught his disciples, "By this all people will know that you are my disciples, if you have love for one another" (John 13:35). If we are not committed to practicing Christian love in our church family, why would anyone ever want to join our church family? People in the church should be under no illusion that they can successfully minister to the community without seeking first to be in right relationships with one another.

The fourth circle, the outer circle, is our ministry to the world. This takes place in our neighborhoods, at our workplaces and schools, and to the ends of the earth. What can we offer the world if we do not first love God and seek to live out that faith at home and at church?

These spheres of the Christian life enable pastors to have an order and priority to their equipping strategy. First, pastors equip the saints to love God and worship Him. Pastors train the congregation how to worship God in private, how to pray, and how to read the Bible.

As pastors shepherd people in their personal walk with God, they then equip believers to live out their faith at home with their families. Sons and daughters are encouraged and equipped to honor and obey their parents, and to care for them in their old age. Siblings are encouraged and equipped to love, pray for, and prioritize one another. Men and women are trained and equipped to live out the roles God has given them in the Bible as husbands, wives, fathers, and mothers. Pastors with this Bible-driven order of discipleship see every home in the church as a "satellite ministry center" of the church. Pastors are responsible to equip, inspire, and hold Christian families accountable to the mission to which God has called them.

When believers are growing in their personal love relationship with God and doing all in their power to make their ministry to their families their top earthly priority, they are ready to be an extraordinary blessing to the local church. Vibrant local churches are built upon healthy maturing believers and healthy biblically functioning families. The more Christians are called and equipped to prioritize their ministry at home, the more that family will overflow with service in the local church.

Then, from the spiritual strength of a person's walk with God, ministry to their family, ministry in the local church, pastors equip the saints for the work of ministry in the community and beyond. Pastors teach Christians how to share their faith. They don't do it for them. They preach the global call of God. They allocate funds so that church members can be sent as missionaries to the ends of the earth.[7]

PASTORS ARE CHRISTIANS TOO

Satan loves it when pastors pray in staff meetings but never alone, never with their wives, and never with their families. Satan loves it when pastors study the Bible in the church office but never at home by himself, and never with his family beside him. Satan loves it when pastors call the church to be bold in sharing their faith with their neighbors and co-workers, but he never personally invites his unsaved neighbor to his home for dinner.

One of the reasons we are so vulnerable to these spiritual attacks is because we have abandoned jurisdictional thinking. A pastor must first think of himself as a Christian *individual*, called by God to walk in prayer, Scripture, personal holiness, compassion, and filled with evangelistic fervor. Second, a pastor must then live out his faith in the context of his family. Does he have parents? His faith begins with his honor and care for them. Does he have siblings? Does he love them, serve them, and seek to partner with them for the gospel? Is he married? God calls him to love, serve, and lead his wife as his most important ministry. Is he a father or grandfather? God has seen fit to entrust immortal souls into his care, and those souls require His most fervent prayers, evangelism, discipleship, training, and equipping. He opens his home as a place of ministry to his neighbors and to his fellow Christians. He does not do these things because he is a pastor, but because he is a Christian!

When a man's heart is given to all these things, in this order, he is then ready for God to use Him in supernatural ways as a pastor in the local church. He has been faithful with "little" and now God can give him responsibility with more. He has demonstrated Christian maturity and godliness with his spiritual responsibilities, now God can entrust more souls to his care. Now, in his calling as a pastor/elder/shepherd in the local church, his jurisdictional responsibilities are clear and limited: Lead in the proper worship of God, preach and teach the Bible, care for the believers, and equip the believers for works of ministry.

We tend to think of ourselves in our third or fourth sphere roles. Who are you? "Well, I am a pastor at the church down the street." I understand the pragmatic need to answer this way in the context of small talk, but is that the answer of our hearts? I pray God will make me a man who thinks, "I am a Christian, I am a husband, father, son, and brother, and I also serve God as a pastor."

NO FAMOUS CHURCHES

One of the practical results of the jurisdictional differences between individuals, families, and local churches is this: There are few, if any, famous local churches. Take this 10-second quiz. Answer as quickly as you can.

1. Name three local churches from the 1800s that made an impact on the world for Christ.
2. Name three Christians or Christian families from the 1800s that made an impact on the world for Christ.

I don't know about you, but I am completely stumped on #1. I can't name one, let alone three. How did you do? What about question #2? I imagine you were able to come up with a few names.

If we allow ourselves to move into the 20th century, the second question becomes even easier.

So, why it is easy to name Christians and Christian families who have impacted the world for Christ but so difficult to name Christian churches? This is because of the unique jurisdictional callings God has placed on individuals, families, and churches. Local churches, as we have discussed above, are charged with an "inward" mission. God has created the institution of the local church for believers to gather for worship, the ministry of the Word, for care, and for equipping. When the local church does what God calls it to do, it releases trained, passionate, biblical

Christians and Christian families into the world. These Christian individuals and Christian families then engage in externally focused, gospel living in their neighborhoods, nations, and to the ends of the earth!

The point here is not that local churches are not important, but exactly the opposite. For the many thousands of "famous" Christians, and for the many billions of not-so-famous ones, God has created His institution of the local church to secretly nourish them, bless them, equip them, hold them accountable, and partner with them so God's calling on their lives might reach its full measure!

GOD CREATED THE LOCAL CHURCH TO CARE FOR BELIEVERS

It may be said that all we have already discussed falls under this category. A local church that worships rightly cares for the believers. Biblical preaching cares for believers. When elders equip the members of the church for the work of ministry, they are showing their care for them. However, four specific things uniquely fall under this category.

God created the local church to care for believers through:

- Loving fellowship
- Faithful prayer
- Biblical discipline/restoration
- Financial support

These four bullets summarize the fifty-nine "one another" commands of the New Testament.[9]

CARE THROUGH LOVING FELLOWSHIP

The Christians were committed to building Christ-centered relationships with one another. In the infancy of the local church, these relationships were built by "attending the temple together and breaking bread in their homes."[10]

As we move forward through the New Testament, because there were no Christian church buildings at that time, we find a greater emphasis on Christian fellowship in homes. Today, when we hear the phrase "Christian fellowship" we often think of the activities that take place in the church building. The church building is a wonderful place to build community, but in the early church, fellowship flowed primarily through hospitality.

The call to Christian fellowship was not only the jurisdiction of the local church, but a call on every Christian individual and family. Hospitality was practiced. Hospitality was commanded.

"Contribute to the needs of the saints and seek to show hospitality."— Romans 12:13

"Show hospitality to one another without grumbling."—1 Peter 4:9

I can't help but laugh at God's command through Peter. I guess it was just as much of a pain-in-the-neck to prepare for guests two thousand years ago as it is today! God's people are to embrace the oftentimes difficult work of hospitality as an essential part of their Christian ministry and witness.

It is important to note the jurisdictional relationships regarding Christian fellowship. Nowhere in the New Testament does one get any indication that pastors were planning social events for the believers. Most certainly, the pastors planned and led the weekly gathering of corporate worship as well as other discipleship meetings of the church.

But, in the early church the burden for fellowship was on the Christian individuals and the Christian families. The pastors/elders called them to obey God and open their homes to one another. The pastors did not plan parties.

We must return, however, to the principle above where we recognize pastors are Christians too. Pastors, as individual men and leaders of families, are required by God in those jurisdictional roles, to practice Christian fellowship and use their homes for ministry. A pastor who is relationally removed from the congregation is not walking in obedience. A pastor who does not regularly welcome others into his home is not walking in obedience.

In fact, if a man was not in the habit of practicing Christian hospitality in his home, he was not consider qualified to serve as a pastor/elder in the early church. In order to be qualified, he must "be hospitable" (Titus 1:8). On the other hand, if a man's home was already a place of ministry for his family and his neighbors, he could be considered for expanded shepherding responsibilities in the local church.

CARE THROUGH FAITHFUL PRAYER

From the beginning of the local church, believers prayed with each other, and for each other.

"And they devoted themselves to the apostles' teaching and the fellowship, to the breaking of bread and the prayers."—Acts 2:42

"... Praying at all times in the Spirit, with all prayers and supplication. To that end keep alert with all perseverance, making supplication for all the saints."—Ephesians 6:18

When believers in the early church were sick, they were encouraged to call the elders of the church to come and pray for them.

"Is anyone among you sick? Let him call for the elders of the church, and let them pray over him, anointing him with oil in the name of the Lord. And the prayer of faith will save the one who is sick, and the Lord will raise him up. And if he has committed sins, he will be forgiven. Therefore, confess your sins to one another and pray for one another, that you may be healed. The prayer of a righteous person has great power as it is working."—James 5:14–16

CARE THROUGH DISCIPLINE

Biblical church discipline is one of the most important, neglected, and difficult jurisdictional responsibilities of the local church. While all the believers in a local church participate in different aspects of church discipline, the biblical process is to be driven by the elders.

In these short paragraphs, I can only urge you from God's Word to practice biblical discipline in your church. For a more thorough discussion of the theology and practice of church discipline, I recommend *A Guide to Church Discipline* by Carl Laney.[11] Laney's flowchart at the back of the book is particularly helpful in applying the various Scriptures to different situations.

Consider Paul's words to the church in Corinth, and whether you have ever heard such words from our pulpits today:

"I wrote to you in my letter not to associate with sexually immoral people—not at all meaning the sexually immoral of this world, or the greedy and swindlers, or idolaters, since then you would need to go out of the world. But now I am writing to you not to associate with anyone who bears the name of brother if he is guilty of sexual immorality or greed, or is an idolater, reviler, drunkard, or swindler—not even to eat

with such a one. For what have I to do with judging outsiders? Is it not those inside the church whom you are to judge? God judges those outside. "Purge the evil person from among you."—1 Corinthians 5:9–13

Paul was speaking in regards to a man who was in an immoral relationship with his stepmother. The man was unrepentant in his ongoing sexual immorality. What were the elders to do? They were to remove the man from the fellowship of the church. What were the believers in the local church to do? They were not to share meals with him, as if he was a faithful brother and everything was "ok."

Discipline is required to show Christian love to the offender. Sadly, it appears this man had not responded to previous correction and discussion. In the same way God uses a night in jail to bring a drug user to repentance, God uses church discipline to bring the wayward to repentance.

Discipline is required to show Christian love to the rest of the church. When unrepentant sin is given a pass in a local church, everyone suffers for it. The congregation gets the message loud and clear, "If that guy can do it so can I." The holy and righteous law of God becomes mixed with each person doing what is right in his or her own eyes. When the congregation sees such a man in fellowship week after week, they can reach no other conclusion but that their elders do not take God's Word seriously.

Discipline is required to walk in the fear of the Lord. We ought to think more often of Ananias and Sapphira.[12] How rarely we talk and preach about the fear of the Lord! Yes, Scripture says perfect love casts out all fear.[13] Yes, Scripture says there is no condemnation for those who are in Christ Jesus.[14] But, we ignore, "Since we have these promises, beloved, let us cleanse ourselves from every defilement of body and spirit, bringing holiness to completion in the fear of God."[15]

When someone in our local church, who claims to be a brother or a sister, embraces and refuses to repent of continued sin, we should fear the judgment of God on our church.

CARE THROUGH RESTORATION

Two stories of church discipline have been powerful examples to me of how God works when local churches carefully obey His Word.

In one church, an elder committed adultery. He eventually came to the other elders, with his wife, and confessed his sin. Because he was an elder who had engaged in persistent and ongoing sin, the Bible required there be public acknowledgment of his sin (1 Timothy 5:20). The elder who had confessed submitted himself to the discipline of the other elders. Not long after this, stood before the congregation on Sunday morning and confessed his sins.. He asked forgiveness from the church and committed to remaining in the fellowship and under the discipline of the elders. That was more than ten years ago, and God has blessed his marriage and his family. He has not served as an elder again, and may never, but he now leads a ministry in the church for men who are pursuing sexual holiness.

It would have been much easier to sweep this under the rug. How embarrassing! An elder caught in adultery. What will people think? There might be lawsuits. People might not trust the leadership anymore. These are not the relevant issues is these moments. All that matters is being obedient to the Bible. God has given the local church a careful and detailed plan for how to disciple those in unrepentant sin and how to protect the rest of the flock.

In another church, a new senior pastor, after having served for a few weeks, discovered some problems with the church finances. After asking a few questions, he determined that the church's administrative assistant had been embezzling funds for many years. She had stolen nearly half a million dollars!

She was removed from her position and submitted herself to the elders. The elders laid out a plan for her to repay what she had stolen and offered her ongoing discipleship and counseling to help her grow in her character and godliness. Because of her role in the church, the pastor announced to the entire church what she had done, and the elders' plan for restitution and care.

Three months later, at the end of a morning worship service, the woman came up to the front of the church and asked if she could say something. She proceeded to publicly confess her sin and asked the congregation for forgiveness. The congregation overwhelmed her with their love and forgiveness and a huge step was taken toward healing and restoration.

The pastor had to go against the conventional wisdom to keep something like this hush-hush. If people find out about this, they might stop giving to the church! Who else is stealing money in this place? Rather than act on fear and a desire for self-preservation, these elders obeyed the Bible, and it proved not only to be a dramatic act of discipleship for the offender, but a blessing for the entire church family.[16]

A failure to practice biblical church discipline is a failure to disciple. Discipleship, absent from church discipline, fails to keep people in the church truly accountable for their actions, and fails to protect innocent members of the church from sin and abuse.

CARE THROUGH FINANCIAL SUPPORT

One of the most dramatic marks of the New Testament church was that believers cared for one another financially. Because this issue is so important, and because it is often neglected, in a coming chapter we will examine this in more detail.

Questions for Discussion:

1. Why do you think some churches develop a culture where pastors are expected to do the work of ministry, rather than equip the believers to do it with them?

2. When people think of "fellowship" in your local church, do they first think in terms of hospitality in homes or events at church?

3. Can you think of a situation when a church failed to apply biblical church discipline? What was the result?

ENDNOTES

[1] Ezekiel 11:5 and Psalm 51:11.

[2] In the New Testament believers are often referred to as saints, not because they were perfect, but because Christ's perfect righteousness had been imputed to them.

[3] As noted earlier, the New Testament terms of elder, shepherd, pastor, and overseer are used interchangeably.

[4] As noted in the previous chapter unbelievers are present during the preaching, but the believers are the primary audience.

[5] http://www.d6conference.com.

[6] While it is true some have "joined" churches who are not converted, we can agree that if a church membership process functions properly only converted believers would be admitted as members.

[7]1 Corinthians 8–9.

[8]I say "invisible" in the sense that God never intended these local churches to be known to the world. Local churches are temporary institutions God has ordained to build His everlasting Church, by equipping the believers and believing families in those local churches for Kingdom ministry.

[9]Carl F. George, *Prepare Your Church for the Future* (Tarrytown: Revell, 1991), 129–131.

[10]Acts 2:46.

[11]Carl Laney, *A Guide to Church Discipline* (Ada, MI: Bethany House, 1989).

[12]Acts 5.

[13]1 John 4:18.

[14]Romans 8:1.

[15]2 Corinthians 7:1.

[16]The pastor of this church gave me permission to share this story with you.

CHAPTER 10:
SHEPHERDING IN THE CHURCH

"Why do you call me, 'Lord, Lord,' and not do what I tell you?"

—LUKE 6:46

I n the previous three chapters, we have briefly summarized the jurisdictional responsibilities God has given to the local church in the Bible. The institution of the local church was not created to accomplish every aspect of God's will on earth. Rather, the local church—through the ordained practices of worship, preaching, care, and equipping—prepares and empowers Christian individuals and Christian families to advance the gospel in every sphere of life.[1]

Not only has God revealed in the Bible the specific practices and jurisdictional responsibilities for His local church, He has revealed how the local church is to be led.

HOW WE THINK

Allow me to step back for a moment. My goal in this book is not to persuade you all of my conclusions and applications about church and family life are correct. My goal is to persuade you to use the Bible and the Bible alone in every matter of faith and life. At the end of the day, Christians may disagree on *what* we think about a particular issue. But, let it never be that Christians disagree about *how* we think. Do we believe all Scripture is God-breathed and profitable? Do we believe all Scripture can *thoroughly* equip us for *every* good work? Are we willing to lock ourselves in a room with the Bible (figuratively, that is) and then trust what God has said?

Many conversations between Christian brothers and sisters end with disagreement. I can live with that, I hope you can too. But, the nature of the disagreement is of the utmost importance. Consider a conversation that ends like this: "Based on these Scriptures, I believe God calls us to do *this* in the local church," and another believer says, "I disagree, I interpret those Scriptures to mean we should do *that*." While this may not be a happy outcome, it is an acceptable one if both parties are genuinely seeking to rightly interpret what God has said and submit their opinions and plans to His Word, as they understand it. At least in this disagreement, the Bible stands supreme! The Bible is held up as the perfect standard for all issues, for all people, in all places, in all cultures, and in all times. Unfortunately, fallen men and women sometimes fail to understand the Bible and interpret it rightly. But, let us agree there are correct and incorrect interpretations. If two Christians disagree about a biblical doctrine, one or both of them are wrong. His Word is never wrong, and the Christian journey is one in which we continually leave behind the wisdom of man to understand and believe the wisdom of God.

This principle is the essential foundation for the chapters ahead. We will be talking about church leadership, caring for the poor, youth ministry, children in church, men's ministry, women's ministry, singles ministry, and evangelism (just a few, small, non-controversial subjects). *How* should we think and talk about these things? Because I am completely convinced in the doctrine of sufficiency, I believe we can and should use the Bible alone to determine our thinking and practice in each of these areas. Perhaps you will disagree with my interpretation of what God has said. Again, I can live with that. Only let us agree as brothers and sisters in Christ that every Word of God is flawless and we need no other source of truth, guidance, or direction than from our Lord and Savior Jesus Christ! Let us shudder together in holy fear at the thought any one of us might *wrongly handle* the word of truth.[2]

SHEPHERDING THE CHURCH

Let's seek to apply the doctrine of the sufficiency of Scripture to the issue of church leadership. According to the New Testament, how was the early church organized? How was it led and shepherded? What patterns and instructions for its leadership has God chosen to reveal to us? As the creator of the local church, God alone has the right to determine its function and how those functions are to be carried out.

This chapter cannot succeed in exploring the many substantive issues of church leadership in the New Testament. For a thorough examination of what God has said regarding church leadership, there is no better resource than *Biblical Eldership* by Alexander Strauch.[3]

THE TWO OFFICES OF ELDER AND DEACON

Earlier we discussed the doctrine of the priesthood of all believers. In the Christian church, there is no priestly class of people who serve God at a super-spiritual level because of their role in the church. However, God has ordained that some men will serve the local church as *elders* and others as *deacons*.

Please refer to Strauch for a thorough exegetical explanation of how the Greek terms for shepherd/pastor (*poimen*), and elder/overseer (*presbuteros*) are used interchangeably to refer to a single office. As a result, I continue to use the terms "elder" and "pastor" synonymously.

These are the two God-ordained "offices" or "positions" we find in the New Testament.[4] It was of first importance in the local churches of the New Testament to establish multiple elders to lead each local church.

> *"And when they had appointed elders for them in every church, with prayer and fasting they committed them to the Lord in whom they had believed."*—Acts 14:23

> *"This is why I left you in Crete, so that you might put what remained into order, and appoint elders in every town as I directed you . . ."*—Titus 1:5

God also authorized His church to place people in the office of deacon (*diakonos*).

> *"Paul and Timothy, servants of Christ Jesus, to all the saints in Christ Jesus who are at Philippi, with the overseers and deacons."*—Philippians 1:1

> *"For those who serve well as deacons gain a good standing for themselves and also great confidence in the faith that is in Christ Jesus."*—1 Timothy 3:13

In Acts 6, although the specific word for deacon is not used, it can be argued that the selection of the seven men to assist the apostles, were the first to serve the local church in this formal capacity.

In general terms, New Testament elders shepherd, lead, and teach while New Testament deacons care, support, and serve those who are in need.

One of the ways in which some churches have departed from the New Testament model of church leadership is by creating a false differentiation between those who are called *elders* and those who are called *pastors*.

Have you ever experienced strange tensions between pastors and elders? Most ministry leaders have. Could it be these tensions stem from the fact the New Testament church did not have two separate groups of men—pastors and elders—with two separate functions? When a church *separates* the role of elder and pastor, it departs from the New Testament model.

Imagine a situation in which the elder board serves as the governing board for the church. The majority of their conversations focus on the finances, building, and oversight of the pastoral staff. The pastoral staff, on the other hand, functions as the spiritual leaders, teachers, and shepherds for the congregation. In this confusing situation elders are expected to govern, but without the spiritual authority of being "pastors." On the other side, pastors are expected to be the spiritual leaders of the congregation, but do not have final authority to make necessary decisions. And we wonder why there are so many conflicts between pastors and elders!

When we make this distinction between pastor and elder, we introduce unnecessary confusion into the leadership structure of God's church. Elders feel less important because they are not "pastors" and "spiritual leaders." Pastors feel less important because they do not have decision-making authority; and when they are called in to make a presentation at an elder's meeting it reminds them of going to the principal's office.

As we will discuss below, there is biblical precedent for elders/pastors serving alongside one another with different areas of emphasis in accordance with their spiritual gifts. But, the idea of two groups—one group of pastors and one group of elders—with one reporting to the other is foreign to the New Testament.

Deacons, however, serve under the spiritual and overall leadership of the elders. In some churches, this creates tension, competition, and jealousy. This is to be addressed, rather than avoided. It is not a biblical solution to avoid this conflict by establishing a single pastor model or by choosing not to have deacons. These challenges are all but guaranteed if the deacons do not understand and embrace their service as being under the shepherding oversight of the elders.

ELDERS IN THE EARLY CHURCH WERE MEN

Because of the dramatic victory of feminist philosophy in our culture, this has become an explosive issue. The Scriptures are filled with examples of women who served God and made a dramatic impact for Him in their homes, churches, and beyond. Amy and I are continually thankful for our Christian mothers who led us to Christ and raised us in the faith. As we will learn in the next section on family theology, women (wives, mothers, and others) travelled with Jesus and the disciples to support them in their ministry. In the early church, men and women functioned with equal importance, value, worth, and dignity. The notion that Christians teach male dominance and female subservience, male importance and female insignificance, is an unbiblical straw man erected by feminism in an effort to destroy the gospel. In every culture where Christianity takes root, women are elevated, protected, celebrated, and honored more than ever before.[5]

The question here is not whether or not women should have significant ministry in the local church. That question is almost too absurd to answer. Of course, they should! The question here is, "What has God said in the Bible about who should serve in the role of elder?"

In considering this question, we must hold firm to the doctrine of the sufficiency of Scripture. God has given us everything we need for the full and proper leadership of His local church. No other source of truth is necessary. If we were to "lock ourselves in a room with the Bible" and ask this question, what conclusion would we reach?

First, God has given us a consistent pattern of loving, godly, male leaders for His church. We can begin with Jesus, Himself. God incarnated Himself as a man. Jesus then chose twelve men to disciple and train. This pattern continues throughout the New Testament.

Second, the qualifications for the office of elder found in Titus 1 and 1 Timothy 3 specifically address men. To be qualified to be an elder one must be "the husband[6] of one wife" (Titus 1:6 and 1 Timothy 3:2).

Third, biblical elders teach the entire Bible to the entire church. Biblical elders have spiritual authority over the entire church. In 1 Timothy 2:12, God says through Paul, "I do not permit a woman to teach or to exercise authority over a man." If God says women should not preach the Bible to men in the local church, they could not practice the fundamental responsibility of the biblical elder.

As I said earlier, we may not reach the same conclusions, but are we committed to using the Bible and the Bible alone to reach those conclusions? I realize many volumes have been written on this. In college, I was trained in and walked in the principles of egalitarianism. After further study, I am now convinced those principles were rooted in culture rather than Scripture. For a careful exegetical study, I recommend *Recovering Biblical Manhood and Womanhood* by Grudem and Piper.[7]

Because of the spirit of feminism in our culture, when the statement is made "elders should be men" many people hear, "women are unimportant and men can rule the church with an iron fist." We must understand the second statement comes from our godless culture, not from any page of Scripture. God calls men to serve as mature, loving, humble, godly, servant-leaders of the local church, giving their lives if needed for the true proclamation of the gospel and the protection of the flock.

ELDERS IN THE EARLY CHURCH WERE MULTIPLE

Seeking to make church decisions using Scripture alone is treacherous! But, that is what we must do. Not only does God say elders/pastors in the local church must be men, but He also says they must be multiple.

God's local church is to be led by *at least* two pastors. God speaks with one voice on this issue so His people would have no confusion. In every instance where the word *elder* is used to refer to those leading a local church, the word is plural: *elders.* Here are some of the many examples:

> "... *be subject to the elders.*"—1 Peter 5:5

> "*Let him call for the elders of the church, and let them pray ...*"—James 5:14

> "... *appoint elders in every town as I directed you.*"—Titus 1:5[10]

> "*Let the elders who rule well be considered worthy of double honor.*"—1 Timothy 5:17

> "... *sending it to the elders by the hand of Barnabas and Saul.*"—Acts 11:30

> "*And when they had appointed elders for them in every church ...*"—Acts 14:23

Every time God speaks of the pastors/elders in regards to the local church, He speaks of them as plural. This is not to say that individual pastor/elders are not discussed. John speaks of himself as an *elder.*[11] Paul speaks of the qualifications that *each elder* is to have.[12] God also speaks through Paul about how the church should confront *an elder* if he is in sin.[13]

God's pattern and instruction on this issue is clear. His local church is to be led by a plurality of elders. There is no biblical evidence for a formal hierarchy among the pastors/elders or for different titles among the pastors/elders. Every elder is called to lead, protect, feed, and nurture the flock. However, pastoral teams in the early church divided duties among each other based on their gifts. All elders preached, but some preached more than others. All elders provided oversight, but some exercised their gifts in this area more than others did.[237]

While there was no "senior pastor" title in the early church, gifted leaders served as *first among equals.*

> Although elders are to act jointly as a council and share equal authority and responsibility for the leadership of the church, all elders are not equal in their giftedness, biblical knowledge, leadership ability, experience, or dedication. Therefore, those among the elders who are particularly gifted leaders and/or teachers will naturally stand out among the other elders as leaders and teachers within the leadership body.[15]

This pattern emerged with Jesus and his disciples. All the disciples were considered equals, but Jesus chose Peter, James, and John as unofficial yet genuine leaders of the leaders.

> Peter possessed no legal or official rank or title above the other eleven. They were not his subordinates. They were not his staff or team of assistants. He wasn't the apostles' "senior pastor."[16]

In the same way, Philip and Stephen stand out as leaders of the leaders of the seven chosen to serve in Acts 6. They were leaders because of their giftedness, not from a formal role or title. Paul did not have a superior rank to Barnabas, but he was looked to as a leader in the relationship because of his gifting.

> *"Let the elders who rule well be considered worthy of double honor, especially those who labor in preaching and teaching. For the Scripture says, 'You shall not muzzle an ox when it treads out the grain,' and, 'The laborer deserves his wages.'"*—1 Timothy 5:17–18

Some elders in the early church were paid others were not. Some served "full-time" while others were "tentmakers." They complimented each other based upon their gifts, calling, experience, and availability.

I fully realize the implications of what I am saying here. The vast majority of churches today are organized in a different manner than God prescribes in the New Testament. That brings us back to the basic question of this book. Is the Bible truly sufficient for every matter of faith and practice? Should what God has said in the Bible about *how* His local church is to be organized be seen as sufficient and binding for all believers, in all places, in all times? If we answer, "yes," then we must be willing to examine everything we do in light of Scripture alone.

ELDERS IN THE EARLY CHURCH WERE QUALIFIED

The early church identified men from within the church whose lives were marked by certain character traits and abilities to serve as pastors/elders. These character traits and abilities are given to us in 1 Timothy 3 and Titus 1:

> *"The saying is trustworthy: If anyone aspires to the office of overseer, he desires a noble task. Therefore an overseer must be above reproach, the husband of one wife, sober-minded, self-controlled, respectable, hospitable, able to teach, not a drunkard, not violent but gentle, not quarrelsome, not a lover of money. He must manage his own household well, with all dignity keeping his children submissive, for if someone does not know how to manage his own household, how will he care for God's church? He must not be a recent convert, or he may become puffed up with conceit and fall into the condemnation of the devil. Moreover, he must be well thought of by outsiders, so that he may not fall into disgrace, into a snare of the devil."—1 Timothy 3:1–7*

> *"This is why I left you in Crete, so that you might put what remained into order, and appoint elders in every town as I directed you—if anyone is above reproach, the husband of one wife, and his children are believers and not open to the charge of debauchery or insubordination. For an overseer, as God's steward, must be above reproach. He must not be arrogant or quick-tempered or a drunkard or violent or greedy for gain, but hospitable, a lover of good, self-controlled, upright, holy, and disciplined. He must hold firm to the trustworthy word as taught,*

so that he may be able to give instruction in sound doctrine and also to rebuke those who contradict it."—Titus 1:5–9

The first concern for potential elders was their spiritual leadership at home. If he is married, is he a dedicated husband? If he is a father, is he already serving as the pastor and shepherd of his children's souls? Does he already have a track record of teaching the Bible to his family? Is he leading his own home toward peace and godliness, or was his family a place of chaos and disobedience? Is his home a place where believers and non-believers are regularly welcomed for fellowship and ministry?

If a man is being considered for pastor/elder, spend time with his entire family. Spend time with his family at church. Spend time with his family in his home.

Potential elders are to be men already known for their character inside and outside the church.

He must have two particular areas of gifting: leadership[17] and teaching.[18] He must hold firmly to the unchanging gospel message. He must be able to instruct others in sound doctrine.[19] He must be able to rebuke those who contradict it. If a seminary degree equips a man for this kind of teaching, praise God for that training. If, however, because of the discipleship he has received and his love for the Word of God, he is able to do this without a seminary degree, he should not be disqualified.[20]

At first glance, it is easy to be overwhelmed by this list of qualifications. If this is the list, who could possibly be qualified to be a pastor? The answer is more simple than you think. Most men, who love the Lord, who study and believe His Word, and who are growing in godliness are qualified to serve.

Is it a super-human requirement for a man to be a faithful husband? Is it so rare to find a man who is self-controlled? Are most of the men in our churches drunkards? Is it too much to expect the men of our church not to love money more than God?

If you step back, you will see the list of pastoral qualifications are simply the basics of the Christian life. These are not character traits and abilities to which only pastors and elders are to aspire, but these are to be the Christian goals of godliness and ministry for *all* men. Is there any Christian man who is not called to lead his family? Is there any Christian man who is not called to love and be able to share God's Word with others?

The great disconnect in the list of qualifications has to do with family life. As we discussed earlier, the 20th century saw the tragic decline of the biblical family. We face a pastoral crisis in the local church, because in many churches only a minority of men are functioning as spiritual leaders at home. If a church is concerned about preparing future pastors, it must focus on preparing current husbands and fathers.

At the heart of God's plan to advance the Gospel is His creation of the local church. He created it with specific and limited responsibilities that are revealed to us in the pages of Scripture. In our next section we will turn our attention to another Gospel-advancing institution—the family.

Questions for Discussion:

1. What is the leadership structure of your local church? What titles are used? What is the path of authority and oversight?

2. Do you disagree with some of my conclusions in this chapter? What Scriptures lead you to your conclusions?

3. How could your local church begin moving toward the New Testament model of a simple plurality of pastors/elders?

ENDNOTES

[1] As noted in the earlier chapters on jurisdiction, it would be immoral for a local church to try and execute a murderer. Instead local churches are to equip Christians, who will serve as judges and government leaders, who are then charged by God to bring justice against wrongdoers. In this way, the local church equips believers to take dominion (see that God's will is accomplished) in every sphere of life.

[2] 2 Timothy 2:15.

[3] Alexander Strauch, *Biblical Eldership* (Littleton, CO: Lewis and Roth, 1995).

[4] Ephesians 4:12 also mentions apostles, prophets, and evangelists but these roles are not governing offices within the institution of a local church. For instance, an evangelist (which describes a particular type of ministry a Christian is called to) might also serve as a deacon within his local church. His ministry as an "evangelist" does not include formal shepherding responsibilities in the church.

[5]D. James Kennedy, *What if Jesus Had Never Been Born* (Nashville, TN: Thomas Nelson Publishers, 1994).

[6]Marriage was not a requirement for eldership, i.e. Paul.

[7]Wayne Grudem and John Piper, *Recovering Biblical Manhood and Womanhood* (Wheaton, IL: Crossway, 2005).

[8]http://www.auburn.edu/~allenkc/openhse/deaconship.html.

[9]Alexander Strauch, *Minister of Mercy, The New Testament Deacon* (Littleton, CO: Lewis and Roth, 1992).

[10]It appears from this text local churches had been established and were meeting together. Paul instructed the first thing that needed to be done in those churches was for qualified men to begin serving as elders. With this principle in mind, it would be possible for a local church to be established in a new community without first identifying two men to serve as elders. However, it is urgent and necessary that qualified men begin serving as elders as quickly as possible.

[11]2 John 1:1.

[12]Titus 1 and 1 Timothy 3.

[13]1 Timothy 5:19.

[14]1 Timothy 5:17–18.

[15]Alexander Strauch, *The Biblical Eldership Booklet* (Littleton, CO: Lewis and Roth, 1987) 14–15.

[16]Ibid.

[17]1 Timothy 3:1, the term overseer is fundamentally a leadership word.

[18]Titus 1:5.

[19]It is helpful to note the essential difference in the list of qualifications between elders and deacons is elders must be able to teach the whole counsel of God and refute those who oppose it.

[20]There is an increasing openness to men who do not have seminary degrees serving as pastors. On one hand, this is a good thing because there is no New Testament requirement for a man to have a formal degree to serve as a pastor/elder. However, this is often taking place because of a reduced emphasis on expository preaching and refuting false teaching in the church. Whether their training is formal or informal, elders need to be fully trained in the whole counsel of God, able to teach it, and able to refute those who deny it.

SECTION 4:

GOD'S MISSION FOR THE FAMILY

CHAPTER 11:
FAMILY MINISTRY IN THE TORAH

"Only take care, and keep your soul diligently, lest you forget the things your eyes have seen, and lest they depart from your heart all the days of your life. Make them known to your children and your children's children."

—DEUTERONOMY 4:9

In this fourth section of the book, we will focus our attention on the divine institution of family. What is the purpose of family? What connection is there between the Great Commission and the Christian home? How does the temporary institution of the family build God's everlasting Church? We will begin in the Torah, the first five books of the Old Testament.

FAMILY MINISTRY

During the past ten years, family ministry has become a hot topic. The Holy Spirit is on the move! Conferences, books, curriculum, and family programming are popping up everywhere. However, it is easy to begin the journey of family ministry with the wrong foundation.

It is true that the majority of kids growing up in our churches today are leaving the faith when they become adults. It is true some youth and children's leaders are questioning the effectiveness of our modern ministry methods. Yet these are not the primary reasons to begin family ministry and put parents back in the primary role of the spiritual training of their children. We should not embrace a parent-centered model of next-generation ministry because it will work better—but rather because parent-centered, family-integrated ministry comes to us from the pages of Scripture.

Some churches start family ministry because there are one or more people on staff who are passionate about it. They get the ball rolling and make some program changes, but family ministry is just one more thing on the already over-full church calendar. When those staff members leave, or lose their passion for family ministry, the new initiatives are abandoned. Family ministry should not be driven by bad statistics or a passionate leader, but by a thorough, Bible-driven theology of family.

My prayer is that in reading this section you will become convinced that the Great Commission and the institution of the family are inseparable. For the first ten years of my pastoral ministry, I had no theology of family, and as a result, I had an anemic view of God's redemptive strategy.

TOWARD A THEOLOGY OF FAMILY

In the next few chapters, we are going to take a "power-walk" through the Bible, from Genesis to Revelation, to see what God has said about His Kingdom purposes for the family. As we take this journey, three theological foundations will emerge.[1]

Foundation #1: God created families to be discipleship centers.

God did not create the family simply to provide food, shelter, clothing, and companionship. The family is a spiritual institution with a spiritual purpose. God created the family for "disciple making."

There is a lot of talk in the evangelical church today about the importance of discipleship small groups. You have heard the buzz lines:

"We need to do life together."

"Discipleship happens in the context of relationships."

"We need to return to authentic community."

God loves discipleship small groups. He just has another name for them. He calls them families. He wants every person to be born into the ultimate discipleship small group—a Christian family. It is the most powerful "group" where life-change happens. Family is where we "do life" together. God desires the relationships in our families to spur one another on toward Christ. Are you looking for authentic community? Are you looking for people to be real and genuine? You will find those things at home. Family life is the ultimate in authenticity! It may not be good, but it is authentic. God created the family to shape the heart of every member of the family with a deep and abiding love for Christ and for His Word.

Foundation #2: The biblical purpose of parenting and grand parenting is to impress the hearts of children with a love for God.

Many parents have wondered, "God, why did you give me these children?" It is vital we understand the answer to the question. God gives children to human mothers and fathers with the calling on those parents to do all in their power to impress the hearts of their children with a love for God and to equip them to make a difference in the world for Christ. But this mission is not for this world alone. Our greatest desire is to see our children spend eternity with their Heavenly Father!

Foundation #3: God created the family as an essential engine of world evangelization through the power of multi-generational faithfulness.

God's desire is to fill the Earth, and ultimately the New Earth, with worshippers of Christ. The Bible teaches that a primary means of accomplishing this is those who love Him will raise their children to love Him, who in turn will raise their children to love Him. God created the family to advance the gospel and the Great Commission. The Bible paints a picture of larger-generation after larger-generation going forth to fill the Earth with worship and being a blessing to all nations.

These three foundations run throughout the Bible and up until the late 1800s were preached and taught regularly as a "theology of family."[2] We rarely even use that phrase anymore. Let's begin our power-walk in the first five books of the Old Testament (the Torah) and discover what God has said about His special creation of the family.

THE FIRST COMMANDMENT

What were the first words God spoke to Adam and Eve? We find them in Genesis 1:28.

> "And God blessed them. And God said to them, 'Be fruitful and multiply and fill the earth and subdue it and have dominion over the fish of the sea and over the birds of the heavens and over every living thing that moves on the earth.'"

When was the last time you or your pastor preached a sermon on the first commandment? In my experience, this text is rarely mentioned. Here in the beginning, God shares with us His grand plan. He reveals what He wants, the purpose of His creation, and what our role is to be on the earth. What does God want? He wants the earth filled with people who will love Him, and worship Him. God's desire is that His children will take dominion over the entire earth by honoring His sovereign power and holiness in every sphere of life. He wanted this in the beginning, and He wants the same thing today. With God's first words we find a global "Great Commission" and we also find the family. How can the earth become filled with worship? God created marriage, and thereby the family, as the core engine for filling the earth with His people. God's plan is to fill the earth, with each generation larger than the one before.

A RIGHTEOUS FAMILY

Adam and Eve were faithful to God's command and had many children[3], grandchildren, and beyond. But because of their rebellion, and the rebellion of their offspring, ten generations later[4] the earth was not filled with worship, but with evil.

> *"The Lord saw that the wickedness of man was great in the earth, and that every intention of the thoughts of his heart was only evil continually."*—Genesis 6:5

This was the most wicked time in human history and will never be repeated. In God's sovereign plan, He chose to begin again with a righteous family. He chose Noah, his wife, their three sons, and their wives.

God did not begin again with a righteous individual, but with a righteous family. When you read the story of Noah's Ark in a child's story Bible, the pictures are usually wrong. There is old man Noah out in the field by himself building the ark. Perhaps there is a group of people off to the side laughing at him.

But Noah did not serve God alone. Building an ark of that size by himself would have been virtually impossible. God saved Noah and his wife, along with their three sons and their wives. Noah's family is mentioned on ten separate occasions between Genesis chapters 6–9. God called a family of eight, as a righteous remnant, to continue God's plan to fill the earth with His people.

AGAIN, BE FRUITFUL

After Noah's family left the ark, they worshiped God.

> *"And God blessed Noah and his sons and said to them, 'Be fruitful and multiply and fill the earth.'"*—Genesis 9:1

God's will has not changed. He wants the earth filled with His people and filled with His worship. How is this going to happen? Godly families will raise godly children, generation after generation, and fill the earth.

MULTI-GENERATIONAL COVENANTS

When we think of the covenants in Scripture, we tend to think of individual people. (God's covenant with Abraham, God's covenant with Moses, etc.) But God describes many of these covenants as explicitly multigenerational.

> *"Then God said to Noah and to his sons with him, 'Behold, I establish my covenant with you and your offspring after you . . .'"*—Genesis 9:8–9

To Abraham, God said:

> *"I will establish my covenant between me and you and your offspring after you throughout their generations for an everlasting covenant, to be God to you and to your offspring after you."*—Genesis 17:7

Because of our loss of multi-generational thinking, we wrongly reduce these biblical covenants to promises God made with individual men. Look again at Genesis 17:7. Three times in just one verse, God emphasizes that His plan for the world is a family, extended family, and multi-generational plan.

GOD'S MISSION FOR ABRAHAM

Why did God choose Abraham? What mission did He have for him? In Genesis 18 God gives us a beautiful summary.

> *"Abraham shall surely become a great and mighty nation, and all the nations of the earth shall be blessed in him."*—Genesis 18:18

This echoes God's earlier calls to Abraham in Genesis 12 and 15. Abraham will be blessed so that he would be a blessing to the nations! God's mission for

Abraham was a macro, global plan. We, as Abraham's spiritual children, are a part of that same plan today.

But what did God want Abraham to do in response to this global vision? What was Abraham's specific calling? This mission has been in effect for 4000 years. Abraham was alive on earth for a small portion of the mission. What could Abraham do, as an individual man in a particular time in history, to advance the global mission of God? The next verse answers the question.

> *"For I have chosen him, that he may command his children and his household after him to keep the way of the Lord by doing righteousness and justice,* so that *the Lord may bring to Abraham what he has promised him."*—Genesis 18:19[5]

How could Abraham advance this global mission of God? By making his family a discipleship center.[6] His task was to disciple his children and his household and to lead them in righteousness and justice. This was the key assignment, given to Abraham by God, "so that the LORD may bring to Abraham what He has promised him."

THE TEN COMMANDMENTS

In Exodus 20, at Mount Sinai, God writes His Ten Commandments into the rock.

The first four commandments are "vertical" in that they have to do with our relationship with God. The last six commandments are "horizontal" in that they focus us on human relationships. The fifth commandment, therefore, is the first commandment for human/horizontal relationships.

> *"Honor your father and your mother, that your days may be long in the land that the LORD your God is giving you."*—Exodus 20:12

God wrote these commands Himself. He put them into a particular order. I don't know about you, but if I were writing these down, I think I would put "do not murder" and "do not commit adultery" before "honor your father and your mother." Not murdering would be a safe place to start when talking about how we should relate to each other. But that was not what God did. The first command He gave for human relationships was "honor your father and your mother."

I don't pretend to know all the reasons God had for this particular order, but one seems clear. The command to honor parents is the first moral decision we face in our lives. My five-year-old daughter, Milly, is not struggling with the "do not commit adultery" commandment right now. There may as well be nine commandments as far as she is concerned. But she is confronted with the moral choice of the fifth commandment a hundred times a day. Will she honor her mother? Will she honor her father?

Paul says, in Ephesians 6, that the fifth commandment is the first commandment with a promise.

> " 'Honor your father and mother' (this is the first commandment with a promise), 'that it may go well with you and that you may live long in the land.' "—Ephesians 6:2–3

This promise troubled me for many years. This is God's Word. A promise is a promise. This obviously means if a person honors their father and their mother that they are going to live a long life. So, if a person dies young, does that mean they didn't honor their parents? I am not comfortable with that. Can I really stand up in a pulpit and tell young people if they honor their parents, God promises they will live to old age? During my years in youth ministry here is how I solved this tension. I would say something like, "If you honor your parents, God will bless you." Sounds good! You can't argue with that, right?

Unfortunately, I was reducing a promise from God into some sort of general truth or generic proverb. The key in approaching this passage is to understand that the Ten Commandments were not written with an individual mindset, but with a communal mindset.[7] These are commands for the faith community, not just individual followers of God. So the promise is not that individuals who honor their parents are guaranteed long life on earth. Rather, if parents will follow God, and if children will honor their parents, and receive their spiritual heritage . . . God promises that the people of God will live long in the land! If the families within a local church evangelize and disciple their own children, that local church will live long in the land.

This is a lock-tight promise from the Creator Himself. It has been rightly said that Christianity is always one generation away from extinction. Do you want to see the Church of Jesus Christ grow and fill the earth with worshippers of God? It starts with parents loving and following God, and children honoring their parents by following in their footsteps of faith.

THE GREAT COMMANDMENT

In Matthew 22:35–38 a Jewish leader challenged Jesus with a powerful question:

> *"And one of them, a lawyer, asked him a question to test him. 'Teacher, which is the great commandment in the Law?' And he said to him, 'You shall love the Lord your God with all your heart and with all your soul and with all your mind. This is the great and first commandment.'"*—Matthew 22:35–38

What a question! Jesus, if you had to boil down God's Word into one commandment, what would it be? The Lord answered from Deuteronomy 6:5. Here we find the purpose of our lives. We glorify God by loving Him with our whole being!

But what does this Great Commandment look like in everyday life? Where do we start? In the verses that follow the Great Commandment in Deuteronomy 6, God gives His people a Gospel mission and a specific way to put that Gospel mission into action.

> *"You shall love the Lord your God with all your heart and with all your soul and with all your might. And these words that I command you today shall be on your heart. You shall teach them diligently to your children, and shall talk of them when you sit in your house, and when you walk by the way, and when you lie down, and when you rise."*—Deuteronomy 6:5–7

Immediately following the Great Commandment, God focuses our attention on family life. He speaks specifically to parents to live out their love for Him by doing all in their power to pass their faith to their children. Are we serious about loving God? Then we must be serious about teaching God's Word diligently to our children. This is the first mission God gives to us after the most important commandment in the Bible. Here we find the purpose of parenting and grand parenting: to impress the hearts of our children with a love for God. At the heart of the Great Commandment and Great Commission is family discipleship, with parents being the primary spiritual trainers of their children.

But how does this work? How can I, as a sinful man with character problems, pass faith and a love for God to my children? Is there a magic formula or six simple steps?

There are no magic formulas, but God gives us a specific, concrete starting point in verse 7.

"[You] shall talk of them when you sit in your house, and when you walk by the way, and when you lie down, and when you rise."

What can parents do to embrace this mission of impressing the hearts of their children with a love for God? Talk! Specifically, God calls heads of households to bring the family together in the home for what is referred to in Christian history as "family worship." "You shall talk of [the Word of God] when you sit in your house." Family worship is the time when a family gathers for prayer, Bible reading, and spiritual conversation.

In verse 5, God gives us the most important commandment in His Word, to love Him with our whole being. He then makes it practical. If you love Me, you will read and talk about My Word at home with your family.

In 2004, I had to face the reality that my schedule did not allow for regular family worship in my home. This plain instruction from God convicted me that the schedule I had chosen was causing me to sin, and was preventing me from practicing the first specific thing God has required of me in response to the greatest of all His commandments.

God then proceeds to give three more power-packed moments of the day when families have special opportunities to grow in faith together:

- When you walk by the way (during transition times)
- When you lie down (when you end your day)
- When you rise (when you start your day)

We will expand on the centrality of family worship in a later chapter.

MARRIAGE AND THE GOSPEL

In the next chapter of Deuteronomy, God continues to reveal His will and plan to the people of Israel. In Deuteronomy 6, God links His Kingdom plan to parents, their children, and spiritual life within the family. In Deuteronomy 7, God links His Kingdom plan to marriage. The Israelites were preparing to enter the Promised Land. God gave the Israelites specific instructions in regards to how they should relate to the Canaanites and other inhabitants of the land. God said,

"You shall not intermarry with them, giving your daughters to their sons or taking their daughters for your sons . . ."—Deuteronomy 7:3

This commandment is echoed in 2 Corinthians 6:14, when God says His people should not be "unequally yoked." But why was God concerned about the marriages of the Israelites? Doesn't God have larger, big-picture, Kingdom concerns? Are there really dire consequences if the people of God marry outside the faith? According to God, yes! In the next verse, God explained His reason for this particular commandment.

". . . For they would turn away your sons from following me, to serve other gods."—Deuteronomy 7:4

Once again, we see God's heart, passion, and priority for multi-generational faithfulness. He wants the earth filled with His people and for families to pass their faith to their children. The marriage relationship is at the heart of the home, and has powerful spiritual impact on the next generation.

BLESSINGS, CURSES, AND YOUR CHILDREN

Toward the end of the book of Deuteronomy, God lays out the blessings that await His people if they will obey Him, and the curses that await them if they disobey.

"I call heaven and earth to witness against you today, that I have set before you life and death, blessing and curse. Therefore choose life, that you and your offspring may live, loving the Lord your God, obeying his voice and holding fast to him, for he is your life and length of days, that you may dwell in the land that the Lord swore to your fathers, to Abraham, to Isaac, and to Jacob, to give them."—Deuteronomy 30:19–20

God sets before the people life and death, blessing and curse. He shows them the path of obedience, and the path of rebellion. Why should they choose the path of obedience? Is it so they can reap the blessings of God alone? No! "Choose life, that you and your offspring may live." God continues to turn our hearts to His multi-generational mission.

Far too often, we talk about our faith as a "personal relationship with Jesus." This phrase is used to describe the intimacy Christ wants in His relationship with us. But one of the downsides of a phrase like this, is it implies my relationship with God is about me. As a result we think individually, when we should also be thinking multi-generationally. Why should we choose life? Because the souls of our children and grandchildren will be radically affected by our decision! God is filling the earth with His worship, generation after generation, and God says that my decisions will ripple through the generations to come.

MOSES' FINAL PLEA

Moses has reached the end of his mission. God has used Moses most importantly to write down, for all people for all time, the words of God.[78] After all the years of joy, suffering, struggle, and victory, what would Moses say?

> *"Moses came and recited all the words of this song in the hearing of the people, he and Joshua the son of Nun. And when Moses had finished speaking all these words to all Israel, he said to them, 'Take to heart all the words by which I am warning you today, that you may command them to your children, that they may be careful to do all the words of this law. For it is no empty word for you, but your very life, and by this word you shall live long in the land that you are going over the Jordan to possess.'"*—Deuteronomy 32:44–47

Why was it so important for the people of Israel to "take to heart all the words" of God? It was not simply so they would love and serve Him. It was not a personal mission to which they were called. They were called to a multi-generational Great Commission. Moses pleaded with the people to love and obey God's Word so they could lead their children.

If the men and women of Israel didn't know and love the words of God, they could not fulfill their most important spiritual mission, which was to pass their faith to their children and grandchildren.

GOD'S KINGDOM AND THE FAMILY

In the beginning, God revealed His plan to fill the earth with His worshippers. How could this grand plan possibly happen? God created the family. In this chapter, we lightly skimmed over the first five books of the Old Testament. In the next chapter, we will power-walk through the rest of the Old Testament as we continue to explore the relationship between God's Kingdom and the family.

Questions for discussion:

1. When was the last time "the first commandment" from Genesis 1 was preached at your church?

2. What words would you use you describe your "theology of family?"

3. Which Scripture in this chapter was most impactful for you?

ENDNOTES

[1]These chapters are designed to address a few of the key theological foundations of family. I am not attempting a comprehensive treatment of the subject.

[2]We will review this historical evidence in chapter 12.

[3]Genesis 5:4.

[4]Genesis 5 records 10 generations from Adam to Noah.

[5]Italics mine.

[6]God called Abraham in Genesis 12:1 to "Go from your country and your kindred and your father's house to the land that I will show you." Abraham did not wander off alone into the wilderness. It was a family mission. He set out with his wife, his nephew, along with his entire household of servants.

[7]Thanks to my friend Pastor Baucham for helping me understand this exegetical key.

[8]Moses wrote the Pentateuch, the first five books of the Old Testament.

CHAPTER 12:
FAMILY MINISTRY IN THE OLD TESTAMENT

"For Ezra had set his heart to study the Law of the Lord, and to do it and to teach his statutes and rules in Israel."

—Ezra 7:10

I n skimming through the first five books of the Old Testament, we have seen God repeatedly demonstrate His plan for the temporary institution of the family to build His everlasting Kingdom. As we proceed into the rest of the Old Testament, God's mission and methods remain the same.

AS FOR ME AND MY HOUSE

Before Moses died, he pleaded with the people to disciple their children and to live with multi-generational vision. Joshua, Moses' disciple, ended his ministry with the same message.

> *"Now therefore fear the Lord and serve him in sincerity and in faithfulness. Put away the gods that your fathers served beyond the River and in Egypt, and serve the Lord. And if it is evil in your eyes to serve the Lord, choose this day whom you will serve, whether the gods your fathers served in the region beyond the River, or the gods of the Amorites in whose land you dwell. But as for me and my house, we will serve the Lord."*—Joshua 24:14–15

Joshua first turns the people's attention to the spiritual lives of their parents and grandparents. According to verse 23, some of the Israelites were continuing to worship the idols and pagan deities of Egypt. Now they would be tempted to worship the false gods of the Amorites who they had failed to drive out of the Promised Land. The people of Israel had a choice to make. Who would they worship? Who would they serve? But this choice was not to be a "personal" one, as if the community of Israel was made up of individuals. Joshua, as the head of his household, makes a family choice. Does God seek our personal and individual faithfulness? Yes, but our personal faithfulness is a part of His larger plan for family faithfulness, multi-generational faithfulness, and filling the earth with His worshipers.[1]

THE TRAGIC ERA OF THE JUDGES

If only the Israelites had done what Moses had said! If only the people had followed Joshua's example and led their entire families in the worship of God! Not long after Joshua spoke these words to the people, Joshua and his generation died. This began a terrible chapter in the history of God's people. The book of Judges is filled with rebellion, judgment, violence, and despair. God brought seasons of repentance and victory, but they were short-lived. In Judges 2, God explains why this happened.

> *"And all that generation also were gathered to their fathers. And there arose another generation after them who did not know the LORD or the work that he had done for Israel. And the people of Israel did what was evil in the sight of the LORD and served the Baals. And they abandoned the LORD, the God of their fathers, who had brought them out of the land of Egypt. They went after other gods, from among the gods of the peoples who were around them, and bowed down to them. And they provoked the LORD to anger."*—Judges 2:10–12

I feel sick reading these words. God had miraculously led His people out of Egypt and through the wilderness. Moses had pleaded with them to take to heart all the words of God, so that they could disciple their children. Joshua called them to serve God as families and commit themselves to God's multi-generational Kingdom mission. But what happened? Apparently, Joshua's generation did not pass their faith to their children. These were the grandchildren of those who crossed the Red Sea! Yet what does the Lord say about them? "And there arose another generation after them who did not know the LORD or the work that he had done for Israel." This is hard to believe. The grandchildren of Moses' generation did not know the Lord. They didn't know about the plagues. They didn't know about the defeat of Pharaoh. They didn't know about the pillar of cloud and the pillar of fire. They didn't know about the law of God and all the events at Mount Sinai.

In the next verse God tells us the immediate result of this generational disaster. "And the people of Israel did what was evil in the sight of the LORD and served the Baals." The Israelites then enter one of the most difficult and unstable periods in their history.

MULTI-GENERATIONAL VISION IN THE PSALMS

The Psalms and Proverbs are filled with God's words about family life. In Psalm 78, God gives us a powerful picture of parents and grandparents discipling their children.

> *"Give ear, O my people, to my teaching; incline your ears to the words of my mouth! I will open my mouth in a parable; I will utter dark sayings from of old, things that we have heard and known, that our fathers have told us. We will not hide them from their children, but tell to the coming generation the glorious deeds of the Lord, and his might, and the wonders that he has done. He established a testimony in Jacob and appointed a law in Israel, which he commanded our fathers to teach to their children, that the next generation might know them, the children yet unborn, and arise and tell them to their children, so that they should set their hope in God and not forget the works of God, but keep his commandments; and that they should not be like their fathers, a stubborn and rebellious generation, a generation whose heart was not steadfast, whose spirit was not faithful to God."—Psalm 78:1–8*

What a marvelous vision! I want to be a father like this. I want to tell my children all about the glorious deeds of the Lord, so that they would tell their children. Then I pray that their children, who are not even born yet, will tell their children. God wants His Gospel to advance throughout the coming generations of my family. Parents and grandparents are called to passionately tell their children the wonders God has done. We don't want our children to end up like the generation after Joshua.

FAMILY DISCIPLESHIP IN PROVERBS

When I read Proverbs during my devotion time, I often think of what I am reading as God's words of wisdom for me. While this is certainly true, the majority of the book of Proverbs is a picture of family discipleship. Most of the proverbs were written by King Solomon to his sons. How many of us have written down the spiritual lessons we want our children to hold on to? That is what Solomon did. Not only was Solomon supernaturally gifted with wisdom, but also he learned extraordinary lessons through his dramatic obedience and disobedience to God throughout his life. So while these are the eternal words of God, for all people, in all places, and in all times, they are also the words of a real father, written to a real son.

> *"Hear, my son, your father's instruction, and forsake not your mother's teaching."*—Proverbs 1:8

> *"My son, keep my words and treasure up my commandments with you."*—Proverbs 7:1

> *"Buy truth, and do not sell it; buy wisdom, instruction, and understanding. The father of the righteous will greatly rejoice; he who fathers a wise son will be glad in him. Let your father and mother be glad; let her who bore you rejoice. My son, give me your heart, and let your eyes observe my ways."*—Proverbs 23:23–26

Solomon knows the path to godliness for his son is honoring his father and mother. Solomon, the father, asks his son to give him his heart. He knows he can't disciple his son without his heart, without a personal relationship with him. He intentionally sets out to have his son learn the lessons from his life. Observe my ways! Learn from my disastrous sin. Learn from the grace God has given me.

Proverbs 31 stands out as a unique chapter. Most of the previous 30 chapters were written from father to son, but this chapter on "the excellent wife" stands apart. Where did the words of Proverbs 31 come from? This vision of a godly wife was originally given from a mother to her son. Here is how the chapter begins:

> *"The words of King Lemuel, An oracle that his mother taught him."*—Proverbs 31:1

Proverbs 31 provides us with a historical model of a mother who purposefully set out to explain to her son what godly womanhood looked like. Did your mother do this for you? If you are a mother with a son, have you studied what the Bible says about godly womanhood? Have you communicated that vision to your son, so he will be equipped to find a woman like that? Have you communicated that vision to your daughter to guide her toward becoming this kind of woman?

Throughout the book of Proverbs God connects wisdom and righteous living with family life.

THE REFRAIN OF KINGS AND CHRONICLES

The books of 1 and 2 Kings and 1 and 2 Chronicles provide a historical overview of the divided kingdoms of Israel and Judah. The northern Kingdom of Israel fell to the Assyrians in 722 B.C. and the southern Kingdom of Judah fell to the Babylonians in 586 B.C. The historical facts God has given us for this period are structured around the rise and fall of the kings of Israel and Judah.

The true history for each king is given, and then God provides an evaluation of that particular king's reign. Most of the accounts conclude with the same question—how did this king relate to his father? Repeatedly, God shows His priority on generational faithfulness. God cast His multi-generational mission and vision to Solomon:

> *"And as for you [Solomon], if you will walk before me, as David your father walked, with integrity of heart and uprightness, doing according to all that I have commanded you, and keeping my statutes and my rules, then I will establish your royal throne over Israel forever, as I promised David your father, saying, 'You shall not lack a man on the throne of Israel.' But if you turn aside from following me, you or your children, and do not keep my commandments and my statutes that I have set before you, but go and serve other gods and worship them, then I will cut off Israel from the land that I have given them, and the house that I have consecrated for my name I will cast out of my sight, and Israel will become a proverb and a byword among all peoples."*—1 Kings 9:4–7

God calls Solomon to see his faith and his mission in the world in relationship to his father David, and to his own children. Follow in the footsteps of your father! Then do all in your power to lead your children to follow after you! Solomon was called to a multi-generational, Great Commission, Kingdom mission. Sadly, both Solomon and his children fell away from the Lord, and the kingdom was split in two.[2]

In the centuries that followed, many kings came to power in Israel and Judah. Here are the words God chose to judge and evaluate these men.

"And he[Abijam] walked in all the sins that his father did before him, and his heart was not wholly true to the LORD his God, as the heart of David his father."—1 Kings 15:3

"And Asa did what was right in the eyes of the LORD, as David his father had done."—1 Kings 15:11

"He [Nadab] did what was evil in the sight of the LORD and walked in the way of his father, and in his sin which he made Israel to sin."—1 Kings 15:26

"He [Baasha] did what was evil in the sight of the LORD and walked in the way of Jeroboam and in his sin which he made Israel to sin."—1 Kings 15:34

"For he [Omri] walked in all the way of Jeroboam the son of Nebat, and in the sins that he made Israel to sin . . ."—1 Kings 16:26

In speaking of these kings, God repeatedly judges them in contrast to their fathers. God promised His blessings for generational faithfulness. He promised His judgment for generational disobedience, and it was not long before He used the Assyrians and Babylonians to execute it.

WHY GOD HATES DIVORCE

The Old Testament ends with the book of Malachi. In chapter 2, we find a commonly quoted phrase, "God hates divorce." This is the only portion of the text Christians usually mention. I have some personal understanding of why God hates this. My mother was divorced twice, and my father four times. My family tree, needless to say, is a little complicated.

My concern is that Christians do not take the time to look carefully enough at this text to understand why God hates divorce. Why is righteous, one-hearted marriage so important to God? In the three verses that proceed Malachi 2:16, God gives us the bigger picture.

". . . You weep and wail because he no longer pays attention to your offerings or accepts them with pleasure from your hands. You ask, "Why?" It is because the LORD is acting as the witness between you and the wife of your youth, because you have broken faith with her, though she is your partner, the wife of your marriage covenant. Has

not the LORD made them one? In flesh and spirit they are his. And why one?"—Malachi 2:13–15a (NIV, 1984)

God poses the question. Why one? What's the big deal with marital unity? Verse 15 continues:

"Because he [God] was seeking godly offspring. So guard yourself in your spirit and do not break faith with the wife of your youth. 'I hate divorce,' says the LORD God of Israel."—Malachi 2:15b–16 (NIV, 1984)

Marriage is a disciple-making institution. Marriage is all about the Great Commission. Husband and wife are to lead and help each other grow spiritually, and together they are to make it their top mission priority to "make disciples" of their children. In this text, God's concern about divorce is related to the damage divorce does to the next generation.

FINAL WORDS

God concludes His revelation in the Old Testament with Malachi 4:4–6:

"Remember the law of my servant Moses, the statutes and rules that I commanded him at Horeb for all Israel. 'Behold, I will send you Elijah the prophet before the great and awesome day of the LORD comes. And he will turn the hearts of fathers to their children and the hearts of children to their fathers, lest I come and strike the land with a decree of utter destruction.'"—Malachi 4:4–6

Four hundred years before Christ, God speaks through Malachi to prophesy the coming of the Messiah. It is the ultimate expression of the Father's love for His children. Once again, God connects His plan of salvation with the institution of the family. At this time, the Holy Spirit will work in such a powerful way that the hearts of fathers will be turned to their children. Fathers will overflow with love, passion, and commitment to their sons and daughters, and the hearts of children will turn back to their fathers.

BEGINNING TO END

In the beginning, God proclaimed His plan to fill the earth with His worshippers. From the beginning, His institution of the family was connected to this global Great Commission. Here in God's last words for this era of revelation, His "great and awesome" plan of redemption is connected to the discipling power of family, and to the relationship between fathers and their children.

Questions for Discussion:

1. Which Scriptures in this chapter were most helpful to you in understanding the connection between God's plan for the world and His institution of the family?

2. In what ways do you see Satan attacking both the institution of the family, and particular families in the world today?

3. What passage of Scripture from this chapter do you want to go back to and study more carefully?

ENDNOTES

[1] Joshua serves as an example of how a godly man can serve in a position of governmental leadership and encourage faithfulness in a nation. Second, in his role as "governmental leader" of Israel, Joshua provides an example of providing religious freedom. He tells the people they are free to choose whom they will serve, and at the same time announces the decision he has made, with his family, to follow the one true God.

[2] 1 Kings 11:1–8.

CHAPTER 13:
FAMILY MINISTRY IN THE GOSPELS (PART 1)

"When Jesus saw his mother and the disciple whom he loved standing
nearby, he said to his mother, "Woman, behold, your son!"
Then he said to the disciple, "Behold, your mother!"
And from that hour the disciple took her to his own home."

—JOHN 19:26–27

I n the many conversations I have had with people about family ministry, I often hear people say, "Sure, the family was a big deal in the Old Testament, but when we come to the New Testament the role of the family is reduced and the local church takes over."

It is true that after Christ's ascension, God establishes the institution of the local church. But as we will see, God's original purpose and design for the family continues to be elevated throughout the New Testament. This is not to say that the family is more important than the local church. In fact, the local church has jurisdiction over the Christian family, and is required by God to protect, nurture, equip, and keep the family accountable to function as God intended. But just as the institution of the family is a temporary creation of God for the purpose of building His eternal Church, the local church is also a temporary creation of God for the same purpose.

Gospel Fellowship Church, where I serve as one of the pastor/elders, will no longer exist as an identifiable church in Heaven. In the same way, the Rienow family will no longer exist as an identifiable group in Heaven. God has created temporary families and temporary local churches to accomplish different aspects of His Great Commission to build His eternal Church.

As we skim across the New Testament, we will continue to see the Kingdom-power and spiritual importance of the Christian family. In this chapter on the

Gospels, I have chosen to generally follow a Gospel harmony rather than examine each of the four books separately. In this way, we can see the chronological flow of God's words related to family life through this portion of salvation history.

THE SEED OF THE WOMAN

Matthew begins his Gospel with the genealogical record of Joseph. Luke, early in his Gospel, includes the genealogical record of Mary. When we read our Bibles, these are frequently sections we skip over. But "all Scripture is breathed out by God"[1] and "every word of God proves true."[2]

The Gospels bring us face to face with the person and work of the Messiah. Everything in the Old Testament has been moving toward this point. When the spiritual battle was declared in Genesis 3:15, God said the seed of the woman would strike the head of the serpent. The Messiah would come into the world through the human family. He would be a real baby, who would grow into a real man, who would deal the deathblow to sin, death, and the devil.

Matthew begins his account of salvation history with a family history. Take a moment and read through the list. There are some impressive names here: Abraham, Ruth, David, and Josiah. We would expect no less for King Jesus! But a closer look reveals names such as: Rahab the prostitute, Rehoboam the rebel, and Manasseh the murderer[3]. This genealogy is a testament to God's sovereignty and His grace working through a sinful family tree.

LAST WORDS, FIRST WORDS

The first historical event recorded in the New Testament focuses on a member of Jesus' extended family[4], a man named Zechariah. Zechariah was a priest, and one day while he was ministering at the temple, the angel Gabriel appeared to him. Gabriel's words were the first words of divine revelation since God spoke through Malachi 400 years earlier. The angel spoke to Zechariah about the baby who would soon be growing in his barren wife's womb.

> *"And he will turn many of the children of Israel to the LORD their God, and he will go before him in the spirit and power of Elijah, to turn the hearts of the fathers to their children, and the disobedient to the wisdom of the just, to make ready for the Lord a people prepared."—* Luke 1:16–17

Do you remember the last words God had spoken 400 years earlier? He promised one would come like Elijah and the hearts of fathers would be turned to their children. In John the Baptist that promise was fulfilled. When we think of the ministry of John the Baptist, we tend to stick with the big picture, which is that he came to prepare the hearts of people for Messiah. But what was John's method? How did he do this? According to the angel, part of John's mission was to call fathers to turn their hearts to their children. Why? Because when fathers turn their hearts to their children, the hearts of both children and their fathers are prepared for Messiah.

Four hundred years earlier, God made it clear His sovereign plan of salvation history was connected to fathers and their children, and with His first words, here in the New Testament He tells us His plan has not changed.

THE ANCIENT BATTLE

The battle between the seed of the serpent and the seed of the woman was dramatically renewed immediately after the birth of Jesus. How would the forces of evil seek to stop God's plan of salvation?

> *"Then Herod, when he saw that he had been tricked by the wise men, became furious, and he sent and killed all the male children in Bethlehem and in all that region who were two years old or under."—* Matthew 2:16

From ancient times until our present day, demonic evil and a hatred for the fruit of the womb go together. In his attempt to thwart God, Pharaoh killed babies. Here, Herod did the same. Satan and his demons continue to hate babies, and seek their murder through abortion and infanticide. In the beginning God said, "be fruitful and multiply," so it should not surprise us that Satan does all in his power to prevent that from happening.

BROTHERS CALLED TO FOLLOW

In the Old Testament, God often called siblings to partner together to advance His Kingdom.[5] Jesus followed this same pattern in choosing His disciples.

> *"While walking by the Sea of Galilee, he saw two brothers, Simon (who is called Peter) and Andrew his brother, casting a net into the sea, for they were fishermen. And he said to them, 'Follow me, and I will make*

you fishers of men.' Immediately they left their nets and followed him. And going on from there he saw two other brothers, James the son of Zebedee and John his brother, in the boat with Zebedee their father, mending their nets, and he called them. Immediately they left the boat and their father and followed him."—Matthew 4:18–22

Have you ever considered that God might call you and your sibling, or a pair of your children, for a shared Kingdom mission? Not only were James and John brothers, but they were likely Jesus' first cousins as well.

LEAVE YOUR FAMILY?

In Matthew 4:22 above, God says, "Immediately they left the boat and their father and followed him." I have heard a number of sermons over the years that have suggested in order to follow Jesus, James and John needed to leave their families behind. They now had a higher calling! So they said a quick goodbye to dad (note, "immediately,") and followed the Lord.

It is true that James and John began to travel with Jesus. But Jesus and the disciples did not travel alone. There was a group of women who travelled with them.[6] It is true that James and John left their dad back in the boat, but their mother joined them on the road as Jesus ministered throughout Galilee.[7]

In Matthew 20, Jesus and his disciples are on the long journey to Jerusalem via Jericho. They were accompanied, as usual by the women who were helping and supporting them. In a somewhat comical moment, we read;

"Then the mother of the sons of Zebedee came up to him with her sons, and kneeling before him she asked him for something. And he said to her, 'What do you want?' She said to him, 'Say that these two sons of mine are to sit, one at your right hand and one at your left, in your kingdom.'"—Matthew 20:20–21

At this point, maybe James and John had wished momma was not a part of the travelling ministry team! The brothers got a lot of flak from the other ten disciples over this.[8] Their mother, Salome, was also there at the crucifixion.[9] She then accompanied Mary Magdalene and Mary the Mother of Jesus to the tomb on Sunday morning.

"When the Sabbath was past, Mary Magdalene, Mary the mother of James[10], and Salome bought spices, so that they might go and anoint him."—Mark 16:1

My point here is to push back on the unbalanced teaching that following Jesus requires leaving one's family relationships behind or reducing one's commitment to family members.

HATE YOUR FAMILY?

But didn't Jesus teach that following Him meant leaving family behind? Beyond that, didn't Jesus say that loving Him fully means hating our family members? Here is what Jesus said;

"Now when Jesus saw a crowd around him, he gave orders to go over to the other side. And a scribe came up and said to him, 'Teacher, I will follow you wherever you go.' And Jesus said to him, 'Foxes have holes, and birds of the air have nests, but the Son of Man has nowhere to lay his head.' Another of the disciples said to him, 'Lord, let me first go and bury my father.' And Jesus said to him, 'Follow me, and leave the dead to bury their own dead.'"—Matthew 8:18–22

"Now great crowds accompanied him, and he turned and said to them, 'If anyone comes to me and does not hate his own father and mother and wife and children and brothers and sisters, yes, and even his own life, he cannot be my disciple. Whoever does not bear his own cross and come after me cannot be my disciple.'"—Luke 14:25–27

"Brother will deliver brother over to death, and the father his child, and children will rise against parents and have them put to death, and you will be hated by all for my name's sake. But the one who endures to the end will be saved."—Matthew 10:21–22

"For I have come to set a man against his father, and a daughter against her mother, and a daughter-in-law against her mother-in-law. And a person's enemies will be those of his own household. Whoever loves father or mother more than me is not worthy of me, and whoever loves son or daughter more than me is not worthy of me. And whoever does not take his cross and follow me is not worthy of me. Whoever

finds his life will lose it, and whoever loses his life for my sake will find it."—Matthew 10:35–39

Understanding Jesus' words above are essential for a Christian understanding of family life and God's Kingdom purpose for family relationships. We must consider these teachings both in their specific contexts as well as within the full context of God's Word. I will work through these texts by answering three questions.

Question #1: Does following Jesus require leaving family relationships behind?

Following Jesus may require leaving family behind. This was not the case for James and John, as they served Jesus together as brothers, and their mother accompanied them during their travels. If following Jesus meant abandoning one's family, Jesus would not have permitted Salome to travel with her sons. In the case of Jesus Himself, He lived ninety-one percent of his holy, perfect, and righteous life on earth with His family.[11] As we have seen in the Old Testament, and as we will continue to see during the formation of the first local churches, God often uses family members to partner together to advance His Kingdom.

Question #2: What did Jesus mean when He said that brother would kill brother, and father would kill son?

He meant exactly what He said. In the first century, it was a life-threatening decision to worship Jesus. From the Roman perspective, worshiping Jesus as a god was no problem. There were many gods. Take your pick. But to worship Jesus alone as God was unacceptable. Not only would your life be in danger from the political powers, but from your parents and siblings as well. Jesus was simply speaking the truth of what was to come, that if you follow Him, your family might try to kill you. Jesus' words remain true to this day. In many families and countries around the world, particularly in Muslim contexts, to trust Christ means putting one's life in jeopardy. Who would kill you for simply "changing your religion?" Your father. Your brother. In the western world, where we generally enjoy religious freedom because of our Christian heritage, it is hard for us to understand how such things could happen. We read these words of Jesus about family members killing each other and find them difficult to understand, or think Jesus may have been speaking in hyperbole. There was no exaggeration here. This was reality for many Christians in the first century, as it is reality for many Christians around the world today.

Question #3: What did Jesus mean when He talked about following Him and hating our family?

Here again, we have essential doctrine regarding family relationships. The key to understanding this teaching in Luke 14 is the context. Jesus is speaking to the crowds. This is a message to the lost. This is a message to those who are enemies of God.[12] Just as Jesus made it clear following Him might mean your family members will execute you, here He makes it clear following Him might require breaking relationships with a hostile, unbelieving family.

Jesus practiced what He preached. In Mark 3, Jesus' family[13] not only did not believe He was the Messiah, they thought He was crazy. They tried to force Him to come back home. In Mark 3:31–35, Mary and Jesus' brothers were outside a house where Jesus was teaching. They sent someone to bring Jesus out, but He refused to come.

What should we conclude? Do we think Jesus hated his family? Do we want to make the case that Jesus had hatred in His heart toward His mother and His brothers. Such an argument is absurd. To conclude this would be to accuse Jesus of sin. In Matthew 5:44, Jesus said, "Love your enemies and pray for those who persecute you." First John 2:9, which are no less the words of Christ, says, "Whoever says he is in the light and hates his brother is still in darkness." Again Christ speaks in 1 John 3:15, "Everyone who hates his brother is a murderer."[14] Jesus directly quotes from the Old Testament in saying:

> *"For Moses said, Honor your father and your mother; and, Whoever reviles father or mother must surely die."*—Mark 7:10

In Luke 14, Jesus was teaching the truth that following Him may require separating one's self from a hostile, unbelieving family. This is as true today as it was in the first century. This message has nothing to do with Christian families. It has no application to how a Christian should relate to believing parents, siblings, or children. If a text like this is used to call Christians to "put their ministry ahead of their family," it is both an abuse of people and abuse of God's Word.[15]

ENDNOTES

[1] 2 Timothy 3:16.

[2] Proverbs 30:5.

[3] 2 Kings 21:16.

[4] Luke 1:36 records that Jesus' mother Mary and Zechariah's wife Elizabeth were relatives. If Mary and Elizabeth were first cousins, that would make Zechariah Jesus' uncle. Note also that God did not choose random disconnected people through which to bring Messiah into the world. Mary and Elizabeth were part of a family. Jesus and John the Baptist were part of that same family, and God chose them to serve Him together during this, the supreme moment of history.

[5] Such as Moses, Aaron, and Miriam leading the people out of Egypt and David and his brothers fighting the Philistines.

[6] Luke 8:1–3.

[7] Mark 15:40–41.

[8] Matthew 20:24.

[9] Mark 15:40–41.

[10] In this context, Mary, Jesus' mother, is called "Mary the mother of James." James was the brother of Jesus.

[11] Thirty out of his thirty-one years.

[12] Romans 5:10.

[13] Mary and Jesus' brothers. After the age of 12, Jesus' father Joseph is not mentioned and it is assumed he died at some point prior to Jesus beginning His public ministry at age 30. See Mark 3:31.

[14] Note also in 2 Timothy 3 the Apostle Paul encourages Pastor Timothy to appreciate and honor his mother and his grandmother who led him to the Lord. If the Christian duty was to "hate your mother," then Paul most certainly would have communicated that to Timothy. Instead, he did the opposite.

[15] Sadly, I have talked with many missionaries who have told me their sending agencies have told them, "You need to focus on the Kingdom of God and let the Lord take care of your children."

CHAPTER 14:
FAMILY MINISTRY IN THE GOSPELS (PART 2)

*"What do you think? If a man has a hundred sheep, and one of them
has gone astray, does he not leave the ninety-nine on the
mountains and go in search of the one that went astray?"*

—MATTHEW 18:12

JESUS ELEVATED GOD'S CALL TO PRIORITIZE FAMILY RELATIONSHIPS

In the last chapter, we examined Jesus' dramatic teaching on hating one's family, leaving family behind, and even murder within families. When we take these Scriptures out of their context, it is possible to conclude that Jesus minimized the importance of family relationships. In fact, Jesus elevated the value, virtue, and importance of family life.

JESUS ELEVATED MARRIAGE

In the first century, even within the Jewish community, marriage was often viewed as disposable, and women were not treated with dignity and value. Jesus confronted the Pharisees about their low view of marriage.

> *"And Pharisees came up to him and tested him by asking, 'Is it lawful to divorce one's wife for any cause?' He answered, 'Have you not read that he who created them from the beginning made them male and female, and said, "Therefore a man shall leave his father and his mother and hold fast to his wife, and the two shall become one flesh"? So they are no longer two but one flesh. What therefore God has joined together, let not man separate.' They said to him, 'Why then did Moses command one to give a certificate of divorce and to send her away?' He said to them, 'Because of your hardness of heart Moses allowed you to divorce your*

wives, but from the beginning it was not so. And I say to you: whoever divorces his wife, except for sexual immorality, and marries another, commits adultery.'"—Matthew 19:3–9

Jesus immediately turned their attention back to the Word of God. "Have you not read?" He then refers to the history of creation recorded in Genesis 2 where God established marriage as the foundational institution for human life and society. Jesus affirmed the supernatural unity God desires for a husband and wife within their marriage relationship. "So they are no longer two but one flesh." Jesus raises the bar for marriage back to where God set it at the time of creation. He had no tolerance for man watering down, diminishing, or minimizing God's Kingdom-purpose for marriage.

JESUS ELEVATED HONORING PARENTS

In the same way the Jews lowered God's commands for marriage and sexual purity, they watered down His commandment to honor their parents. This set up another major confrontation between Jesus and the Pharisees.

> *"Then Pharisees and scribes came to Jesus from Jerusalem and said, 'Why do your disciples break the tradition of the elders? For they do not wash their hands when they eat.' He answered them, 'And why do you break the commandment of God for the sake of your tradition? For God commanded, "Honor your father and your mother," and, "Whoever reviles father or mother must surely die." But you say, "If anyone tells his father or his mother, 'What you would have gained from me is given to God,' he need not honor his father." So for the sake of your tradition you have made void the word of God. You hypocrites! Well did Isaiah prophesy of you, when he said: 'This people honors me with their lips, but their heart is far from me; in vain do they worship me, teaching as doctrines the commandments of men.'"*[1]—Matthew 15:1–9[2]

Why did Jesus accuse the Pharisees of having their hearts far from God? They were enabling the people to dishonor their parents, and profiting from it. We need to do a little digging to understand the wicked thing that was happening here.

God had commanded the people to honor their fathers and their mothers. Honor in the family was so important to God that the penalty for dishonor was death. As a part of this commandment, it was expected that sons and daughters would do all they could to care for their parents in their old age. This Old Testament principle was explicitly repeated by God in 1 Timothy 5, which we will look at in the next chapter.

However, the Pharisees had developed a complicated set of human traditions, which provided loopholes for sons and daughters to avoid God's commandment. If a child were to say, "I have decided to give my money to the Lord (to the synagogue, to the poor, etc.)," the child would not be held accountable to provide for their needy parents.

In today's terms, we might picture a Christian man who has aging parents who are no longer able to provide for themselves. This man has thousands of dollars in his savings, but rather than do what he can to help his parents, he "promises God" that his money will be set aside for "supporting missionaries." In the first century, the Pharisees were teaching that this was an acceptable practice and that he was "off the hook" to obey God's law.

The Pharisees had watered down the commandment of God to honor parents through their foolish human traditions, and they were encouraging others to do the same. Jesus "reset" the bar regarding God's holy and righteous command for His people to honor their parents. Jesus made it clear that our financial responsibility to care for our parents comes before our financial responsibility to be generous with others.

Not only did Jesus restore the command to honor parents to its proper place, but He practiced what He preached. His last act in His earthly ministry was to provide and care for Mary, His mother.

> "When Jesus saw his mother and the disciple whom he loved standing nearby, he said to his mother, "Woman[3], behold, your son!" Then he said to the disciple, "Behold, your mother!" And from that hour the disciple took her to his own home."—John 19:26–27

Jesus had never stopped loving His mother. With His thoughts on all the sons and daughters who would be saved through His sacrifice, His final concern was for His mother. He asked John (the disciple whom he loved) to take care of Mary. It is fair to conclude that Joseph had died prior to this time. John accepts this important mission from His Lord and "from that hour" he took Mary into his home[4] and provided for her in Jesus' stead.

JESUS NURTURED FAITH IN CHILDREN

Jesus went against the popular and religious culture of His day and prioritized children.

> *"And they were bringing children to him that he might touch them, and the disciples rebuked them. But when Jesus saw it, he was indignant and said to them, "Let the children come to me; do not hinder them, for to such belongs the kingdom of God. Truly, I say to you, whoever does not receive the kingdom of God like a child shall not enter it." And he took them in his arms and blessed them, laying his hands on them."*—Mark 10:13–16

Note Jesus' emotions here. He is indignant with the disciples. This was not meek and mild Jesus. Why? Because Jesus understood the Great Commission begins with the souls of the little ones. The Great Commission is not just personal, but multi-generational. The disciples were standing in the way of parents and grandparents, and Jesus quickly put an end to it.

Notice also Jesus was not married, nor did He have children. Jesus set the example for every believer, regardless of their family situation, to intentionally nurture faith in children, and participate in God's multi-generational Great Commission. We are all called to "next generation" ministry.

JESUS CALLS US TO PURSUE LOST CHILDREN

As Jesus was teaching His disciples, He asked a child to stand next to him[5] while He was teaching. He wanted them to see a real child standing before them, as He explained God's heart for children.

> *"See that you do not despise one of these little ones. For I tell you that in heaven their angels always see the face of my Father who is in heaven. What do you think? If a man has a hundred sheep, and one of them has gone astray, does he not leave the ninety-nine on the mountains and go in search of the one that went astray? And if he finds it, truly, I say to you, he rejoices over it more than over the ninety-nine that never went astray. So it is not the will of my Father who is in heaven that one of these little ones should perish."*—Matthew 18:10–14

Jesus wanted the disciples to have the same heart for children that God had for children. He wanted them to understand the urgency and passion of God for children to believe in Him, follow Him, and not wander off. We must reclaim this urgency and passion in the church today. The most optimistic opinions tell us we are losing nearly half of our own children to the world![6] Who is sounding the alarm? Who is declaring a Great Commission crisis? Where are the fathers, mothers, grandfathers, and grandmothers who are willing to drop everything and do all in their power to go in search of the ones who are astray?

JESUS' WARNINGS ON SIN AND CHILDREN

Some of Jesus' strongest language focused on God's desire to see children follow Him and obey Him. He issued grave warnings against anyone who influenced a child to sin. In the same sermon noted above, Jesus, with a child standing beside Him said:

> *"Whoever receives one such child in my name receives me, but whoever causes one of these little ones who believe in me to sin, it would be better for him to have a great millstone fastened around his neck and to be drowned in the depth of the sea."*—Matthew 18:5–6

The seriousness of sin is set in the context of the effects of our sin on the next generation. God's purpose is to bring glory to Himself by filling the earth with worship, and from the very beginning God declared His mission would be accomplished through the generations.

THE GREAT COMMISSION AND THE FIRST COMMANDMENT

At the end of Matthew's gospel, we find Jesus' Great Commission to His disciples.

> *"And Jesus came and said to them, 'All authority in heaven and on earth has been given to me. Go therefore and make disciples of all nations, baptizing them in the name of the Father and of the Son and of the Holy Spirit, teaching them to observe all that I have commanded you. And behold, I am with you always, to the end of the age.'"*—Matthew 28:18–20[7]

God's desire from the creation of the world is unchanged. He wants this earth, and the New Earth, filled with worshippers. With this in mind, we can see the first commandment from Genesis 1:28 echoed here in the Great Commission.

Jesus parallels, reiterates, and expands His first commandment to Adam and Eve.

FIRST COMMANDMENT	GREAT COMMISSION
Genesis 1:28	Matthew 28:19–20
Be fruitful and multiply	Make disciples
Fill the Earth	Of all nations
Subdue it	Teach them to observe all I have commanded

In the first commandment, God calls us to multiply physically and spiritually through having and raising godly children. Jesus calls His followers to "make disciples" and thereby multiply! Jesus called His disciples to be disciple-makers. In the beginning, God established His plan to "fill the earth." Jesus repeats His own words[8] from Genesis 1 when He calls His disciples to "all nations." In the beginning, God called Adam and Eve to subdue the world, and take dominion over it. This meant far more than taking care of the garden and the animals. Adam and Eve, and their descendants were called to establish the righteous and holy reign of God in every sphere of life. Jesus reiterates this call by saying "teach them (all nations) to observe all I have commanded you."

Am I arguing that the Great Commission is all about marriage, the family, and raising godly children? No, the Great Commission is much greater and broader. But as we have seen throughout God's word, marriage, the family, and raising godly children are all connected to the Great Commission.

Like you, I have heard many sermons on the Great Commission. The typical pattern in these sermons is to preach through the text and then challenge the congregation to think about (1) our non-Christian neighbors, and (2) unreached people groups (global missions). Are you praying for and reaching out to your non-Christian neighbors, and are you involved in global missions? These are certainly proper challenges, and appropriate application points from Matthew 28.

But our adult friends and those on the other side of the world are not the first ones we are called to evangelize and disciple. If we are married, encouraging faithfulness and godliness in our spouse is where our ministry begins. If we are parents or grandparents, God has chosen to entrust immortal souls into our care. God has given us spiritual responsibilities with our children who are a higher priority than our spiritual opportunities with our neighbors.

As a pastor and preacher, God has graciously given me many opportunities to share the gospel and see people repent and trust Christ. None of these conversions came about because of my flowery words or persuasive presentation. The Holy Spirit simply uses His Word and brings people to repentance. I have had the thought, "What if God used my sharing the gospel to lead 1,000 people to repent and trust Christ . . . but I lost one of my six children?" I am thankful and humbled for any fruit God brings about in my public ministry, but my greatest desire is to spend eternity with my wife[9] and children. For many years, I was passionate about making disciples of those in my community and around the world, while I neglected my most important calling, leading my wife and children to know and love God.

SUMMARY

God's plan has been the same from the beginning. He is filling the earth with His worship and He has chosen His temporary institution of the family as an essential component to carry out His plan. In every chapter of the four gospels, except for Mark 4, God refers to family relationships or gives us spiritual truths using a family analogy. There is a divine ordering to our Great Commission ministry in the world.

Questions for discussion:

1. Have you, or someone you know, had to leave their spiritually hostile family in order to follow Christ?

2. Why do you think Jesus warns us so strongly not to lead children into sin?

3. Is your local church a welcoming place for children? When children walk in the door of your church, do they receive an enthusiastic welcome?

4. In what ways does your family show honor to parents and grandparents? In what ways could your family grow in this essential Christian attitude and practice?

ENDNOTES

[1] Isaiah 29:13.

[2] See also Mark 7:1–13.

[3] In the parallel account in John 19, John records that Jesus called Mary "dear woman," which is another indication of His love and honor for His mother.

[4] The disciples travelled with Jesus, but were not homeless.

[5] Matthew 18:2.

[6] The most optimistic number I have found cites "only" 40% of young people growing up in our Christian home and churches leaving the faith as adults (http://www.youthministry.com/busting-drop-out-myth). This article uses this number to help us "calm down" a little about the crisis regarding the next generation. As noted in the introduction, I believe we are losing far more than half of our sons and daughters by the time they enter college. In fact, while they may be physically in our churches during junior high, many of them are "already gone" in that they have little or no Christian worldview. For a serious look at this serious issue take a look at *Already Gone*, by Ken Ham.

[7] There is one imperative verb here, "make disciples." There are three participles that describe how disciples will be made: by going, by baptizing, and by teaching.

[8] We can rightly refer to all the words of the Bible as the words of Jesus, the second person of the Trinity. Matthew 28 is a central text for Trinitarian theology. When Jesus says, "baptizing them in the name of the Father and of the Son and of the Holy Spirit," the word "name" is singular, yet He speaks of the three persons of the Godhead.

[9] In a future chapter we will talk about Jesus' teaching that there will be no marriage in Heaven.

CHAPTER 15:
FAMILY MINISTRY IN THE NEW TESTAMENT

"For the promise is for you and for your children and for all who are far off,
everyone whom the Lord our God calls to himself."

—ACTS 2:36-39

A s we move into the book of Acts, God does something new. He creates, establishes, and ordains a new institution, the local church. God's creation of the local church did not eliminate His purpose for the family. Rather, in the New Testament, He lays out specific ways in which the family and the local church are to relate to one another and accomplish different aspects of His plan to build His Church. The local church is built on the health and spiritual life of families. The local church has the extraordinary and vital responsibility to equip the family and keep it accountable to its purpose and function according to God's Word.

In this chapter, we will look at God's plan for the family in the New Testament (following the Gospels).

THE LOCAL CHURCH LAUNCHED WITH MULTI-GENERATIONAL VISION

Throughout the Old Testament, God called His people to a multi-generational mission. Nurturing faith in the hearts of their children was to be a top priority for the people of God. The local church in the New Testament was launched with this same vision.

In Acts 2, the Holy Spirit fell on the believers and they were supernaturally empowered to preach the gospel in languages, which were unknown to them. Peter wrapped up the day with a dramatic evangelistic sermon. Here is how he concluded:

> *"Let all the house of Israel therefore know for certain that God has made*
> *him both Lord and Christ, this Jesus whom you crucified." Now when*
> *they heard this they were cut to the heart, and said to Peter and the rest*

of the apostles, "Brothers, what shall we do?" And Peter said to them, "Repent and be baptized every one of you in the name of Jesus Christ for the forgiveness of your sins, and you will receive the gift of the Holy Spirit. For the promise is for you and for your children and for all who are far off, everyone whom the Lord our God calls to himself."—Acts 2:36–39

Peter proclaimed the three-fold move of the Gospel communicated cover-to-cover in the Scriptures: You, your kids, and the world! First, God calls *you* to repent and trust Christ alone for salvation. Then God calls you to do all in your power to lead your children to do the same. Then, as you are seeking to disciple your children, God calls you *and* your children to share the gospel with all who are far off.

Unfortunately, in many parts of the modern church, the sermon each Sunday contains two predictable points. Point #1, "Get right with God." Point #2, "Go make a difference in the world." In one form or another, this is what we hear week after week. It is not that these messages are wrong, but rather that they are incomplete. We need to return to a more radical, Bible-driven call for discipleship. Get right with God by grace alone through faith alone! Get right with your spouse! Get right with your children! Get right with your local church! Now, together with your family and with your brothers and sisters in Christ, go make a difference in the world!

We have functionally replaced the top priority of the Christian life, which is to serve, minister to, and make disciples of our families, particularly our own children. As a result, we have many well-intentioned Christian men and women who give their hearts and souls to help lead the programs at church and in the community but never sit down to read the Scriptures at home with their own children. I know this sort of Christian very well. It used to be me. I gave my best to my full-time pastoral ministry at church but my wife and children got the spiritual leftovers. I was neglecting my most important calling, while at the same time receiving accolades for my public ministry.

YOU AND YOUR HOUSEHOLD

As the Gospel spread through the book of Acts, God continued to call people to a multi-generational vision. God not only saved individuals, but entire families.

"And he told us how he had seen the angel stand in his house and say, 'Send to Joppa and bring Simon who is called Peter; he will declare to you a message by which you will be saved, you and all your household.'"—Acts 11:13–14

"One who heard us was a woman named Lydia, from the city of Thyatira, a seller of purple goods, who was a worshiper of God. The Lord opened her heart to pay attention to what was said by Paul. And after she was baptized, and her household as well, she urged us, saying, "If you have judged me to be faithful to the Lord, come to my house and stay." And she prevailed upon us."—Acts 16:14–15

"Then he brought them out and said, "Sirs, what must I do to be saved?" And they said, "Believe in the Lord Jesus, and you will be saved, you and your household." And they spoke the word of the Lord to him and to all who were in his house. And he took them the same hour of the night and washed their wounds; and he was baptized at once, he and all his family. Then he brought them up into his house and set food before them. And he rejoiced along with his entire household that he had believed in God."—Acts 16:30–34

Every Word of God is flawless.[1] All Scripture is God breathed.[2] God wanted to be sure, as He inspired Luke to write the book of Acts that His people would keep the Great Commission, their families, and their children connected. God did not build local churches on converted individuals alone but converted families.

SEX, MARRIAGE, AND SINGLENESS

In the books of 1 and 2 Corinthians, Paul instructs and confronts the church leaders in Corinth regarding the proper functioning of their local church. Paul instructs as to how the local church should be addressing and responding to issues of sexuality, marriage, and singleness.

In 1 Corinthians 5:1–12, Paul instructs the Corinthian church to remove from their fellowship a man who was in a sexually immoral relationship with his stepmother. This man was engaging in ongoing, unrepentant sexual immorality. Therefore, for the ultimate good of the man[3] and for the protection of the church, Paul instructs the leaders to "purge the evil person from among you."[4]

Here we see the intersection of a person's private sexual life, the family, and the local church as being interconnected. The mission of the local church depends on and is connected to the spiritual health of the marriages and families within it.

In chapter 7, Paul then seeks to correct the confusion and error in the Corinthian church regarding marriage and singleness. Verse 1 of chapter 7 may be one of the most misused passages in the Bible. Here are two translations:

"Now concerning the matters about which you wrote: "It is good for a man not to have sexual relations with a woman."—1 Corinthians 7:1 (ESV)

"Now for the matters you wrote about: "It is good for man not to marry."—1 Corinthians 7:1 (NIV, 1984)

This verse is often used to teach that singleness is *better* than marriage. This is accomplished by only using the second part of the verse. "God says in 1 Corinthians 7:1 that it is good for a man not to marry." But that is *not* what God said. That is what the Corinthians said. In this section of Paul's letter, he is responding to a previous letter they had written to him. This is why he begins this section with, "Now concerning the matters about which you wrote." It was the Corinthians who said "It is good for a man not to have sexual relations with a woman," not God. In the remainder of chapter 7, God speaks through Paul to respond to this assertion. The first thing God says is:

"But because of the temptation to sexual immorality, each man should have his own wife and each woman her own husband."[5] —1 Corinthians 7:2

The primary theme in this chapter is both marriage and singleness are gifts and callings from God. As soon as we begin to pit marriage against singleness, and argue about which one is better, we have distorted the biblical way of thinking. God says:

"But each has his own gift from God, one of one kind and one of another."—1 Corinthians 7:7

Paul had the gift of singleness. He was called to it. He was passionate about his ability to advance the gospel through his singleness.[6] In the same way, those who are married or desire marriage are called to advance the gospel through marriage.

In a later chapter, we will talk about the application of these doctrines for singles-ministry within the local church.

GOD'S CALL TO CHILDREN

In the New Testament, God speaks directly to children. Children were considered full persons, and were called by God to live faithfully. Not surprisingly, God's primary call to children focused on their relationship with their parents.

> *"Children, obey your parents in everything, for this pleases the Lord."*—Colossians 3:20

> *"Children, obey your parents in the Lord, for this is right. "Honor your father and mother" (this is the first commandment with a promise), "that it may go well with you and that you may live long in the land."*—Ephesians 6:1–2

How were children called to live out their faith? What was God's first concern for them? Children were called to demonstrate their love for Christ by obeying and honoring their parents. The same is true for children today. How can we evaluate a child's spiritual health? Look at how well the child honors and obeys his or her parents.

God speaks to children in the same way He speaks to adults throughout the Bible. He calls all His people—men, women, boys, and girls—to begin their life of faith at home. When children hear Jesus' words to "love your neighbor," their first thought should be, "How can I show love to my parents?" Father and mother are the child's first and closest "neighbor."

GOD'S CALL TO HUSBANDS

While God calls some men, like Paul, to serve Him through singleness, He calls the majority of men to serve Him in and through marriage. God created men and women with equal value, worth, dignity, and importance. But He also created us differently—physically, emotionally, and spiritually—because He has given men and women different roles in the context of the family and the local church.

In Ephesians 5, God gives husbands their divine job description.

> *"Husbands, love your wives, as Christ loved the church and gave himself up for her, that he might sanctify her, having cleansed her by the washing of water with the word . . ."*—Ephesians 5:25–26

The world accuses Christianity of teaching male dominance and female subservience. Some go so far as to say that the Bible is abusive to women. This is absurd on every front. For starters, get out your history book and look what has happened to the value and dignity of women in every culture where Christianity has taken root. The more Christian a culture becomes, the more women are honored, blessed, liberated, cherished, and protected.[7]

What is God's first command to husbands? Love your wives. What does it mean for a man to love his wife? God answers that question in 1 Corinthians 13 where He defines love.

> *"Love is patient and kind; love does not envy or boast; it is not arrogant or rude. It does not insist on its own way; it is not irritable or resentful; it does not rejoice at wrongdoing, but rejoices with the truth. Love bears all things, believes all things, hopes all things, endures all things."*—1 Corinthians 13:4–7

These are the attitudes and actions to which God calls husbands. Unfortunately, I fall short of this every day. I do not have the strength of will or quality of character to love Amy like this. This drives me to my knees! The only chance I have of obeying God's holy and righteous command to love my wife is if the Holy Spirit supernaturally empowers me every day.

God gives the husband his second mission and purpose in the next phrase from Ephesians 5:25: we are to give ourselves up for our wives. This is what Christ did for His bride, the Church; and therefore this is what we are to do for our brides as well. To put it simply, God calls a husband to serve his wife.

Don't miss the theological connection that God makes between the mission of the husband and the work of Christ. God wants us to understand how we treat our wives is a reflection of the gospel and of Christ Himself. When Christian men demand to be served rather than serve, the gospel is perverted and Christ's work on the cross is obscured. In the same way, when Christian men are servants and follow in the footsteps of Christ as they give themselves up for their wives, the gospel is visible and Christ is honored.[8]

But why are husbands called to love and serve their wives? What is the ultimate purpose?

> "Husbands, love your wives, as Christ loved the church and gave himself up for her, *that he might sanctify her*…"[9]—Ephesians 5:25–26

Here we find the ultimate purpose for the husband. He is called to lead his wife in becoming more like Christ. He is to nurture faith, godliness, and holiness in her. Marriage is connected to the Great Commission. It is a "disciple making" institution.

The husband's divine job description is clear: Love, serve, and lead. Not only is it clear, but it is precisely ordered. If a husband tries to lead his wife without first loving her and serving her . . . well, good luck with that! A woman's heart will likely not be led by a man who doesn't first love her and serve her. In fact, if a husband tries to lead his wife without first demonstrating his love for her and laying his life down for her, she will resent him. Leadership, no matter how good and right it may be, without a heart of love and sacrifice, will be received by the wife as domination and control. On the other hand, when a wife experiences love and service from her husband, she increasingly opens her heart to him, trusts him, and responds to his spiritual leadership.[10]

If a man is married, and he desires to be a Great Commission, externally focused, missional Christian, he begins his ministry with the soul of his wife. There is to be no higher earthly love and priority in his life. He is to love her with an ultimate love, just as Christ loved His Church. God created the temporary institution of marriage to build His everlasting Church.

GOD'S CALL TO FATHERS

In the next chapter of Ephesians, God gives a Great Commission calling to fathers.

> *"Fathers, do not provoke your children to anger, but bring them up in the discipline and instruction of the Lord."*—Ephesians 6:4

Fathers are to take the lead in passing faith and character to their children. What is God's primary plan for children to be evangelized and discipled? Fathers. God did not create the institution of the local church to take over or replace His calling for fathers to disciple their children at home. Rather, the early Christian churches trained and equipped fathers for their "disciple making ministry" at home. Ephesians 6 is a specific example of this training. Ephesians, along with the other letters of the New Testament, were read as sermons in first century churches. These words were spoken from the pulpit to fathers: calling, challenging, and instructing them how to embrace their mission to disciple their children.

God gives men two vital words here if they want to impress the hearts of their children with a love for God. Fathers are to bring their children up in the *discipline* and *instruction* of the Lord.

The word *discipline* here means far more than correcting wrong behavior. It is a word that connotes systematic training and action. One might think of teaching a child the "discipline" of karate. The child engages in wide variety of training activities, which in the end lead him toward becoming an expert in karate. In the same way, God calls fathers to take the lead in the spiritual training of their children. Fathers are to pray *with* their children, worship in church *with* their children, and serve their neighbor *with* their children. Fathers are to practice the *disciplines* of the Lord *with* their children.

But fathers are not only commanded to practice their faith with their children, they are commanded to bring them up in the *instruction* of the Lord. Echoing the Great Commandment in Deuteronomy 6, God calls fathers to talk with their children about the things of God. Where can a father find the "instruction of the Lord?" There is only one place: in His Word. Fathers are to lead regular family worship in the home: reading, studying, and discussing God's Word at home.

Once again, God connects the Great Commission with the family. If a man wants to impact the world for Christ and he is a father, he should think first of the souls of children, the souls that God has uniquely entrusted to his care.

GOD'S CALL TO WIVES AND MOTHERS

In the New Testament, God calls husbands and fathers to live out their faith primarily in the context of their families. God gives the same call to wives and mothers. They are called to a world-changing mission for the glory of God! Sadly, our culture has accused Christianity of offering a vision of male-dominance and woman-subservience. This is not the biblical vision. Consider God's word to wives in Ephesians 5:

> *"Wives, submit to your husbands, as to the Lord. For the husband is the head of the wife even as Christ is the head of the church, his body, and is himself its Savior."*—Ephesians 5:22

> *"However, let each one of you love his wife as himself, and let the wife see that she respects her husband."*—Ephesians 5:33

These are dangerous words in our culture today. Again, the world accuses Christians of treating women as secondary and less important than men. Rather than stand up and proclaim God's wonderful picture of marriage and family, which gives dignity and purpose to both men and women, we often remain silent.

The two calls for wives from Ephesians 5, to submit to and respect their husbands, are connected to God's first definition of "wifehood." Here is what God said in Genesis 2 when He created Eve, and with Eve, the institution of marriage.

> *"Then the LORD God said, "It is not good that the man should be alone; I will make him a helper fit for him."*—Genesis 2:18

God created the wife as a *helper* for her husband. Things are going from bad to worse. Submit? Respect? Help? It all sounds so demeaning, doesn't it? We know the term "helper" is not a derogatory or minimizing term. God takes this term for Himself![11] God calls wives to come alongside their husbands, to *help* them become more like Christ, and to *partner* with them in impressing the hearts of their children with a love for God.

The husband is to lead his wife toward increased faith, godliness, and increasing Kingdom impact. The wife is to help her husband grow in faith, godliness, and increasing Kingdom impact. No one has more spiritual influence on a man than his wife does. God then speaks to wives, giving them two essential attitudes and actions, which they will need if they want to help their husbands become godly men: respect and submission. In the same way a woman will not be led by a man who does not first love her and serve her, a man will not be helped by a woman who will not respect him.

Just as a Christian man is called to begin his ministry for Christ at home with his family, the Christian woman is called to love God by prioritizing her family. In Titus 2, God provides us with a picture of a spiritually mature woman. The specific context for Titus 2 is women's ministry in the local church. We will expand on this in a later chapter. As women disciple other women, what is the goal? What does a "discipled" woman look like?

> *"Older women likewise are to be reverent in behavior, not slanderers or slaves to much wine. They are to teach what is good, and so train the young women to love their husbands and children, to be self-controlled, pure, working at home, kind, and submissive to their own husbands, that the word of God may not be reviled."*—Titus 2:3–5

Older women in the local church are called to disciple younger women. What is the end goal of this discipleship? What areas of Christian life should the older women give particular attention to? First, they are to train the younger women to love their husbands. Second, they are to train them to love their children. Out of the seven key areas of discipleship, four focus on the family.

If a woman is married, her most important ministry in the world is loving her husband, and helping her husband grow in godliness. When a married woman hears "love your neighbor," she thinks of her husband first.

If she is a mother, her next priority is loving her children, and impressing their hearts with a love for God. My mother came to Christ when I was three months old. My father was a functional atheist. My mother did not have a believing husband to partner with. In a practical way, she was the spiritual head of our household. She prayed with me, read the Bible to me, and led me to repent of my sins and trust Christ.

Timothy, a young pastor in the early church, was also discipled by his mother and grandmother.[12] Motherhood is a Great Commission calling. It is an invitation by God into His plan to fill the earth with His worship. The early church understood if a woman was a mother, her Great Commission calling was to begin with the souls of her children.

PASTORS MUST PUT THEIR FAMILIES FIRST

Throughout the New Testament, God weaves together His purposes for the Christian family and the local church. Both temporary institutions were created to build His everlasting Church, and God gives them distinct functions under that singular purpose.

A major issue in the first century was the selection of elders to lead in local churches. I am persuaded the New Testament term *elder* is interchangeable with the terms pastor, overseer, and shepherd.[13]

God gave specific instructions to the first churches about what qualifications a man needed to have in order to serve as a pastor/elder. Here are a portion of those qualifications.

> *"The saying is trustworthy: If anyone aspires to the office of overseer,*
> *he desires a noble task. Therefore an overseer must be above reproach,*
> *the husband of one wife, sober-minded, self-controlled, respectable,*

hospitable, able to teach, not a drunkard, not violent but gentle, not quarrelsome, not a lover of money. He must manage his own household well, with all dignity keeping his children submissive, for if someone does not know how to manage his own household, how will he care for God's church?"—1 Timothy 3:1–5

"This is why I left you in Crete, so that you might put what remained into order, and appoint elders in every town as I directed you—if anyone is above reproach, the husband of one wife, and his children are believers and not open to the charge of debauchery or insubordination."—Titus 1:5–6

A prerequisite for spiritual leadership within the church was effective spiritual leadership in the home. In the early church, if a man was a husband or father and desired to be a pastor/elder, he needed to demonstrate he was dedicated to shepherding his wife and children before he was allowed to shepherd the greater body. A man would never be entrusted with overseeing the souls of others, if he was not first already faithfully seeking to oversee the souls in his home.

He had to demonstrate he was spiritually managing his own household. God asks, "If someone does not know how to manage his own household, how will he care for God's church?" The Christian life is ordered. Our first calling as believers is our ministry at home.

God reiterates this principle even more strongly in Titus 1:6 where we read, "his children are believers . . ." The NIV translates this as, "a man whose children believe." How are we to understand this? Does this mean that if a man has a child who is not converted then he is disqualified from serving as a pastor? We cannot make that case because anyone with an infant (an unconverted child) would be disqualified. We may not have all the answers we would like here. Some translate this word as "faithful" and focus on the honorable behavior of the children. The Greek word refers to children who are in the home, which means this may not apply to adult children.

Regardless of one's interpretation, we must take this powerful text seriously. Why would God say a man cannot serve as a pastor if his children are not believers or not "faithful"? I believe it is because if a man has a son or daughter who is far from God, he has little extra time to minister to others. One of his own is lost! Does he have time to pray? He should pray for his lost son. Does he have time to share the gospel? He should share it with his lost daughter.

God's qualifications for pastors reinforce the divine plan He gave us at creation. He has created the temporary institution of the family to fill the earth with worship and build His Church. Nothing has changed. God calls the local church to equip and train families to engage in this Kingdom mission.

HEAVEN AND THE FAMILY

As one reads the book of Revelation, God's temporary institution of the family fades away. God's purpose for the family will have been accomplished! Earthly marriage is eternally replaced with the marriage between Christ and His Church.[14] Earthly parenting is eternally replaced with our Heavenly Father directly caring for all His sons and daughters.[15]

This is the hope and purpose for the Christian family. God created the family as a vital engine of world evangelization through the power of multi-generational faithfulness. Until the trumpet sounds, God's mission for the family will not change.

Questions for Discussion:

1. Do you see your local church as made up of individuals or made up of families? Why might this be important?

2. Why do you think people tend to pit "marriage" against "singleness"? What are the results when this kind of thinking gets into a local church?

3. When it comes to a potential elder/pastor for your local church, do you carefully examine his family life, in particular the spiritual maturity of his children? In your opinion, why do some churches fail to do this?

4. Which Scripture in this chapter had the greatest personal impact on you?

ENDNOTES

[1] Proverbs 30:5.

[2] 2 Timothy 3:16.

[3] 1 Corinthians 5:5.

[4] 1 Corinthians 5:13.

[5] Italics mine.

[6] 1 Corinthians 7:6.

[7] D. James Kennedy, *What if Jesus Had Never Been Born* (Nashville, TN: Thomas Nelson Publishers, 1994), 14–16.

[8] Rob Rienow, *Visionary Marriage* (Nashville, TN: Randall House, 2010), 23.

[9] Italics mine.

[10] Ibid 32.

[11] Psalm 30:10.

[12] 2 Timothy 1:5.

[13] Alexander Strauch, *Biblical Eldership: Revised and Expanded Edition* (Colorado Springs, CO: Lewis and Roth, 1995).

[14] Revelation 21:2.

[15] Revelation 21:7.

CHAPTER 16:
FAMILY MINISTRY THROUGH CHURCH HISTORY

"And the word of God continued to increase, and the number
of disciples multiplied greatly in Jerusalem . . ."

—ACTS 6:7

I n conversations over the years about family ministry, I have had some friends tell me I have gone "a little overboard" with all this "family stuff." I am sure there have been times in which I have overstated things out of my passion to see the Christian family engage in the Great Commission. However, I am convinced God has spoken clearly in His Word about His Kingdom purposes for the family. In addition, these biblical teachings have been echoed, reinforced, and applied through Christian history.

At the beginning of chapter 7, I said, "These [theological] foundations run throughout the Bible and, up until the late 1800s, were preached and taught as a theology of family." In this chapter, we will discover that many Christian theologians and pastors during the 1900 years after the resurrection, boldly proclaimed the biblical connection between the Great Commission and family life.[1]

FAMILY MINISTRY IN THE EARLY CHURCH

During the first few centuries after Christ's resurrection, believers practiced family worship in their homes. This was separate from the worship gathering of the local church. During the early decades there were no church buildings, so local churches were all "house churches." But family worship and church worship were distinct from one another, as the different jurisdictions of local church and family were upheld. Consider how the early church fathers spoke about the connection between the family and the advance of the gospel.

[Fathers and mothers] you must not forsake the Commandments of the Lord! You must not slay the child, by procuring abortion! Nor, again, must you destroy it—after it has been born! You must not withdraw your hand from your son, or from your daughter. But you shall teach them the fear of the Lord—from their infancy.—Epistle of Barnabas, 19:5[2]

When you go home from [your local church], lay out with your [physical] meal a spiritual meal as well. The father of the family might repeat something of what was said [in church]; his wife could then hear it, the children too could learn something . . . In short, the household might become a church, so that the devil is driven off and that evil spirit, the enemy of our salvation, takes to flight; the grace of the Holy Spirit would rest there instead, and all peace and harmony surround the inhabitants [of the home.]—John Chrysostom[3]

The early church fathers continued in the teaching of the Old and New Testaments, calling believers to live out their faith in their homes. Chrysostom makes an important theological point (which we will develop more in this chapter) that the family has been created by God to be *like* a small church, just as the church was created by God to be *like* a family. The family, the local church, and the universal Church are inseparable.

Chyrsostom strongly addressed the issue of "men's ministry" in the local church. He confronted the men for not taking the lead in discipling their families, but rather expecting the pastors to do it all for them. Chrysostom claims that this pattern is preventing the pastors from being faithful and increasingly effective in their ministries:

But you hold me riveted fast here. For, before the head [of the household] is set right, it is superfluous to proceed to the rest of the body. You [men] throw everything upon us [pastors]. You alone ought to learn from us, and your wives from you, your children from you; but you leave all to us. Therefore our toil is excessive.[4]

He also cast a beautiful multi-generational vision for the ministry of mothers:

Mothers, be specially careful to regulate your daughters well . . . For if you form them in this way, you will save not only them, but the husband who is destined to marry them, and not the husband only, but the children, not the children only, but the grandchildren. For the root being made good, good branches will shoot forth, and still become better, and for all these you will receive a reward.[5]

FAMILY MINISTRY IN THE MIDDLE AGES

As the Christian community moved toward the Middle Ages, there was an increasing centralization and professionalization of religious life. The physical building of the local church became the primary place where faith was lived and expressed. As a result, there was a slow departure away from the Great Commission ministry of family, which God gave us in His Word.

However, there were important voices calling God's people back to God's plan for the family, and its unique jurisdiction. Augustine of Hippo called heads of households to function as if they were pastors for their families.

Accordingly, brethren, when you hear the Lord saying, Where I am, there shall also my servant be, do not think merely of good bishops and clergymen. But be yourselves also in your own way serving Christ, by good lives, by giving alms, by preaching His name and doctrine as you can; and every father of a family also, be acknowledging in this name the affection he owes as a parent to his family. For Christ's sake, and for the sake of life eternal, let him be warning, and teaching, and exhorting, and correcting all his household; let him show kindliness, and exercise discipline; and so in his own house he will be filling an ecclesiastical and kind of episcopal office, and serving Christ, that he may be with Him forever. For even that noblest service of suffering has been rendered by many of your class; for many who were neither bishops nor clergy, but young men and virgins, those advanced in years with those who were not, many married persons both male and female, many fathers and mothers of families, have served Christ even to the laying down of their lives in martyrdom for His sake, and have been honored by the Father in receiving crowns of exceeding glory.[6]

Augustine was concerned about those who were laymen feeling as if they were second-class spiritual citizens. How true this is for many Christians in our churches today! I have lost track of the number of times I have heard people tell me, "I am only a teacher," "I'm just a business man," "I'm just a mom." As if some of our time is for secular purposes and some for spiritual purposes! Augustine emphasized the biblical teaching if a man desired to serve as a pastor in the church; he must first serve as a pastor in his home.

Augustine's warnings were not heeded. In A. D. 430, church leaders began to speak of Deuteronomy 6:6–7 in regards to life in monasteries *rather* than life in families. God's words for the home were wrongly applied to the professional clergy.[7] Later in A. D. 600, Gregory the Great, Bishop of Rome (Pope), began to transfer God's words for children and parents to the role of the clergy. He used Colossians 3:21, "children, obey your parents in the Lord" to mean that congregation members should obey their priests.[8] This set into motion ongoing jurisdictional confusion between the local church and the Christian family. Imagine the confusion this caused for children as they called two persons "father and mother" in their home, and other persons (priests and nuns) "fathers and mothers" at church. God's Great Commission jurisdiction for the natural family had been downgraded.[9]

FAMILY MINISTRY IN THE REFORMATION

God sparked a global spiritual reformation in the 14th and 15th centuries. Wycliffe translated the Bible into English, making it possible for "regular Christians," not just the clergy class, to have access to God's Word. Luther then translated the Bible into German, and the Guttenberg press enabled the masses to read and be transformed by the Bible.

With the availability of God's Word to families, and the call to return the church back to the doctrine of the sufficiency of Scripture and obedience to biblical jurisdictions, the Christian family was once again unleashed for Great Commission ministry. In particular, family worship was revived and prioritized as the starting point for Christian living.

John Calvin boldly called the Church back to a biblical view of family and the need for the Great Commission to begin within the jurisdiction of the home. This book could be filled with Calvin's exposition of the Bible related to family life.

> Indeed, the scope of God's purpose must be carefully noted. His will, as made known to Abraham, bound all Abraham's descendants. Certainly God does not make his will known to us with the intent

that the knowledge of him should perish with us. He requires us to be his witnesses to the next generation so that they in turn may hand on what they have received from us to our remoter descendants. Therefore it is a father's duty to teach his sons what he himself has learned from God. In this way we must propagate God's truth.[10]

In 1556, John Knox wrote, "You must [share with] your children in reading Scripture, exhorting, and in prayers, which I believe should be done in every house once a day, at least."[11]

It became common practice for church leaders in the 1600s to regularly visit the home of each family in the church to assess whether or not the parents were discipling their children through the regular practice of family worship. In 1647, believers in Scotland published the Directory for Family Worship in which they wrote:

> The assembly requires and appoints ministers to make diligent search and inquiry, whether there be among them a family or families which neglect the duty of family worship. If such a family is found, the head of the family is to be admonished privately to amend his fault; and in case of his continuing therein, he is to be gravely and sadly reproved by the session; after which reproof, if he is found still to neglect family worship, let him be, for his obstinacy in such an offense, suspended and debarred from the Lord's supper, until he amend.[12]

Family worship was a major issue of church discipline. Why did these churches take it so seriously? Why did they invest so much time going from home to home to encourage and ensure family worship was taking place? Family worship was a top priority because they were passionate about the Great Commission. They wanted to see the gospel of Christ advance locally and globally. They knew the Great Commission to make disciples began with the souls of their sons and daughters. They knew God had spoken clearly in the Bible that parents and grandparents were to take the lead in the spiritual training of their children and grandchildren. For them, a church could not be serious about the Great Commission if it was not serious about family worship.

Jonathan Edwards frequently taught on the biblical doctrines of family life. In 1750, in his "Farewell Sermon," he said:

We have had great disputes [about] how the church ought to be regulated; and indeed the subject of these disputes was of great importance: but the due regulation of your families is of no less, and, in some respects, of much greater importance. Every Christian family ought to be as it were a little church, consecrated to Christ, and wholly influenced and governed by his rules. And family education and order are some of the chief means of grace. If these fail, all other means are likely to prove ineffectual. If these are duly maintained, all the means of grace will be likely to prosper and be successful.[13]

Edwards preached the biblical vision for the Christian family. He called Christian families to function as if they were "little churches." Families are to be filled with worship, evangelism, discipleship, fellowship, discipline, and service. These are words we usually associate only with life in the local church, but they belong just as much to the Christian home. Edwards also preached what continues to be true today, if children grow up with active discipleship in the home, it is likely they will follow God all the days of their lives. However, if children's spiritual training consists only of what they receive in church, that spiritual training is "likely to prove ineffectual."

FAMILY MINISTRY IN MODERN TIMES

In the late 1800s, our nation moved from a largely agricultural society to an industrial society. Rather than working near the home as a part of the family business, men moved away from home to work in factories. Kids also left home more than ever before as public schools were built. In the 1900s, women increasingly began to work outside the home as well. More and more parents delegated the training of their children to the "professionals" at school and at church. All these factors resulted in the cry we frequently hear from families today, "No one is ever home!"

Charles Spurgeon was deeply concerned about the changes that were occurring in Christian culture during this time. Christians were once again thinking "religious activities" took place in the church building, and "secular activities" took place out in the world. In his article, "The Kind of Revival We Need," he wrote:

We deeply want a revival of family religion. The Christian family was the bulwark of godliness in the days of the puritans, but in these evil times hundreds of families of so-called Christians have no family worship, no restraint upon growing sons, and no wholesome instruction or discipline. How can we hope to see the kingdom of our Lord advance when His own disciples do not teach His gospel to their own children? Oh, Christian men and women, be thorough in what you do and know and teach! Let your families be trained in the fear of God and be yourselves 'holiness unto the Lord'; so shall you stand like a rock amid the surging waves of error and ungodliness which rage around us.[14]

Spurgeon's message is desperately needed today! Godly men and women in growing churches receive the constant call to get involved in "ministry." Often "ministry" is synonymous with "volunteering at a church program." The Christians of the Reformation sought to reclaim the biblical doctrines of family life. It is time to "reform" again and return to the sufficiency of Scripture for every matter of faith and life. It is time to return to the practice of the early Christians and embrace the truth that "ministry" begins in our homes.

Family worship is rare in Christian homes today. In the family conferences I do at churches around the country, I regularly ask the attendees how many of them grew up in a home that practiced some sort of family worship or family devotions. The response is consistent. 10–15% of adult Christians in our churches today experienced family worship when they were growing up. Predictably, even fewer practice it themselves. In a scientific survey, George Barna found that "Fewer than one-twentieth of churched households ever worship God outside of a church service or have any type of regular Bible study or devotional time together during a typical week."[15]

A few centuries ago, this lack of disciple making in the home would have resulted in 19 out of 20 people in our congregations being under discipline, and being barred from communion! We must reform again and restore the Christian family to its God-ordained role for the advance of the Gospel.

The Holy Spirit is on the move! Toward the end of the 20th century, God began stirring the hearts of men, women, and church leaders around the world to return to His revealed plan for the family. Here are but a few examples of how this reformation of family life is taking place across diverse denominations and theological traditions:

- Men's ministries such as Promise Keepers[16] and Iron Sharpens Iron[17] have risen up to call men to their biblical responsibilities as servant leaders in their homes.

- Ministries such as Focus on the Family[18] and Family Life[19] were born, supporting both families and local churches in an effort to reclaim the Christian family.

- A dynamic network of family-integrated churches has been growing across the world.[20]

- The home education movement began because parents turned their hearts toward their children for the purpose of Christian education and family discipleship.

- National conferences on family ministry, such as AMFM (Association of Marriage and Family Ministries)[21] and the D6 Conference[22], are meeting a vital need in training church leaders toward biblical family ministry.

- The global 4/14 movement is elevating the importance of reaching people with the Gospel while they are young and that God's plan for reaching them is family discipleship.[23]

- Voddie Baucham's *Family Driven Faith* has inspired many parents to take the lead in discipling their children.[24]

- Kurt Bruner's "HomePointe Model" is equipping churches to strengthen families and equip parents.[25]

- Ben Freudenberg's book The Family-Friendly Church has helped many churches transition toward a home-centered, church-supported model.[26]

- Brian Hayne's Shift has helped equip churches with strategies to engage parents in home discipleship,[27] and his book The Legacy Path is giving parents practical tools to pass faith to their children.[28]

- Mark Holmen's ministry has helped churches around the globe catch a vision for "faith at home."[29]

- Richard Ross' "Turning Hearts" events for parents and teenagers have been used by God to bring reconciliation and healing in thousands of families.[30]

- Randy Stinson and Timothy Paul Jones' "Family Equipping Model" is giving large churches a blueprint for engaging parents in home discipleship.[31]
- Scott Turansky and Joanne Miller's Book, Parenting is Heart Work, is providing parents with tools for reaching the hearts of children, not just changing their behavior.[32]
- Eric Wallace, through his ministry Uniting Church and Home, has helped both established churches and new church plants to build on the biblical model for church and family.[33]

These are just a few examples of how God is on the move! God is always seeking to reform, and re-reform His church. He is calling His people back to His Great Commission plan for the family.

CONCLUSION

We have finished our brief study of God's eternal purpose for the temporary institution of the family. Volumes would be required to plumb the depths of all the ways God has chosen to reveal Himself in and through the context of the family. As we conclude this section, consider the words of Jacob Abbott (1890):

> God has grouped men in families. Having laid the foundation of this institution so deep in the very constitution of man, that there has been no nation, no age, scarcely even a single savage tribe that has not been drawn to the result which he intended. For thousands of years, this institution has been assailed by every power which could shake it. By violence from without, or undermined by treachery from within. Lust and passion have risen in rebellion against it. Atheism has again and again advanced the attack, but it stands unmoved. It has been indebted to no human power for its defense. It has needed no defense. It stands on the firm, sure, everlasting foundations which God has made for it.
>
> Wars, famine, pestilence, and revolutions have swept over the face of society, carrying everywhere confusion, terror, and distress. Time has undermined and destroyed everything which it could touch and all human institutions have thus been altered or destroyed in the

lapse of ages. But the family lives on; it stands firm and unshaken. It finds its way wherever human beings go. It survives every shock, and rises again unharmed after every tempest which blows over the social sky. It is a contrivance for human happiness, and God has laid its foundations too deep and strong to be removed.[34]

God's purposes for the family, which He established in the beginning, remain in place today. The family is a divine institution with divine purposes: the evangelization of the lost, the discipleship of the believers, the worship of God, and the love of neighbor.

Questions for Discussion:

1. Did you grow up in a home that practiced family worship? What about your home today? In your opinion, how many families in your church regularly pray and read the Bible together at home?

2. How would your church be different if pastors sought to train and equip heads of household to disciple their families?

3. Which of the historical examples of family ministry surprised you the most? Why?

ENDNOTES

[1] As noted earlier, this is not an attempt to romanticize an earlier era of the Christian church. There is no "golden age" other than the principles and precepts given for the early church in the New Testament. We do not follow human leaders of the church, or seek to become disciples of them. We seek to follow Christ and His Word, and seek to become His disciples.

[2] As translated by Lightfoot, www.earlychristianwritings.com/text/barnabas-lightfoot.html.

[3] Robert C. Hill, trans., *Fathers of the church Volume 1 of Homilies on Genesis, St. John Chrysostom*, (Washington CD: CUA Press, 1999), 34.

[4] John Chrysostom, *Homily 9 on Colossians*, www.newadvent.org/fathers/230309.htm.

[5] John Chrysostom, *Homily 9 on 1 Timothy*, www.newadvent.org/fathers/230609.htm.

[6] Augustine of Hippo, *Tractate 51 on the Gospel of John*, www.newadvent.org/fathers/1701051.htm.

[7] John Cassian, *Second Conference of Abbot Isaac, Chapter 10*, www.newadvent.org.

[8] Gregory the Great, *Pastoral Rule Book 3: Chapter 4*, www.newadvent.org/fathers/36013.htm.

[9] Francis Nigel Lee, *Daily Family Worship*, (South Africa: Signposts Publications and Research Center, 2000), 143.

[10]Joseph Haroutunian, ed. trans., *Calvin: Commentaries*, (Grand Rapids, MI: Christian Classics Ethereal Library, 1958), 247.

[11]John Knox, *Letter of Wholesome Counsel*, www.swrb.com/newslett/actualNLs/ltrwhole.htm.

[12]www.reformed.org.

[13]www.ccel.org/ccel/edwards/works1.i.xxvi.html.

[14]www.spurgeon.org/revival.htm.

[15]George Barna, *Transforming Children Into Spiritual Champions*, (Ventura, CA: Regal, 2003), 125.

[16]www.promisekeepers.org.

[17]www.ironsharpensiron.net.

[18]www.focusonthefamily.com.

[19]www.familylife.com.

[20]www.ncfic.org.

[21]www.amfmonline.com.

[22]www.d6conference.com.

[23]http://4to14window.com/.

[24]Voddie Baucham, *Family Driven Faith* (Wheaton, IL: Crossway, 2007).

[25]Kurt Bruner and Steve Stroope, *It Starts At Home* (Chicago, IL: Moody, 2010).

[26]Ben Freudenberg, *The Family Friendly Church* (Colorado Springs, CO: Group, 1999).

[27]Brian Haynes, *Shift: What it Takes to Finally Reach Families Today* (Colorado Springs, CO: Group, 2009).

[28]Brian Haynes, *The Legacy Path* (Nashville, TN: Randall House, 2011).

[29]www.faithathome.com.

[30]www.richardaross.com.

[31]Timothy Paul Jones, *Family Ministry Field Guide: How Your Church Can Equip Parents to Make Disciples* (Indianapolis, IN: Wesleyan, 2011).

[32]Joanne Miller and Dr. Scott Turansky, *Parenting is Heart Work* (Colorado Springs, CO: David C. Cook, 2005).

[33]www.unitingchurchandhome.com.

[34]Jacob Abbott, *Training Children in Godliness*, ed. Michael J. McHugh, (Arlington Heights: IL, Christian Liberty, 1992), 117–118.

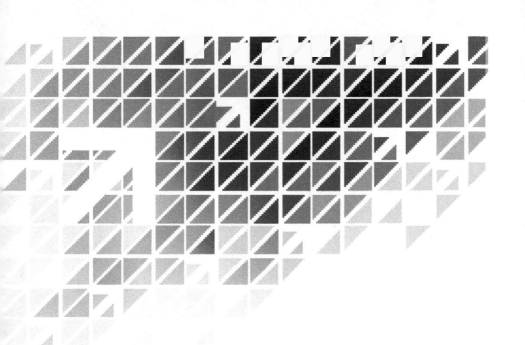

SECTION 5:

UNITING CHURCH AND FAMILY IN THE GREAT COMMISSION

CHAPTER 17:
CARING FOR THE POOR

"If a brother or sister is poorly clothed and lacking in daily food, and one of you says to them, 'Go in peace, be warmed and filled,' without giving them the things needed for the body, what good is that?"

—JAMES 2:15–16

THE FOUNDATION

I n this, the final section of the book, we will seek to apply the doctrines of sufficiency and jurisdiction to discover how God has created the family and the local church to partner together to advance His Kingdom.

Let us take Christ's words (the Bible)[1] and apply them to every matter of faith, practice, and ministry! Will Scripture alone shape our thoughts on caring for the poor? Will Scripture alone shape our thoughts on children's and youth ministry? Men's ministry? Women's ministry? Evangelism?

This is our path ahead.

CARING FOR THE POOR

When we think of "ministries in the church," caring for the poor is not the one we usually think of first. Here are a few reasons why I have chosen to begin the final section of the book on this subject. First, caring for the poor is a major emphasis in the Bible as a whole, and the New Testament in particular. Second, ministry to the poor is often a low or non-existent priority. Third, God is on the move in this essential area of Christian life. From my perspective, the Holy Spirit is moving in this area of ministry today, but little attention is being paid to what God has said in the Bible of *how* Christians are to care for the poor, and *who* should be doing it.

If we are going to seriously engage in the biblical *mission* to care for the poor, we must begin by examining the Bible to learn God's *methods*. We can do the right thing with the right intentions; but if we do it the wrong way, or through the wrong jurisdiction, it becomes wrong. When it comes to caring for the poor, *what* does God want? *How* does He want it done? *Who* is supposed to do it?

I am sure you have heard the term "war on poverty." This was a phrase coined by President Johnson in 1964. Many would argue the government is losing that war. Rather than look to human government for a plan to deal with poverty, let's look to the King of Kings. He has declared His own "war on poverty" and in the Bible He lays out His strategy.

GOD'S WAR ON POVERTY IN THE CHURCH

In the Bible, God lays out a strategy to defend His people against poverty. His children are His top priority in this battle. The majority of Scripture on the issue of poverty provide God's instructions for how *believers* are to care for *other believers*. Because of this emphasis, we will first consider the war against poverty in the church (ministry to believers), and later broaden the scope to consider the war against poverty in the world (ministry to non-believers). These are two separate battlefronts, and are treated differently in Scripture.

In the Bible, God lays out four "lines of defense" to guard His people from poverty.[2]

THE FIRST LINE OF DEFENSE: INDIVIDUAL WORK

When it comes to the issue of poverty in the church, where should we begin? God starts with the jurisdictional responsibilities of the individual. It begins with each person choosing to be a producer, not just a consumer. God commands believers to work.

> *"Six days you shall labor, and do all your work . . ."*—Exodus 20:9

> *"For we hear that some among you walk in idleness, not busy at work, but busybodies. Now such persons we command and encourage in the Lord Jesus Christ to do their work quietly and to earn their own living."*—2 Thessalonians 3:11–12

God speaks strong words through Paul! The brothers were commanded and encouraged in the Lord Jesus Christ *to do their work and to earn their own living.* Working hard to provide for one's self and one's family was a Christian duty and virtue in the early church. A few verses earlier, God speaks even more strongly against those who are unwilling to work.

> *"Now we command you, brothers, in the name of our Lord Jesus Christ, that you keep away from any brother who is walking in idleness and not in accord with the tradition that you received from us. For you yourselves know how you ought to imitate us, because we were not idle when we were with you, nor did we eat anyone's bread without paying for it, but with toil and labor we worked night and day, that we might not be a burden to any of you. It was not because we do not have that right, but to give you in ourselves an example to imitate. For even when we were with you, we would give you this command: If anyone is not willing to work, let him not eat."*—2 Thessalonians 3:6–10

First, God instructs believers to "keep away from any brother who is walking in idleness." Laziness was considered a serious sin and God made it clear to the Christians of the early church a lazy person should not be included in ongoing, warm, loving fellowship. This was not meant to punish the lazy person, but to elevate the importance of hard work and motivate anyone who might be tempted by sloth.

God's final instruction through Paul is both 100% clear and 100% against the wisdom of our age. "If anyone is not willing to work, let him not eat." This is one of the many places in the Bible where God gives us a *methodological* instruction regarding caring for those who are poor or hungry. As a reminder, God is speaking here about how Christians are to care for hungry Christians. In the Bible, the term "brother" is exclusively used to refer to believers, or in the case of the Old Testament, those who were part of the faith community. The term "brother" is never used in the Bible in terms of "the brotherhood of mankind." As noted above, the overwhelming focus of poverty care in the Bible is focused on believers caring for other believers who are in need.

My tendency is to think, "This person is hungry. Jesus wants me to love this person. I should give this person some food." But here in 2 Thessalonians, Jesus says He does not want His people to give food to believers who will not work. In this particular situation, their hunger pangs are a gift from God to motivate them to work. If well-intentioned believers take away those hunger pangs, all they have succeeded in doing is rewarding the lazy person's sloth and temporarily removing the hunger God wanted to use for good in the person's life.

Because our twisted culture has infiltrated the church, the truth I am about to write has become anathema. Some people are poor and hungry because they are under the judgment of God. Please notice I said, "Some." We have lost our fear of God. We have forgotten He says we will reap what we sow. We have ignored His promises of blessings and curses. Some of the suffering in the world is the direct result of the judgment and punishment of God on those who have sinned against Him!

> *"How long will you lie there, O sluggard? When will you arise from your sleep? A little sleep, a little slumber, a little folding of the hands to rest, and poverty will come upon you like a robber, and want like an armed man."*—Proverbs 6:9–11

It is for this reason it is unbiblical to talk about "eradicating all poverty." While I completely share the heart of that goal (you may find that hard to believe at this point), the only way it could be accomplished is if we eradicated all sin. Some poverty is due to the sin of the poor person (i.e., laziness). Other poverty is due to the sin of others (i.e., corrupt governments). So as long as we have sin with us, we will have poverty with us.

FAMILIES AND CHURCHES THAT "WORK"

When families and churches embrace God's command for individual work and responsibility, they seek to build cultures where hard work is considered virtuous. Men, in particular, are looked to and leaned on to provide for their families. Young sons are given the opportunity to work, encouraged to pursue entrepreneurship, and contribute as teenagers to the financial needs of their families, with the vision toward providing for their own family in the future.

BUT WHAT IF THE PERSON CAN'T WORK?

God's first line of defense against poverty is individual work and personal responsibility. However, sometimes people who want to work can no longer provide for themselves or their families. Many become sick and cannot work. Local economies collapse, reducing the number of available jobs. Wars break out, creating economic chaos. Many terrible things can happen which make it difficult or impossible for a brother or sister in Christ to fend off poverty.

God understands all these things and therefore He created a second line of defense to protect His sons and daughters against poverty.

THE SECOND LINE OF DEFENSE: THE CHRISTIAN FAMILY

When individuals cannot provide for themselves, God calls families to do what is necessary to help them. God explains the details of this "line of defense" in 1 Timothy 5:

> *"Honor widows who are truly widows. But if a widow has children or grandchildren, let them first learn to show godliness to their own household and to make some return to their parents, for this is pleasing in the sight of God. She who is truly a widow, left all alone, has set her hope on God and continues in supplications and prayers night and day, but she who is self-indulgent is dead even while she lives. Command these things as well, so that they may be without reproach. But if anyone does not provide for his relatives, and especially for members of his household, he has denied the faith and is worse than an unbeliever."*—1 Timothy 5:3–8

God provides us with a series of vital *methods* for how poverty in the church should be addressed. The Lord speaks through Paul, instructing Timothy and the elders in his local church *how* they were to care for the poor widows among them. These widows could not provide for themselves. The first "line of defense" of individual work had been breached. Now what?

God calls families to use their resources to care for members of the family who are in need. In the particular case of the widow, or more broadly aging parents, God says children and grandchildren must "first learn to show godliness to their own household and to make some return to their parents."

God broadens the scope in verse 8 where He says, "If anyone does not provide for his relatives, and especially for members of his household, he has denied the faith and is worse than an unbeliever." When we think of caring for the poor around us, we must first think about those in our immediate and extended families who may be in need. This is not to say believers are commanded to give money to any family member who needs it. In this text regarding widows, God establishes criteria of character. If parents have a son who is poor and addicted to drugs, it may be unwise and destructive for them to give him money, even if he is "in need."

Christian families who catch this vision share their resources with one another, to meet their needs and help everyone in the family avoid debt. I appreciate the story shared with us by our friend Jean Fisher. Jean's family seeks to embrace this biblical vision of family sharing and generosity. When it came time for Jean to go to college, her immediate family did not have the needed funds. Jean was invited to share the need with her uncles, and the decision was made among the members of the extended family to provide the needed funds so Jean would not have to incur debt. Christian families do not think of the resources God has given them in individual or "nuclear family" terms, but in terms of multi-generational vision and multi-generational generosity.

Paul instructs Pastor Timothy to "command these things" of the believers in the local church. God takes the mission of caring for the poor seriously, and He wants it done His way.

Does this mean parents should not bother to save for retirement? Of course, not. That would be a violation of God's first line of defense against poverty. God's plan A is for men to provide for their families, be good stewards of their resources, save for their own retirement, and leave a generous inheritance to their godly children and grandchildren. That is "the way things ought to be."

> "A good man leaves an inheritance to his children's children, but the sinner's wealth is laid up for the righteous."—Proverbs 13:22

As believers this is what we should pray for and this is what we should work for. But because of our fallen world, plan A doesn't always work out. Every parent I know wants to able to leave an inheritance for their children's children, rather than have their children provide *for them* in their old age. But sometimes this is necessary. It is part of God's war against poverty.

It is the Christian responsibility of children to provide needed financial help to their parents in their old age. Amy and I are thankful and blessed to have six different 401(k) plans. When we use the letter (k) we mean (k)ids. Our desire is to be good stewards with what God provides for us so our children will not need to care for us financially. It is also our desire to disciple our children so they will be eager and prepared to care for us if necessary. This is not selfish or demanding. This is part of God's revealed plan to keep believers from poverty.

BUT WHAT IF THE FAMILY CANNOT HELP?

Unfortunately, just as there are many situations which prevent an individual believer from working and providing for themselves, there are many instances when an entire family is in poverty. As much as they would like to help the individual member in need, they cannot. Because of this reality, God established a third line of defense.

THE THIRD LINE OF DEFENSE: THE LOCAL CHURCH

The institution of the local church has jurisdictional responsibility to care for church members who (1) cannot provide for themselves, and (2) who do not have family members who can or will provide for them.

Following God's command for families to "provide for their own," God instructs pastors how to handle situations when a family cannot help. One of the purposes of the local church is to be a safety net to keep believers out of poverty. When individuals and families cannot provide for themselves, pastors in a local church are authorized to take a portion of the funds freely given to them by the congregation and give it to those who are in need.

The early church practiced this principle.

> *"There was not a needy person among them, for as many as were owners of lands or houses sold them and brought the proceeds of what was sold and laid it at the apostles' feet, and it was distributed to each as any had need."*[3]—Acts 4:34–35

Individual Christians and Christian families freely gave of their resources to the apostles (the first elders). The apostles were then responsible to provide for those in the local church who were in need. We see this take place in Acts 6.

> *"Now in these days when the disciples were increasing in number, a complaint by the Hellenists arose against the Hebrews because their widows were being neglected in the daily distribution. And the twelve summoned the full number of the disciples and said, "It is not right that we should give up preaching the word of God to serve tables. Therefore, brothers, pick out from among you seven men of good repute, full of the Spirit and of wisdom, whom we will appoint to this duty."*—Acts 6:1–3

In keeping with the principles revealed later through Paul in 1 Timothy 5, the apostles used monies freely given to them by the believers, and used it to provide food for widows who were in need.

> "Let a widow be enrolled if she is not less than sixty years of age, having been the wife of one husband, and having a reputation for good works: if she has brought up children, has shown hospitality, has washed the feet of the saints, has cared for the afflicted, and has devoted herself to every good work."—1 Timothy 5:9–10

The early church had a "list of widows." These widows were "truly widows," in that they could no longer provide for themselves and they had no family or children who were able or willing to take care of them. Those that were on the list of widows were fully supported by the local church on an ongoing basis. This was a big budget operation, and as we saw in Acts 6, it required extensive organization and leadership. The early church was heavily invested in caring for their poor in general, and their widows in particular, because they understood it was a vital jurisdictional responsibility of the local church.

God established other criteria for a widow if she was to be fully supported by the local church. She had to at least 60 years old. She had to be a faithful wife (when her husband was living). She had to have a reputation for good works. What sort of good works would qualify a woman for such massive financial support? Imagine what it would take in your community to fully support a widow. In many communities this would be at least $30,000 per year. What would qualify a woman for such generosity? Big stuff! First, she had to be a woman who engaged in the overwhelming difficult kingdom ministry of bringing up children. Second, she had to be a woman who did the difficult and time-consuming ministry of hospitality. Third, she needed to show care to other Christians. Fourth, she needed to care for the afflicted.

Only serious, dedicated, Kingdom-minded widows were to be enrolled on the list. This meant being a good mom, opening your home, caring for other believers, and helping the hurting. Are those the things you would include on the list of ingredients for a dedicated, godly life? Doesn't seem very dramatic does it? These are dramatic things in the eyes of God.

BACK TO THE SECOND LINE OF DEFENSE: THE CHRISTIAN FAMILY

Pastors must not be hasty to use money from the church's bank account and give it to a poor member of the church. The first step is to make careful inquiry to determine if the believer in need has family members who are able and willing to provide for them. But what if there are family members in the local church who could help, but refuse to do so? In that case, the pastors should instruct the family to obey God and provide for the person in need. If they are unwilling to obey what God has said, they should be subject to a process of church discipline.

> *"If any believing woman has relatives who are widows, let her care for them. Let the church not be burdened, so that it may care for those who are truly widows."*—1 Timothy 5:16

It is a jurisdictional violation for the local church to use its monies to provide for a poor widow, or a poor member, if the person in need has believing family members who can help.

CHRISTIAN GENEROSITY

While the institution of the local church is authorized to use money freely given by the congregation to help the poor within the body, the majority of poverty alleviation in the New Testament comes through individual Christians and Christian families helping one another. These acts of generosity may be taking place apart from any direct knowledge or involvement of the pastors.

In each of the following texts, God speaks specifically to the need for believers to help *one another* financially.

> *"What good is it, my brothers, if someone says he has faith but does not have works? Can that faith save him? If a brother or sister is poorly clothed and lacking in daily food, and one of you says to them, "Go in peace, be warmed and filled," without giving them the things needed for the body, what good is that? So also faith by itself, if it does not have works, is dead."*—James 2:14–17

> *"Then the King will say to those on his right, 'Come, you who are blessed by my Father, inherit the kingdom prepared for you from the foundation of the world. For I was hungry and you gave me food, I was thirsty and you gave me drink, I was a stranger and you welcomed me, I was naked and you clothed me, I was sick and you visited me, I was in prison and you came to me.' Then the righteous will answer him,*

saying, 'Lord, when did we see you hungry and feed you, or thirsty and give you drink? And when did we see you a stranger and welcome you, or naked and clothe you? And when did we see you sick or in prison and visit you?' And the King will answer them, 'Truly, I say to you, as you did it to one of the least of these my brothers, you did it to me.'"—Matthew 25:34–40

"By this we know love, that he laid down his life for us, and we ought to lay down our lives for the brothers. But if anyone has the world's goods and sees his brother in need, yet closes his heart against him, how does God's love abide in him?"—1 John 3:16–17

If we fail to think jurisdictionally, and fail to pay careful attention to the words God has given us, we are in danger of misunderstanding and misapplying His Word. Both of these texts are commonly misused and applied toward the Christian responsibility to care for the *unsaved poor in their communities*. We will talk about that responsibility later in the chapter. However, these texts specifically address caring for the poor *within* the body of Christ. James says, "If a brother or sister is poorly clothed . . ." Jesus says, ". . . as you did it to one of the least of these my brothers . . ." John says, ". . . sees his brother in need . . ." As noted earlier, there is no example in Scripture when "brother" or "sister" is used to refer to humankind in general. These words always refer to either (1) literal siblings, or (2) fellow believers in the family of God.

PREACHING GOD'S PLAN

When a local church applies the sufficiency of Scripture to God's call to care for the poor, it is reflected in the preaching. Pastors present a unified, Bible-driven message to the congregation.

- *Message #1:* Work hard. Take responsibility for yourself and your family. Be responsible, and do all your work as unto the Lord.

- *Message #2:* Provide for your family. Take care of your parents. As far as it depends on you, let no faithful member of your family be in need. This is your Christian duty and responsibility.

- *Message #3:* If you cannot provide for your needs, and your family is unable or unwilling to help you, this church is here for you. We refuse to allow anyone in our church to be on government aid. We take care of our own. God commands us to do this, and we are committed to doing it. Not only is "the church" here for you, but your brothers and sisters are here for you as well. God wants our church to be filled with secret acts of generosity the pastors may never know about.

BUT WHAT IF THE LOCAL CHURCH CANNOT HELP?

In the same way individuals and families are sometimes unable to provide for themselves, it is possible for an entire church to be unable to provide for one another. What then? God has ordained a fourth line of defense.

GOD'S FOURTH LINE OF DEFENSE: MORE LOCAL CHURCHES

Many of God's commands for *how* to care for the poor are being ignored. He has ordered for specific lines of defense to be established, yet his soldiers often ignore His instructions. God's fourth line of defense may be the one we ignore the most. When a particular local church cannot provide for the poor within the body, God calls on other local churches to send the money necessary to enable the local church in need to fulfill its jurisdictional responsibility. This was modeled by the local churches in the New Testament.

> *"So the disciples determined, every one according to his ability, to send relief to the brothers living in Judea. And they did so, sending it to the elders by the hand of Barnabas and Saul."*—Acts 11:29–30

> *"At present, however, I am going to Jerusalem bringing aid to the saints. For Macedonia and Achaia have been pleased to make some contribution for the poor among the saints at Jerusalem."*—Romans 15:25–26

Follow the money! Christians voluntarily gave their money, through their local elders, to the elders of a needy church, so those elders could distribute it properly to the poor in their body. This is often practiced today when there is a disaster in a particular community.

A COMPREHENSIVE PLAN

God thought of everything! Four lines of defense to keep His children out of poverty: individual work, the family, the local church, and more local churches. Why are we seeing so little results from the "war on poverty?" Because we are not following God's plan. We love the divine mission (care for the poor), but we don't practice the divine methodology.

BUT WHAT ABOUT THE POOR OUTSIDE THE CHURCH?

As noted above, God's first concern regarding poverty is providing for the needs of believers. I don't intend that to sound heartless. I encourage you to examine every text which deals with caring for the poor, and you will see that the majority, both Old and New Testament, focus on poverty alleviation within the faith community. There is an important reason for this! If we do not first take care of our own, and do all in our power to ensure there are "no poor among us," we *cannot* overflow with generosity to those who are in need outside the church. How it must grieve God when a local church is helping meet the needs of a poor community a few miles away when a single mother in the church is on food stamps! Christians cannot care for the poor around them if they are in poverty themselves.

In the same way God has a plan to care for the poor within the church, He has a plan to care for the poor who are outside the church. Once again, we appeal to the doctrines of sufficiency and jurisdiction.

God has ordained two institutions to take responsibility for caring for the poor in the world: the Christian individual, and the Christian family.

Here are three of *many* Scriptures we can turn to where God calls individuals to care for the poor:

> *"Whoever is generous to the poor lends to the LORD, and he will repay him for his deed."*—Proverbs 19:17

> *"Whoever closes his ear to the cry of the poor will himself call out and not be answered."*—Proverbs 21:13

> *"Religion that is pure and undefiled before God, the Father, is this: to visit orphans and widows in their affliction, and to keep oneself unstained from the world."*—James 1:27

In Luke 10, Jesus tells the story of the good Samaritan. Which jurisdiction was Jesus speaking to? It was a call to *individuals* to show compassion, offer mercy, and give care to those around them.

God also calls godly *families* to engage in caring for the poor outside the church. In the Old Testament, God instructed families not to harvest all of their crops, but to leave the edges of their fields untouched. In this way, families helped the poor around them.

> *"And when you reap the harvest of your land, you shall not reap your field right up to its edge, nor shall you gather the gleanings after your harvest. You shall leave them for the poor and for the sojourner: I am the LORD your God."*—Leviticus 23:22

Note the consistent principles God gives us to govern generosity and benevolence. The New Testament principle of "if a man is not willing to work, let him not eat" is applied in the *gleanings* principle. Godly families were commanded by God to generously allow the poor to have the opportunity to work for their own food. Those who were able-bodied were not to be robbed of the dignity of harvesting their own food and bringing it home to their families who were in need.

Godly families are also called to minister to the poor through hospitality in their homes.

> *"Is it not to share your bread with the hungry and bring the homeless poor into your house; when you see the naked, to cover him, and not to hide yourself from your own flesh?"*—Isaiah 58:7

Consider the words of righteous Job:

> *"[If I have] eaten my morsel alone, and the fatherless has not eaten of it ... then let my shoulder blade fall from my shoulder, and let my arm be broken from its socket."*—Job 31:17, 22

Job says, if I have not had the poor in my house, you can rip my arm off!

These calls to care for the poor are not made to the pastors at your local church. I cannot find a single example in the New Testament in which the pastors in a local church took the money which was given by the believers, and directly distributed it to non-believers. Why is this? Because God created different jurisdictions with different responsibilities. God has called Christian individuals and Christian families to care for the poor outside the church.

TWO THOUSAND YEARS OF CHRISTIAN COMPASSION

We can see God's plan at work during the two thousand years of Christian history. Have you ever wondered where hospitals came from? Christian men and women put their money together and built them. Why are there organizations like the Red Cross and YMCA? Christian men and women embraced God's call on their lives to use their resources to care for the poor.[4] Where did the idea come from to rescue children in crisis? Who is standing up to save babies in the womb from being slaughtered? These and the vast majority of ministries of compassion around the world come from Christians seeking to obey God. "So also the secular agencies of our time have inadvertently taken pages from the Bible and used them to create many of today's charities."[5]

Why are there Christian para-church ministries all over the world seeking to care for the poor? The standard answer (which drives me nuts) is, "If the local church was doing its job, we would not need all those para-church ministries." No! In the Bible, God gives a limited mission to the local church. He gives a much broader mission to Christians and Christian families. The local church is to *equip the believers* for the work of the ministry. Perhaps we need a better title than "para-church organizations," but generally speaking these ministries are the result of proper jurisdictional thinking. These organizations were founded by passionate Christians and Christian families, voluntarily coming together to meet a need.

UNBIBLICAL METHODS OF CARING FOR THE POOR

As if this chapter has not been controversial enough, I want to conclude by addressing two unbiblical methods of caring for the poor which are yielding catastrophic results.

If you remember the section on jurisdictional theology, you will recall not only are individuals tempted to sin, but entire institutions are tempted to sin as well. Larger institutions (jurisdictions) are continually tempted to usurp the God-given responsibilities of lesser jurisdictions in order to secure more power.

During the 20th century, the United States government violated its biblical jurisdiction and took over the responsibility to care for the poor. Let's consider Social Security as one example of this jurisdictional violation.

What happens when a jurisdiction usurps responsibility from the lesser jurisdictions? The results are always the same: (1) the crisis will not be solved and

(2) the institutions which are responsible for responding properly to the crisis will be robbed of motivation, time, and resources—making it more difficult for those institutions to respond in the future.

So we now live in a day where the government has taken over the jurisdictional responsibility to provide for the elderly. This is done through forced taxation, and it is doomed to economic collapse. The government cannot perpetually take money from the young, and simultaneously borrow money from those not yet born, and give it to those who are currently in need. At some point, the game is up.

So what has happened? First, the crisis has not been solved, and many would argue it has been made worse. Second, the institutions which God created to care for the aged (the individual, family, and local church) are robbed of motivation, time, and resources to do the job. As a result, virtually no one in my generation even thinks about planning to financially care for their parents. That's the government's job!

I'll never forget a conversation I had with an 82 year-old woman. I had been preaching about jurisdictional theology and she met me in my office and said, "Pastor Rob, I feel as if you were saying that it was wrong for me to take my social security check. You don't understand. I need that money from the government to live!" I responded by saying, "Of course you should get your check. It's your money. Where did you get the idea it was the government's money? They forcibly taxed your husband for forty years, and now they are giving you back a *small portion* of what you paid in." We then proceeded to figure out how much the government had robbed her through the unbiblical jurisdictional violation of Social Security. We figured that if her husband had been able to keep and invest the 15% of his paycheck the government took from him to put into social security, she would have over $3,000,000 in a retirement account![6] She came into my office a little upset with me. She left righteously furious at the unbiblical system of government we have elected in our country.

Not only has the government violated God's jurisdictions in caring for the elderly, but every other kind of poverty as well. The results have been tragic. Can you name a single "government project" community which has thrived, flourished, and "graduated" itself from needing government assistance?

The poor are suffering! What can Christians do about it? First, we practice biblical compassion as individuals, families, and local churches. But if we are to take seriously God's call to care for the poor, not only must we follow God's methods when caring for individuals in need, but we must do all in our power to combat socialism in our nation. To care for the poor without fighting back socialism is like picking up a rock in a raging river, drying it off, and tossing it back in only to get wet again. We must do all in our power to re-route the entire river and lead our nation back to proper jurisdictional responsibilities. Only then will we see a dramatic positive change in the "war on poverty."

I appreciate one of the ways Grace Family Baptist Church in Houston, TX seeks to help the poor in their community. They call their members to care for the poor in their own neighborhoods! There have been situations when a believer in the church has had a neighbor with such an urgent emergency the believer came to the pastors to ask them for help. In those situations, the pastors could chose to give church funds *to the Christian family* who were then equipped to give it to their neighbor. The Christian family was meeting a need through genuine relationship, and the local church was helping the family succeed.

Every pastor has had the experience of a person in need walking in off the street and asking for help. I received many of these visits over the years, and even though I tried to help, I often walked away in tears. The pain and brokenness was overwhelming. These are not easy situations. Is this person telling me the truth? Is the church getting scammed here? These are complicated situations, but here are a couple of thoughts. First, it may be appropriate for the pastor to help the person as a *personal* ministry. "I believe you have a genuine need, and I want to help you. But know this is not money from the church. This is my money, and as a Christian I want to do what I can to help." Second, it may be appropriate for the pastor to call some members of the church to come to the church, or join in by phone, to talk with the person who is in need, so they could consider whether or not they, *as Christian individuals and families,* could help.

AN URGENT CRISIS

God's people must rise up with a holy urgency regarding God's call to care for the poor! God has laid out a careful strategy in the Bible for *how* Christians are to care for the poor. If we will faithfully commit ourselves to fighting this war *His way,* we will see lives and communities transformed as never before.

Questions for Discussion:

1. Why do you think people are so resistant to the idea some poverty in the result of God's judgment?

2. In what ways does your local church follow the New Testament jurisdictional model of caring for the poor?

3. As an individual Christian (and as a Christian family), in what ways do you care for fellow believers who are in need? In what ways do you care for the poor outside your family and your church?

ENDNOTES

[1] Romans 10:17 and Colossians 3:16.

[2] While I do not believe God wants all Christians "healthy and wealthy," I do believe He promises to supply all His children's needs. I believe that in the Bible, God gives us a radical and thorough plan for how He wants His children to provide for one another.

[3] The early Christians were generous with one another and generous in their giving to their local church. However, they did not create communes or socialist economic structures. The early Christians held private property and private assets. However, they viewed all their material things as blessings from God. They understood God commanded to use their material blessings to provide for themselves, to provide for their families, to freely (not under compulsion) provide for one another, and to freely give to their local church.

[4] Tragically, some ministries of compassion that began as explicitly Christian organizations have now abandoned their Christian roots.

[5] Kennedy, 34.

[6] We reached this number by considering her husband's forty years of employment, at an average of $40,000 per year. Social security takes 15% of every pay check. We calculated the investment results if she and her husband had been able to keep that $6,000 each year and invest it into a basic index fund for that time period.

CHAPTER 18: TRANSFORMING YOUTH AND CHILDREN'S MINISTRY

"He established a testimony in Jacob and appointed a law in Israel, which he commanded our fathers to teach to their children, that the next generation might know them, the children yet unborn, and arise and tell them to their children, so that they should set their hope in God and not forget the works of God, but keep his commandments."

—PSALM 78:5–7

FROM MY HEART

I love youth and children's ministry, because I love youth and children. God gives us different passions and gifts, and since I was in high school He has given me a love for the next generation! I served as a student leader in my youth group and was grateful for my youth pastor, Ken Geis, who was a spiritual father for me. Ken encouraged me to go to Wheaton College to prepare to serve in full-time youth ministry. At the beginning of my sophomore year, I began volunteering in the youth ministry at Wheaton Bible Church with Pastor Bob Johnson. That was the start of 19 years of pastoral ministry with youth, children, and families. I am thankful for the many hours of coaching and mentoring I received from Pastors Gary Dausey and Rob Bugh. I get excited about all the things we are exploring in this book, but nothing is more exciting to me than reaching the next generation for Christ.

By many standards, I was a "successful" youth pastor. There were a number of years when we had nearly 500 high school and junior high students actively involved in our ministry. More than 200 students and staff participated in our short-term mission trips around the country each year. The parents in our church, more often than not, encouraged me about the job I was doing. And we were seeing spiritual fruit in the lives of the students.

In fact, this morning, as I was preparing to write this chapter, I received an email from a woman who was in my youth group when she was a teenager. She wrote, "Thank you for all that you have done for my life. I cannot begin to thank you enough for being such a positive influence on me in middle school and high school." Millions of young people have been blessed, encouraged, and impacted by youth pastors and caring youth volunteers.

But as I crossed my first decade in youth ministry, I became increasingly concerned. I didn't want to admit it, but the facts were right in front of me. The majority of the students who seemed to be "on fire" for the Lord when they were in high school, were now no longer following the Lord as adults. I hate writing that word *majority*. But to use another word would be lying. These are not numbers or statistics to me. These are young men and women I love! I think back to the first small group I led for high school boys. Eight boys. Four years. Bible study every week. Today, one is at home with the Lord. Six are no longer practicing Christians. Just one is still serving the risen Christ with all his heart. Millions of empty nest parents around our nation are grieving over their prodigal children!

THE MESSAGE AND THE METHOD

Part of my philosophy of youth ministry was encapsulated in the phrase: "We have an unchanging message in a constantly changing package." What I meant by this was the message of the gospel was unchanging and God's Word was unchanging; but the *methods* we would use in youth ministry would be constantly changing to meet the changing tides of youth culture.

It sounded so good, deep, and "missiological." I was blind to the huge problem right in front of me. What was so wrong about my philosophy? In the Bible, God is not silent on the method. God does not say, when it comes to next-generation ministry, "Here is the gospel, get it to kids and teens however you want." As we have explored throughout this book, God has filled the Bible with His divine methods. He tells us *what* He wants (in this case, we can all agree God wants us to do all in our power to evangelize and disciple children), but He also tells us *how* to do it, and *who* should do it.

Because I didn't understand or believe the doctrine of the sufficiency of Scripture and was ignorant about the theology of jurisdiction, I was not doing youth ministry *God's way*. I was doing it my way, using the latest creative approaches, new ideas, and human innovations. I accepted His mission (disciple the next generation), but ignored His methods.

THE NEW EXPERIMENT

In the late 1800s and early 1900s local churches began a new experiment. In order to reach the next generation for Christ we developed an age-segregated, church-building based ministry model. Over time, in many churches this ministry model became the primary tool for ministering to children, while their parents became secondary.

We are not losing the majority of our children because children's and youth ministry has been done poorly. We are giving it our best! We are not losing the majority of our children because our leaders are not passionate and loving. The youth and children's ministry leaders I know are pouring themselves out for the sake of the kids and teens they love. It isn't fundamentally a problem with our resources and curriculum. There are some powerful, Bible-driven resources being used in many churches.

The reason why we are seeing true Christianity in the United States decline from generation to generation is we have turned away from God's *method* of passing faith to children. The message here is not, "The stats are bad. Here is a model that will work better." God's people are not to be governed by what works best. We are to be governed by Scripture and Scripture alone.

LOCK THE DOOR

So what should youth and children's ministry look like? We must "lock ourselves in a room with the Bible" and inquire of God's Word, "What plan have You revealed for how children and youth are to be evangelized and discipled?" If we used the Bible alone to answer this question, what would we conclude? God has given us two primary *methods* for the spiritual training of children.

First, God has filled the Bible with His call to parents and grandparents to be the primary disciplers of their children. If a person is a parent or grandparent, their Great Commission calling begins with the souls of their own children. This mission to disciple our children is a 24-7 calling and God calls His people to the specific practice of family worship in the home. Heads of households are to lead their families in prayer and reading Scripture.

The biblical basis for this is not simply Deuteronomy 6, Psalm 78, and Ephesians 6. As we have already seen, God's call to parents to disciple their children, and for the family to function as a discipleship center, is found throughout the Bible.[1]

(If you have not already done so, please go back and read section four. I realize some of you may have flipped straight to this chapter because of your interest in youth ministry.)

Who has God called to evangelize and disciple children?

Parents.

How are parents to do this?

Through comprehensive family discipleship which flows out of family worship in the home.

Second, God entrusts the local church with the mission to disciple the next generation. But it is not enough to say the local church should disciple children. The local church must not only accept the divinely-revealed mission, it must practice the divinely-revealed methods. The local church and the Old Testament faith community were entrusted with two primary responsibilities in regard to the discipleship of children.

First, the local church was entrusted with the jurisdictional responsibility to train and equip parents to disciple their children at home. Pastors were charged with the mission to "equip the saints for the work of ministry" (Ephesians 4:12), and for those who are parents and grandparents, their "ministry" begins with the souls of their children. A pastor's primary impact in the life of a child comes through his impact in the lives of the child's parents.

Second, children were included in the weekly corporate worship service. The corporate worship service was a place for everyone, regardless of their age, to come together for the worship of God and to grow through the preaching of His Word. In the context of the corporate worship service, pastors lead whole families together in worship and teach them the Bible. Because this is such a critical issue in the church today, I will seek to offer a detailed biblical examination of this in an upcoming chapter.

In addition to parents, *who* has God called to evangelize and disciple children?

The local church.

How is the local church to do this?

(1) By training and equipping parents to disciple their children at home, and

2) By including entire families in the corporate worship service.

MEALS AND VITAMINS

Think of family worship in the home, and corporate worship with their parents at church as two essential "spiritual meals" for children. These were ordained by God and not man.

We might consider other discipleship opportunities as vitamins. Youth group. Retreats. Sunday school. Sadly, millions of young people in our churches today never eat any meals! The only spiritual nourishment they receive comes from vitamins—and we wonder why they are malnourished.

MODERN YOUTH MINISTRY CONFIRMS THE BIBLICAL MODEL

During my years as a youth pastor, there were a number of things that were continual frustrations for me. Year after year, I worked with my staff team to address them, but we never made the kind of progress I felt was needed. I realize now the dysfunctions I was seeing with the modern model were all pointing back towards God's design.

Ratio Problems

If you are a children's pastor with five kids in the ministry, you can run things all by yourself. But what happens when thirty kids show up? Time to recruit some volunteers! As ministries grow, doing it alone is simply not an option. Most next-generation ministries end up with some kind of small group structure. Leaders are assigned to a group of children for the purposes of follow up, Bible study, prayer, and discussion.

Have you ever led a discipleship small group for children or teens? For the sake of discussion, let me assume you had eight kids in the group. As you think about that group, with how many of those eight did you have a closer, personal relationship? With how many did you have a strong sense of trust, warmth, and vulnerability? I have asked these questions to thousands of youth pastors and volunteers and the response is a consistent, "two or three." With that close relationship comes increased influence. But what about the other five or six kids in the group? They don't have that same bond with you and often experience less impact. We have ratio problems.

Turnover Problems

It's the end of August. Fall programming is starting up next week. Where are you going to find the last ten volunteers you need to be fully staffed? For some this annual number is ten, for others it is one hundred. Many volunteers engage with us for only a year. Others commit for even less than that. Recruitment is often a leadership nightmare, but stop and consider this problem from the perspective of the child. Many children receive a new "discipler" every year as they grow up in the church. I call it the "discipleship roller coaster." In first grade, little Mike loves his teacher! He enjoys going to Sunday school. Then he moves up to second grade, and his new teacher, Mr. Jones is not so hot. He isn't as fun or as good a teacher as Mr. Smith. What is little Mike supposed to do? What will his parents say? He just has to stick it out, and hope that third grade will be more like first grade. We have turnover problems.

Heart Problems

I don't mean this to be critical, but the simple fact is that many of the volunteers working with our children and students do so with a heart of love, while others are "just volunteering." I don't mind those who are "just volunteering" because sometimes we just need more adults for crowd control. But if we have any hope of helping young people grow in their faith, we need to approach them with a genuine attitude of love. It sounds harsh, but some who are working with youth care a lot, others only care a little. We have heart problems.

Training Problems

As a youth pastor, I realized in order to disciple students, I had to disciple my volunteers. There was no way I was just going to send a bunch of teenage girls over to a woman's apartment to be discipled without getting that leader trained. Here was the process I followed. When people expressed interest in serving in the youth ministry I met with them personally. After getting to know them during that hour, if we decided to take the next step, I would run a criminal background check on them. We would also follow up with two references. So, if the hour interview went well, you were not a criminal, and two people gave you a good reference, you were good to go. I would now entrust a small group of immortal souls into your spiritual care. But not before you came to my small group leaders training class. It was an intense three hours of small group principles, Bible study principles, and classic do's and don'ts. If you sat there for three hours, you were now considered "trained."

I used to view this process as rich, thorough, and deep. I now look back and wonder how I could have been so naïve. Many of the volunteers I worked with were godly, mature, and dedicated people. Others (and I don't say this with a critical attitude) had no business being a spiritual influence on children or teaching the Bible. We have training problems.

Obedience Problems

As a youth ministry team, we spent a lot of time talking about how to encourage spiritual accountability in the lives of the students. We wanted to see students living out what they believed. What I didn't realize, however, was our modern ministry model separates obedience from sanctification.

I believe as we respond to God's grace and obey God, we grow spiritually. In the same way, when we choose to disobey God, we "shrink" spiritually. Spiritual growth and obedience cannot be separated from one another.

Imagine a fourth grade girl confesses to you that she has been cheating on her tests at school. You talk with her, share some Scripture with her, and encourage her to pray hard and study hard—and not to cheat on her tests this coming week.

She goes home prepared to do the right thing! Next week, you follow up with her and ask, "How did you do with your tests this week?" Sadly, she confesses to cheating again.

If you were sharing this story with a fellow leader would you say, "I told this girl last week that she should not cheat on her tests, but she disobeyed me." Is that the language you would use? Would you say that the girl "disobeyed" you when she cheated on her tests again? I would not. I would say, "she didn't follow my advice," or "She didn't follow through on my encouragement to her." To say, "She didn't obey me," sounds creepy. As children's and youth leaders we are mentors, supports, and encouragers to young people. But we have separated obedience from spiritual growth, and as a result we have generations of spiritually-stunted men and women. We have obedience problems.

SO WHAT HAVE WE LEARNED?

Through the last century of modern youth and children's ministry we have learned what we are really looking for is:

- A low "leader-to-child ratio"

- A person who will disciple a child for the long haul

- A person who loves the child with all their heart and is willing to sacrifice everything to lead them toward godliness

- A person who has day-in, day-out experience and skills working with this age of child

- A person who has authority from God to require obedience from the child.

Does this sound like someone we might know? A parent! All the things we are looking for in our church-based ministries God has already built into the institution of the family, and the parent-child relationship.

BUT WHAT ABOUT KIDS WHO DON'T HAVE CHRISTIAN PARENTS?

I can hear you. "Rob, this whole model where the church equips Christian parents to disciple their kids is great for all the Christian families, but what about all the unsaved kids who don't have parents to disciple them?" This question is of the utmost urgency and importance.

As a first response, I need to address the assumption in the question. The assumption is that our modern ministry model *is* radically effective evangelistically.

I once gathered together my team of ten paid youth ministry staff and asked them a question, "Can you give me the names of students who have come to Christ in this last year?" I didn't want names of students who checked a box on a card. I didn't want names of students who were on fire for a month and disappeared. I wanted the names of students who a year ago were lost, in families that were lost, and who were now converted, walking with Christ, and meaningfully connected with the church.

The response? At first, silence. Everyone was racking their brain trying to think of a student who was a new believer. This was in the context of five hundred active students from 7th-12th grade. This was in the context of a ministry dedicated to outreach and evangelism. We were blowing the doors off. Many events were standing room only. Yet, we were struggling to come up with specific students who we *knew* had been converted. After more thought, we identified five students who we believed were new converts. Five out of five hundred.

So my first response to the question of reaching unsaved youth is to challenge the assumption that what we are currently doing *is* effective. While God uses fallen people and flawed methods (thank you, Lord) to advance His Kingdom, we should not be at all satisfied with the evangelistic effectiveness of our current ministry model. People are dying apart from Christ and going to hell, and through our ministry model we see precious few saved! We must return to God's methodology, not only because it is His, and not only for the sake of our own children, but for the sake of the lost as well.

I set out to interview these five new believers. I wanted to find out what happened to them. What was their story? How did God take them from darkness to light? Many of their answers would not surprise you. God brought them a Christian friend. They attended a couple youth group events. They heard some portions of Scripture. But there was a common thread. Each of these five (and I realize this was not a Barna study) not only had a Christian friend, but they were meaningfully involved in their Christian friend's family life. They went on trips with them. They frequently were over for meals. They could walk in the front door without knocking, because they were so welcome in that home. They saw love, forgiveness, grace, joy, and the gospel in action.

I asked them, from their perspective, what had the greatest impact on their journey toward Christ. They all said in their own words, "being a part of that family." At the time I didn't understand the doctrines of sufficiency and jurisdiction, but my view of "child and youth evangelism" changed forever. Before that time, I thought the responsibility for reaching unsaved youth rested with Christian young people (through peer-to-peer evangelism) and with the local youth ministries.

I am now convinced the responsibility for child and youth evangelism is an "all-hands-on-deck" mission for every family in the local church. As a father, it is not my job to simply say to my children, "You need to be sharing Christ with your friends." Instead, God calls us to minister together as a family by opening our home to children in the neighborhood. Our family is a powerful evangelism and outreach center. This is not because we are super-spiritual, but simply because we are Christians.

If we are going to get serious about reaching children who don't have Christian parents, we need to unleash every single one of the local church's "satellite ministries." But Rob, we don't have any satellite ministries. Yes, you do! They are called homes.

My second response to the question of reaching unsaved children is we have dramatically over-estimated the evangelistic impact of church programs, and dramatically under-estimated the evangelistic impact of the Christian family. Imagine if the parents and grandparents in your church stopped looking to the youth ministry to reach the unsaved students in the community, but took the responsibility to intentionally welcome their children's friends into their homes with the goal of reaching not only them, but their entire family for Christ!

Here is a third response. One of the reasons we do not see many unsaved students coming to Christ is because the majority of our focus in Sunday school and youth group is on Christian students. If your church is like most, the majority of children in Sunday school are from church families. The majority of students on your youth group retreat are from church families. The leadership of the church, along with the parents, are expecting the youth and children's leaders to disciple the church kids! As a result, most next-generation ministry leaders are overwhelmed with all of their relationships and discipleship with children who come from Christian homes. This leaves precious little time for serious outreach to the unsaved.

This seems counter-intuitive, but an essential key to accelerating youth evangelism is for a church to embrace the biblical model of home discipleship. When this happens, the youth and children's ministry team is no longer expected to disciple the Christian children from the Christian homes! Instead, in accordance with God's Word, parents are trained and equipped to disciple their own children at home. When this happens (1) every Christian home grows in its mission of becoming a discipleship and evangelism center and (2) the youth and children's ministry staff at the church are freed up to get out of the church building and launch evangelistic initiatives out in the community. We cannot wait any longer to embrace the biblical model, for the sake of our own children, *and* for the sake of the lost.

A CLASSIC JURISDICTIONAL DISASTER

The history of youth and children's ministry could be a "poster child" to illustrate the biblical principles of jurisdiction and what happens when God's jurisdictions are ignored.

In the early 1800s, Robert Raikes led the Sunday school movement in England. Then "Sunday school" swept across the United States during the 1800s, driven primarily by the American Sunday School Union.[3]

One of the mistakes we make when studying history is assuming that words maintain their same meaning over time. Every Christian today would define the term "Sunday school" as a gathering of children in the church building on Sunday morning. We see "Sunday school" as a ministry organized by the local church to help Christian children grow in their faith and help lead lost children to Christ.

In the 1800s, the term "Sunday school" referred to something completely different. I encourage you to read the official historical record of the American Sunday School Union by Wm. H. Levering.[4]

Here were the essential characteristics of "Sunday school" in the 1800s.

- "Sunday school" programs were not led by pastors, but by passionate Christians and Christian families who wanted to reach out to lost children and families in the community. Did some pastors participate? Of course, but they did so out of Christian love, not out of pastoral duty.

- "Sunday school" gatherings were not held in local churches or administrated by local church leaders. Meetings were held in homes, schools, outdoors, and in places of business.

- The purpose of the "Sunday school" was to provide Christian care for needy children and their families and, above all, to give Christians the opportunity to share the gospel with the lost.

- It was their mission to establish "Sunday schools" in towns and neighborhoods *where there were no Christian churches*, in hopes that enough people would come to Christ and a local church could then be established.

Don't take my word for it. Here is how the American Sunday School Union described the first century of their ministry (written in 1888).

Reaching out to unsaved children in the community was led by compassionate Christians, not organized as a "program" in the local church:

> On December 19, 1790, a meeting was held in the city of Philadelphia, by a few pious men, among them Wm. White, D.D., Benjamin Rush, M.D., Matthew Carey, Thomas P. Cope, and others of like prominence, for the purpose of taking into consideration the establishment of Sunday Schools in this city.[5]

Their strategic priority was to call Christians to engage in sharing the gospel with children in unreached areas. Their strategy was to call Christians to boldly evangelize unreached neighborhoods in hopes a local church might be established. For them it was "Sunday school" should start churches, not churches should start "Sunday schools."

> [We] seek to plant a Sunday school in every neglected place, and to maintain it until it becomes self-sustaining; ripens into a church

to be attached to whatever denomination predominates in that neighborhood.[6]

There was never a thought "Sunday school" should be developed to disciple Christian children from Christian homes.

> The American Sunday School Union is doing a work which no other association can successfully begin to approach. It goes in the "high-ways and hedges" and gathers in the children of all denominations, for it is non-sectarian, to teach them the Bible and the need of a Saviour, in all parts of this great land. Its efficient and consecrated missionaries establish Sunday Schools where no church organizations can as yet be maintained, and are the means of bringing into the Church of Christ on earth thousands who otherwise would have been deprived of all religious privileges, of all knowledge of even the Bible itself . . .[7]

The original "Sunday school" usually included adults and was run by Christians rather than professional clergy. They gathered in homes and other community locations.

> The immediate result of this house-to-house visitation was that on Sunday, June 8, over 70 people gathered at the house of Mr. Robinson. With varied histories, and for many different causes, had these families left their homes elsewhere; but all had come here with one aim in common, the getting of land from which they hoped to earn their daily bread. And now, for the first time on this new scene of their labors, they gathered together in public meeting to worship the Father of all, and to make plans and promises to meet regularly to study the book that speaks of Him. That day the Fairview Union Sunday School was organized, and arrangements made to meet each Sunday afternoon at a new school house near the center of the settlement.[8]

> Wherever a faithful missionary of this society goes, be it in the older states or in the new West, he finds more destitute children than he can possibly reach ; and in every case, without a known exception, conversions follow the opening of God's word in the homes of the people.[9]

But what did they do? When we think of "Sunday school" we are mentally locked in to the 60 minute slot on Sunday morning. Here is what the original "Sunday school" movement did:

> [Sunday school workers] establish schools, visit families, distribute Bibles, Testaments, lesson helps and good literature, and, by so doing, cause people to see the need of help to overcome the evil of this world, and accept Christ as the only sure help in time of need.[10]

> The American Sunday School Union is doing good work in the needy localities of our state, organizing Sunday Schools and supplying the people with Bibles, Testaments, libraries, papers and elementary books, so that all may be able to read God's Word.

Today we call it "community outreach," in the 1800s they called it "Sunday school." As noted above, their vision was that "Sunday school" ministries would eventually lead to church planting.

> At a meeting of the Sunday School, held Aug. 10, 1884, a movement for the organization of a Congregational Church was initiated.[11]

> Sunday school is the forerunner of the church.[12]

> The church which grew out of your Sunday school here is to have its house of worship dedicated and its minister ordained next Sunday.[13]

> Jeremiah Kimball, who has labored in central Dakota as a missionary of the American Sunday School Union for several years reports 144 new Sunday schools formed, and 67 churches having grown out of his schools.[14]

> If the study of the Bible by the young who have no church to attend does not prepare them for the church when it does come, then we know not what will prepare them, for the Bible is the text-book of every Sunday School that lays any claim to being Christian.[15]

THE LOCAL CHURCH "TAKES OVER"

As we learned earlier, larger jurisdictions are always tempted to take over the responsibilities of smaller jurisdictions. Many aspects of the "Sunday school movement" began with proper jurisdictional theology. Christians and Christian families had Christ's heart for the lost and they came together, shared resources, and organized and launched ministries of evangelism and compassion in communities that did not have local churches. Praise the Lord! This is exactly what God calls His people to do.

This began to change toward the end of the 1800s. Slowly but surely, programs grew inside church buildings rather than out in the community, and parents were gradually marginalized in the discipleship process.

These changes have brought predictable results.

I talk with Christian parents *every week* who have little passion in their hearts to personally lead their children to Christ, to teach them His Word at home, and to prepare them for a life of godliness. How could this be? They don't have to worry about these things. They can drop them off at children's church or youth ministry. The professionals at church will teach my kids the Bible. The jurisdictional violation predictably robs Christian parents of the motivation to disciple their own children.

They are also robbed of time. For many families, after friends, sports, activities, social media, eating, and sleeping, there are only a few moments in a day to connect with their children. When the local church calls parents to drop off their children for an hour of discipleship on Sunday, and then two more hours on Wednesday, there is even less time for parents to disciple their children.

Unsaved children in the community also suffer from the jurisdictional violation. In the same way Christian parents are robbed of motivation to disciple their own children, Christians are robbed of the motivation to reach the lost children in their neighborhoods. I don't need to invite that lost family to my home. The youth group offers some great outreach programs! Because the institutional local church has wrongly taken over the mission of "youth evangelism," Christians and Christian families have stepped back, and the result is *fewer* people reaching out to unsaved families.

WHAT CAN BE DONE?

Is it too late for us to return to the biblical model for discipling the next generation? Never! In the next chapter, we will talk about steps local churches can take to increasingly equip parents, build a culture of family discipleship, and reach *more* unsaved families with the gospel.

Questions for Discussion:

1. Did you grow up in a Christian education ministry? What was your experience?

2. If you grew up in church, did your family have an intentional plan to disciple you and teach you God's Word at home? If so, what did that look like?

3. What was most interesting to you about the "Sunday school" ministry of the 1800s?

4. What results do you see from the local church taking over the discipleship of children? Can you see the results of the principle of jurisdictional violation in your context?

ENDNOTES

[1]In the Bible, children are never described as wards of the state. Nor are they ever described as wards of the local church. In Scripture, when we read "our children" or "your children" the jurisdictional context is always in terms of parents and the family.

[2]The Scriptural base for this will be developed in chapter 20.

[3]http://www.youthministryinstitute.org/Files/Research/Historical%20Timeline%20in%20 Youth%20Ministry.pdf.

[4]Wm. H. Levering, *The American Sunday School Union*, (Brown and Pettibone: Chicago, 1888).

[5]Ibid, 2.

[6]Ibid, 5.

[7]Ibid, 11.

[8]Ibid, 12.

[9]Ibid, 24.

[10]Ibid, 14.

[11]Ibid, 17.

[12]Ibid, 18.

[13]Ibid.

[14]Ibid, 20.

[15]Ibid, 23.

"Oh that my ways may be steadfast in keeping your statutes! Then I shall not be put to shame, having my eyes fixed on all your commandments."

—PSALM 119:5–6

The issue of next-generation ministry is serious and urgent. Multi-generational faithfulness is at the heart of God's local church, at the heart of our homes, and is literally a life-and-death matter for our children.

Thank God for His mercy and grace! He is patient with us, and His Holy Spirit continues to sanctify and conform us into the image of Christ. In the same way, the Holy Spirit leads and guides His local churches to continually reform and return to doing His will, His way.

WHERE DOES CHANGE BEGIN?

For Christians, the first step of change is simple, but often times the most difficult. It was terribly difficult for me. After more than a decade in youth ministry, I had become convinced the model I was leading was not found in Scripture. Beyond that, God had clearly laid out a proactive and intentional model to evangelize and disciple children, and that model centered around parents and families. I knew something had to change. I didn't know what to do or how to do it. But I knew where I needed to start. I needed to repent, and I did.

I simply confessed to God, that though my intentions were all good, I had not allowed His words on youth ministry to guide and shape my ministry. I had gone my own way and done my own thing. Repentance is always the first step, and it has extraordinary spiritual power.

God used His Word to lead Pastor Arthur Jenkins (St. James Episcopal Church, Charleston, SC) to this same place. He recognized they had built their next-generational discipleship strategy around the church building, rather than around parents and families. What could he do to turn things around? He didn't have all those answers (none of us do), but he knew what to do first. He stood up in front of his congregation on a Sunday morning and repented. He confessed to them he had not led the church according to God's revealed plan in His Word. He invited parents and grandparents to repent with him. He pledged to the church he would seek to lead a transformation back to the biblical model of family discipleship.[1] Praise the Lord!

BEGIN WITH THE RIGHT CONVERSATIONS

I have seen many churches begin the family ministry journey with all the wrong conversations. "We need to do a better job connecting with parents." "Families are falling apart all around us, and the church needs to help." "Kids are impacted more at home, so we need to focus more on families." These are all important conversations but this is not where we start.

As a leadership team, take all the time needed to wrestle with the doctrine of the sufficiency of Scripture and jurisdictional theology. Wear your Bibles out. Take a year. Take two. From the top down, seek doctrinal unity about what God has said about the unique roles of His family and His local church.

I would encourage your pastors/elders to consider writing a short document offering theology of "church and home." What role should the family play in passing faith to the next generation? What role should the local church play? Once you have doctrinal unity, based on the Bible alone, you are then prepared to lead with courage and conviction.

LEADING CHANGE: FIRST STEPS

For most churches the process of moving from "church-centered, home-supported" to "home-centered, church-supported" takes time.[2] In the same way it takes time to disciple a church toward biblical worship or biblical evangelism, it takes time to disciple a church toward family discipleship.

Here is a tool that may help you take some initial steps toward equipping parents to disciple their children and uniting families in spiritual growth.

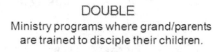

DOUBLE
Ministry programs where grand/parents
are trained to disciple their children.

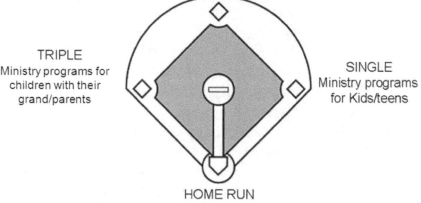

TRIPLE
Ministry programs for
children with their
grand/parents

SINGLE
Ministry programs
for Kids/teens

HOME RUN
Church helps Grand/parents provide spiritual
training and discipleship in the home

Copyright 2007
Rob Rienow
www.visionaryparenting.com

In baseball, there are different "hits" that have different levels of impact on the game. Doubles make a bigger impact than singles. Triples accomplish more than doubles. Home runs are most powerful of all. In the same way, some things make a bigger spiritual impact in the lives of children than others. If you share my passion for youth and children's ministry, you want to see a big impact! So what can the local church do to evangelize and disciple the next generation?

Forgive me for using the word "program" in this section. Many pastors have told me, "Rob, we are not a program church, we are discipleship church." I get that. When I use the word "program" I am simply referring to whatever things the local church does to accomplish its ministry.

Hitting Singles: Ministry Programs for Children and Teens.

Sunday school. Youth group. Awana. Retreat weekends. God uses these events for spiritual impact in the lives of children. But often parents and grandparents are effectively removed from the discipleship process.

Hitting doubles: Ministry programs where parents and grandparents are trained to disciple their children.

At Wheaton Bible Church, I worked for many years with Jeremy Tullis who served as our Student Ministries Pastor. Pastor Tullis made an important change to how he approached the issue of teaching teens about sexuality. When I was leading the youth ministry, I would simply schedule a guys retreat and teach them what I thought the Bible said about sex. Jeremy wanted to equip parents to have these conversations with their teenagers. So he scheduled a parent meeting in February, and over the course of two hours sought to equip them with the biblical principles of sexuality for *them* to share with their sons and daughters. He explained to parents that later that spring there would be a youth ministry event for students (guys and girls separated) in which these same principles would be taught. This event was designed to *reinforce* what the students had already learned from their parents at home. This programming shift was a small step in the right direction.

Perhaps your church offers a mid-week children's ministry event such as Awana. One of the first steps you could take would be to move away from the model where parents drop their kids off and head out for coffee, and replace it with a model where parents stay and receive training and equipping on home discipleship.[3]

If you spend an hour with children, they get one hour of ministry. If you spend an hour training and equipping parents, your hour multiplies itself into hundreds of hours of ministry in the home. When the local church trains and equips parents it is functioning biblically, following God's jurisdictions, and ministering more effectively than ever before.

Hitting triples: Ministry programs for children with their parents and grandparents.

If you were a junior high pastor, which of the following do you think would make a bigger impact? A Friday night Bible study with ten boys, or that same ministry time with the boys and their dads? If possible, we would love to have the dads there. Why? Because we know if the fathers and sons could grow together the spiritual impact would multiply.

One of the first things to do is continually invite parents to all your ministry events. Don't just say, "You are welcome to come and check things out if you want to." In every promotional piece, make it clear parents are always invited. Turn your youth retreat into a family retreat. Turn your youth mission trip into a family mission trip.

This is *especially* important for those children and teens who may not have parents who are able or willing to participate. Children from struggling or unsaved families don't need to connect to a peer culture; they need to connect to a family culture. They need other moms and dads in the church who will take them under their wing.

Here is the best news about *hitting triples*. You don't need to run a single new program to get this started. You have a powerful family ministry event in your church every week. It is called *church*. The corporate worship service is the weekly spiritual meal for everyone in the local church, from the youngest to the oldest.

Hitting home runs: Church helps parents and grandparents provide spiritual training and discipleship in the home.

What is the most powerful "program" a child or teenager can "attend?" The most important spiritual meal in the life of a child is family worship in the home. As we learned in the previous section on family theology, family worship in the home is the centerpiece of the Christian family and is the first action step for parents who want to disciple their children.

These few minutes of family prayer and reading the Bible together are supernatural moments of discipleship. Can you imagine if every child had the blessing of seeing their father or their mother open the Bible each day and read it with a humble, believing heart? For the first ninety years of my father's life he was an atheist. I am so grateful God saved my mother when I was a baby and she prayed with me and my brother and read the Bible to us.

This may sound strange, but I want to challenge you to think of family worship in the home as a "program" you are trying to run. Take one hour with your leadership team and brainstorm together how you could get the program of "family worship" up and running in your church. In the same way you think about your other programs, how could you get the maximum participation? How could you run this program with excellence? How could you structure this program to have the maximum spiritual impact?

One of the first steps we took at Wheaton Bible Church to increase family worship was in our children's ministry. For many years, when parents would pick up their children from Sunday school we would give them a sheet of paper which told them about what their child learned that morning. We then encouraged them to have follow-up conversations with their child at home. We realized the *message* of this take-home paper was backwards. We were telling parents Sunday school was in the lead, and you should support Sunday school. We needed to flip the process. We took a baby step in the right direction by taking *next week's* handout sheet and passed it out to parents this week. We titled the handout, "Take the Lead," and then communicated (as an example), "Next week in Sunday school we will be talking about prayer. Here are the Scriptures we will be studying. Please take the lead this week and read and discuss these Scriptures together as a family."

Some churches also apply this principle in relationship to the corporate worship service. They give parents the sermon text and worship songs for *next week* so families can read the Bible and sing together at home.[4] This is particularly effective in preparing children and teens to get the most out of the corporate worship service. It is a small but valuable step in becoming "home-centered and church-supported."

Is your ministry hitting for power?

In an upcoming leadership meeting, sketch out a baseball diamond and write singles, doubles, triples, and home runs by each base. Then make a list under each heading of what your ministry is doing in that area. With many of the churches I have consulted the end result of this exercise is the realization that all of their ministries are in the "single" category.

Pray and talk as a staff about how you can increase the impact of your ministry by putting your time, resources, and money into the more powerful discipleship environments.

ARE PARENTS REALLY QUALIFIED TO DO THIS?

As discussed in the last chapter, the most common response I hear to the biblical vision for family discipleship is, "What about kids who don't have Christian parents?" After we talk through that one the second question is, "Most of the parents in our church are not spiritually mature enough to disciple their kids, so how does it make any sense for them to try and do it?"

I may be off base on this, but I think this is the only area of the Christian life where pastors tell people in the church they can't do something God commands.

Let's say we have a brand new believer. Do we encourage that "baby Christian" to wait to start tithing until they are more spiritually mature? Do we encourage that "baby Christian" to wait to start singing in church until they feel more comfortable? No! We invite them to rest in the grace and power of God and follow Him fully right now!

God commands parents to disciple their children. Is there anything in His Word that says parents need to reach a requisite level of holiness before they can obey? I completely agree parents cannot lead a child in a direction they are not going themselves. But if we have men and women who have been in our church for five or ten years, and they are not sufficiently discipled to shepherd their children at home, that is a church crisis of epic proportions!

Another key response to this question is family worship is not just for the children. Family worship is not a Bible class being led by the parent. Because this is our mentality we think, "This parent can't teach the Bible. Family worship is Bible class at home. This parent can't lead family worship." All that is required is a parent who wants to love and obey, and wants his or her children to love and obey Him too. Parents like this, with all their problems and immaturities, pray alongside their children. They read the Bible to their children with a humble, believing, and obedient spirit. They confess their sins to their children and listen as their children confess their sins in return.

If a man is an immature Christian, God will use family worship as a powerful discipleship tool in his life. He will be reading the Word to the family. He will be asked questions for which he *must* go out and seek answers. The living Word of God will change him from the inside out.

Here is the bottom line. God never calls us to do something and then abandons us when we seek to be obedient. God has called all parents in the local church to be the primary spiritual trainers for their children in the home. All God is looking for is our obedience. The Holy Spirit then brings spiritual transformation, not only for the child, but for the parent as well.

LEADING CHANGE: SECOND STEPS

Adding more power to your programming strategy is only a first step. Many churches are taking a more dramatic step toward the biblical model by unifying ministries around family discipleship.

At Wheaton Bible Church, we knew we needed to unify our discipleship strategy across our children's, junior high, and high school ministries. For many years, each of these ministries did their own thing. They taught what they wanted. They had separate strategies. Outside of trying not to conflict with each other on the calendar they were autonomously functioning "silos."

Over the course of a year we developed a plan to have our entire next-generation team partner together and to wrap our discipleship model around the family. At the heart of our strategy was a new approach to how we taught the Bible. We committed to three principles:

Principle 1: Unified

We wanted each child in the church to be learning and growing in the same Scriptures at the same time. If you walked into the high school room on Sunday and the lesson was on Romans 12, you could walk down the hall to the 1st grade room and know that they were studying Romans 12 as well. This was necessary because for families with multiple children, it was crazy to think they were going to be having multiple tracks of family Bible reading and discussion at home. Parents get in the car after church and ask the kids in the back, "What did you learn in Sunday school today?" If they have three children, they usually hear three completely different answers. It prevents the family from having a shared discipleship path.

Principle 2: Bible-Driven

What can we give to children that will lead them to repentance, help them grow in faith, and equip them for every good work? The Bible. Stories don't change hearts. Testimonies don't change hearts. Videos don't change hearts. Only God's Word, through the Holy Spirit, changes hearts. Those other things can help us engage with the Bible, but if we are not careful they can quickly crowd out the Bible, resulting in only a few moments of our teaching time being spent in reading and carefully explaining what God has said.

We decided on a plan to walk through the Bible every four years. What would we do after the first four years? Do it again. After that? Do it again. Our "super secret strategy" was to teach through the Bible. If a child went through 1st-12th grade, they would have had the opportunity to walk through the Bible three times!

Special emphasis was given to teaching Bible doctrine before practical application. Far too often we use the Bible like Aesop's fables—we share a story with a moral. Our primary purpose in teaching Scripture is to teach doctrine, from which application flows.

Principle #3: Parents first, church second

If God created parents to disciple children at home, then our ministry structure must wrap and revolve around family worship in the home. Toward this end, we wrapped our unified, Bible-driven curriculum around family worship.[5]

Each month we wrote and distributed a Family Worship Guide, which equipped families to set aside one family worship time each week in order to prepare for that coming Sunday. In the guide, we provided parents with an activity that prepared them for the Bible reading, worship songs, the Scripture reading, discussion questions, and prayer response. We also included a special section for parents of teens to dig deeper, a Scripture memory verse, and a progressive series of catechism questions.[6]

As noted above, it was essential to us for parents and their children to study the Scripture at home during the week *prior* to learning more in Christian education. Our ministry strategy should have the goal that children never hear anything at church they have not first heard from their parents at home. To move in this direction, we need to increasingly equip parents for home discipleship.

The Family Worship Guide was not homework for parents, nor did we want it to be viewed as curriculum that needed to be followed point by point. Instead, it was a resource for parents to modify, adapt, change, and improve to best fit the spiritual needs of their families.

Parents who are a part of churches who take this second step of family ministry never have to ask, "So what did you learn in Sunday school?" They already know because they talked about the Scripture for that day in family worship earlier that week. The question changes to, "What else did you learn about Romans 12?"

God is working in many churches to lead them in this next step of increased unity around family discipleship and building faith in and through homes. A diverse range of movements including HomePointe[7], Faith@Home[8], Legacy Milestones[9], D6 Family[10], and Treasuring Christ[11] all take steps toward unifying the ministries of the church with a vision for family discipleship.

LEADING CHANGE: GOING ALL THE WAY

Leading change in a church is fraught with peril! It requires godly pastors/elders who patiently, loving, and firmly lead with united biblical convictions. In this chapter, we have explored some powerful early steps a church can take to better equip parents and accelerate family ministry.

While these are first steps, they may take many years to implement. It may take months for your leadership team to align your doctrinal convictions on the question of *how* God has ordained in the Bible for children to be evangelized and discipled. If after that doctrinal work, some leaders fall on their knees in repentance, but others see no need to do so, that division may eventually fracture your church. This issue of ministering to the next generation is at the heart of God's plan to fill the earth with His people! If a pastoral staff does not see *this* issue the same way from God's Word, it may prove impossible to find unity in other areas as well.

What would it look like if we exploded the vision all the way? There may be months or years of "first steps," but where does it end? What would youth and children's ministry look like if we fully embraced the model God gives us in the Bible?

It might seem that to go "all the way" would mean we fire all of the next-generation ministry staff and bulldoze the Christian education wing of the church! Jobs don't need to be lost and buildings don't need to be demolished to embrace this vision. But jobs would be *radically* transformed and buildings would be used very differently.

A RADICAL NEW JOB DESCRIPTION

If God has given jurisdictional responsibility to parents to disciple their children at home, what is a youth pastor supposed to do? His job description has to be overhauled.

We need to address a potential difficulty at this point. The role we are talking about is of a full-fledged "pastor" in the church. The qualifications for this role are found in Titus 1 and 1 Timothy 3. I am not trying to take anyone's job away, but it may be that someone currently serving as a youth pastor may not be biblically qualified to serve as a pastor/elder. As difficult as it would feel, there might be a need to have the current youth pastor "reapply" for the new position.

To all my friends in youth ministry, I want you to imagine sitting before the elders/pastors of your church as they proceed to lay out the following vision for your ministry. I will write this as if the pastors/elders were speaking directly to you.

LIVE IT

The most important thing in this new role is you live like a Christian at home. We are counting on you to spend personal and private time with God, studying His Word, and in prayer. Your relationship with your wife needs to be your highest earthly priority. When you think of "loving your neighbor" and "making disciples" we want you to think of her first. Your next spiritual priority must be the discipleship of your children. We need you to lead family worship in your home. You will not be able to lead the church in things you are not practicing yourself. Spiritually leading your family is a foundation and prerequisite to serving as a pastor in the local church. We are here to love you, encourage you, and keep you accountable to this, your most important Kingdom ministry.

TRAIN THE TRAINER

God has called parents to be the primary spiritual trainers of their children at home. If you are going to minister to children and youth, you need to spend time with parents. Have lunch with them. Have coffee with them. Talk with them before and after church. Invite them over to your home. Accept invitations when you are invited to their homes. God has given you a gift and expertise in communicating biblical truth to young people! We need you to give all of that expertise to the parents and grandparents in our church, so they can be as effective as possible in shepherding their children.

In regard to the curriculum you are using, I want you to go through it with a fine-toothed comb and be sure it is teaching biblical doctrine, simply and clearly. Then, instead of putting that curriculum in the hands of volunteers to teach the youth, I want you to put it into the hands of parents. To do this, you may need a team of volunteers, and they need to join you in this key mission to "train the trainer."[12]

BRING THEM TOGETHER

Include parents in everything you do. Youth retreats become family retreats. Youth mission trips become family mission trips. Youth group service days become family service days. Youth group night becomes family night. Small groups in homes become family groups in homes.[13] Right now most parents just drop their kids off for you to minister to them while a few stay around as volunteers. We need you to turn that around! We want you to develop a ministry where the default setting is families come together. Then we will be equipped and prepared to care for the students who do not have Christian families because they will not just connect with peers, but with entire families from our church. When new students come, your mission is to connect them with a godly family in the church.[14]

Now instead of splitting everyone up by age and putting them in different Christian education rooms, we need you to fill those rooms with people of all ages—parents, grandparents, singles, and their children of all ages.[15] A key part of your pastoral role is to lead our church so all ages come together for worship and discipleship.

GET OUT OF HERE

Our community is filled with children and teens who are lost and they come from families who are lost. This is a matter of the utmost importance and urgency. We need you, as a Christian man, to set the example for other believers and the Christian families in the church. Do you remember what they called "Sunday school" in the 1800s? Christians and Christian families went out into the neediest parts of the community, not to run a local church program, but to bring Christian love and share the gospel. Invite other Christians to join you in coaching a sports team through the park district or YMCA. Pull families together to serve and build relationships at the homeless shelter. Volunteer to help with after-school tutor programs and pray God will enable you to build relationships with unsaved families. Equip the saints in our church for this vital ministry!

Unsaved students and their families aren't here in the church building. If you are going to lead the families of our church to reach them, you have to get out of here.

WRAP UP

I love children, youth, and next-generation ministry more than ever before. If we are going to reverse the generational spiritual decline in our nation, we must return to the *methods* God has given us in the Bible for the evangelism and discipleship of the next generation. The methods He has given us in Scripture not only are what is needed to disciple our own children, but also to reach the millions of children and teens from unsaved homes.

Questions for Discussion:

1. Every church leader makes mistakes. When was the last time you repented over a wrong decision you made as a church leader?

2. Turn back to the picture of the baseball diamond. How is your church doing when it comes to hitting doubles, triples, and home runs?

3. To what degree have the leaders in your church wrestled with the Bible and developed shared doctrines related to next-generation ministry?

4. If you are a youth or children's leader, what was your response to the radical new job description at the end of the chapter?

ENDNOTES

[1] Read more of Pastor Jenkin's story here: http://diosc.com/sys/images/documents/jubdeo/feb_mar07_jub_deo.pdf.

[2] Ben Freudenberg and Rick Lawrence, *The Family Friendly Church*, (Group: Colorado, 2009).

[3] *The Visionary Parenting* book and DVD series are designed to be used by churches to equip and inspire parents to take the lead in discipling their children at home. Learn more at www.VisionaryFam.com.

[4] There are an increasing number of resources out there to equip parents for family worship. Free Family Worship Guides through books of the Bible are available for download at www.Visionaryfam.com. Homelight resources give parents creative ideas for spiritual conversations (www.myhomelight.com). Our family also enjoys *Seeds Family Worship* (www.seedsfamilyworship.net), and *Family Time Training* (www.famtime.com). The catechism found in *Truth and Grace: Memory Book 1* (Tom Ascol, Founders Press: Cape Coral, FL, 2000) is also excellent.

[5] One of the family ministry curriculums that seeks to prioritize these three principles is the D6 curriculum from www.d6family.com.

[6] These *Family Worship Guides* are available for free download at www.VisionaryFam.com.

[7]www.drivefaithhome.com.

[8]www.faithathome.com.

[9]www.legacymilestones.com.

[10]www.d6curriculum.com.

[11]www.treasuringchristonline.com.

[12]I love what Pastor Greg Braly, from New Hope Church in New Hope, MN tells parents. When he shares the vision of their ministry he says, "We want to be your best friend and greatest support in your parenting journey.

[13]My family is a part of a "generational" small group. Six families, with children ranging in age from 16 to 1, meet together in each other's homes for worship, fellowship, fun, and Bible study. Each night includes a family worship time, as well as a time for the adults to meet and pray with one another. Age-integrated small groups are a powerful way to build generational discipleship in your church. Generational groups are particularly effective for single parents. They can bring their children to the group, no babysitters needed. Their children build relationships with other children the parent knows. The single parent is supported by the other families in the group.

[14]Many youth in the community are in unstable homes. They do not need to be brought into a peer culture which is often even more unstable. They need to be connected to godly families.

[15]I have appreciated how Awana through their new Awana@home initiative is helping churches move away from a "drop off" ministry to a family-integrated ministry.

CHAPTER 20:
CHILDREN IN CHURCH

"And they offered great sacrifices that day and rejoiced, for God had
made them rejoice with great joy; the women and children also
rejoiced. And the joy of Jerusalem was heard far away."

—Nehemiah 12:43

S hould children be a part of the corporate worship service in the local church, or will children benefit most from a discipleship environment designed specifically for them?

For nineteen hundred years of Christianity this question was rarely asked, because there was a universal answer and universal practice. Beginning with the early church and through the Christian centuries, children worshiped with their families in the weekly worship service. But Christian history is not a sufficient base upon which to make this decision. This is a significant question and how we answer it shapes our understanding of worship and the purpose of the local church.

In this chapter, we will seek to answer the question, "Do children belong in the corporate worship service of the church?" through the lens of *Sola Scriptura*. If we were to use the Bible, and the Bible alone, to answer this question, what would we conclude? This question is too important to rely on the words of men. We need the Word of God.

WHERE ARE ALL THE HIGH SCHOOL STUDENTS?

For the first twelve years of my pastoral ministry, I didn't think much about this question. My senior pastor pressed me to deal with it. During one of our meetings he expressed his concern to me that many of our high school students were not attending the corporate worship service. (Perhaps this was because I was offering a worship service for high school students . . .) He gave me an assignment. He wanted me to put together a Bible overview on the question, "Do children belong in church?"

I confess, I thought the assignment was a bit unfair. It was not that I minded getting an assignment from him, but rather I didn't think I would find anything. I truly didn't think God had said anything about this particular issue. I could not have been more wrong. What I found through that research permanently transformed my perspective.

A GROWING TREND

Here is something I have observed in many churches. Perhaps you have seen it too. Children grow up through our children's ministries and they love it! They move into the cool junior high group and once again, they love it! Then, it is off to high school with all the events, retreats, and trips. It is a mountain top experience!

After they graduate high school, these young men and women ask, "Where do I go now?" In many churches the answer is, "You go to church now and get involved with the whole faith community!" I have lost track of the number of high school graduates who have responded, "Well, OK, but I really don't feel that connected with the whole church service thing. Isn't there some kind of college group I can get involved with?" So what do we do? We whip up a college ministry for them. Four years later, when college group is "over" they come and ask, "Where do I go now?" We say, "You go to church now and get involved with the whole faith community!" Again the response comes, "Uhhh, I appreciate that and everything, but I don't really connect in that kind of worship, can we start some kind of new worship service on Saturday nights?" We whip up a new Saturday night "cutting edge" worship service. Then after a couple months or years, they don't come back and ask, "Where do I go now?" They just disappear.

One of the things I had to repent of as a youth pastor was working so hard to win the hearts of students to the youth group. I wanted the youth group to be the place where they found their connection, community, and identity. What I should have done was sought to win their hearts to their families and to our entire church. My mission should have been to help them find their connection, community, and identity at home and with our entire church family, not only with their peers.

Let's walk through the Bible to see what God has said to us about this question: "Do children belong in church?"

God Commanded Parents to Celebrate Passover with Their Children

The Passover celebration was held both in homes and in the larger community of faith. God gave the people specific commands for how Passover was to be celebrated, and He had created Passover for the inclusion and spiritual training of children.[1]

> *"You shall observe this rite as a statute for you and for your sons forever. And when you come to the land that the LORD will give you, as he has promised, you shall keep this service. And when your children say to you, 'What do you mean by this service?' you shall say, 'It is the sacrifice of the LORD's Passover, for he passed over the houses of the people of Israel in Egypt, when he struck the Egyptians but spared our houses.'"*—Exodus 12:24–27

God Commanded Israel to Worship with Their Children in the Feast of Weeks

> *"You shall count seven weeks. Begin to count the seven weeks from the time the sickle is first put to the standing grain. Then you shall keep the Feast of Weeks to the LORD your God with the tribute of a freewill offering from your hand, which you shall give as the LORD your God blesses you. And you shall rejoice before the LORD your God, you and your son and your daughter, your male servant and your female servant, the Levite who is within your towns, the sojourner, the fatherless, and the widow who are among you, at the place that the LORD your God will choose, to make his name dwell there."*
> —Deuteronomy 16:9–11

God Commanded Israel to Worship with Their Children in the Feast of Tabernacles

The first text for this is found in Deuteronomy 16:13–14.

> *"You shall keep the Feast of Booths seven days, when you have gathered in the produce from your threshing floor and your winepress. You shall rejoice in your feast, you and your son and your*

daughter, your male servant and your female servant, the Levite, the sojourner, the fatherless, and the widow who are within your towns."
—Deuteronomy 16:13–14

Later in Deuteronomy, God gives more detailed instructions regarding how the Feast of Tabernacles was to be celebrated. Not only were the children of Israel to be participants in the worship gathering, but the children of the aliens living in the land were specifically encouraged to attend to hear the words of the law.

> *"Then Moses wrote this law and gave it to the priests, the sons of Levi, who carried the ark of the covenant of the LORD, and to all the elders of Israel. And Moses commanded them, "At the end of every seven years, at the set time in the year of release, at the Feast of Booths, when all Israel comes to appear before the LORD your God at the place that he will choose, you shall read this law before all Israel in their hearing. Assemble the people, men, women, and little ones, and the sojourner within your towns, that they may hear and learn to fear the LORD your God, and be careful to do all the words of this law, and that their children, who have not known it, may hear and learn to fear the LORD your God, as long as you live in the land that you are going over the Jordan to possess."—Deuteronomy 31:9–13*

Families Worshiped Together During the Time of Joshua

Despite what appears to be an unusually long worship event, children were present for the entire reading of the Torah.

> *"And afterward he read all the words of the law, the blessing and the curse, according to all that is written in the Book of the Law. There was not a word of all that Moses commanded that Joshua did not read before all the assembly of Israel, and the women, and the little ones, and the sojourners who lived among them."—Joshua 8:34–35*

Families Repented Together During the Time of Ezra

> *"While Ezra prayed and made confession, weeping and casting himself down before the house of God, a very great assembly of men,*

women, and children, gathered to him out of Israel, for the people wept bitterly."—Ezra 10:1

God Commanded Israel to Worship with Their Children During the Time of Joel

The Lord called His people to gather together for a fast and a "solemn assembly." This was a serious spiritual gathering for a serious spiritual purpose. It was God's expressed will for all His people to be there, even the infants.

> "Blow the trumpet in Zion; consecrate a fast; call a solemn assembly; gather the people. Consecrate the congregation; assemble the elders; gather the children, even nursing infants. Let the bridegroom leave his room, and the bride her chamber."—Joel 2:15–16

Children Were Included in the Church Services in the Book of Acts

In many churches, people start getting antsy when the clock hits twelve noon. Time to wrap it up pastor! On one occasion in the book of Acts, Paul preached all the way till midnight.

> "On the first day of the week, when we were gathered together to break bread, Paul talked with them, intending to depart on the next day, and he prolonged his speech until midnight. There were many lamps in the upper room where we were gathered. And a young man named Eutychus, sitting at the window, sank into a deep sleep as Paul talked still longer. And being overcome by sleep, he fell down from the third story and was taken up dead. But Paul went down and bent over him, and taking him in his arms, said, "Do not be alarmed, for his life is in him." And when Paul had gone up and had broken bread and eaten, he conversed with them a long while, until daybreak, and so departed. And they took the youth away alive, and were not a little comforted."—Acts 20:7–12

He preached so long that the boy[2] fell asleep, fell out of the window, and died. Paul had to take a break from his sermon to pray for God to raise him from the dead, which God did. After that was taken care of, he was able to continue teaching until daybreak.

Children Were Included in the Church Services in Ephesus and Colossae

In Paul's letters to these churches, he specifically speaks to children. These letters were intended to be read to congregations in these cities. Paul knew he could speak directly to the children because he knew they would be with their parents in church, and would hear the sermon along with everyone else. It is also reasonable to conclude Paul had no problem with the children being exposed to the entire content of the letter. There is no indication the children were brought in to the church service to hear the part that was for them and then escorted out.

God spoke to children in the early church with these words:

> *"Children, obey your parents in the Lord, for this is right. 'Honor your father and mother' (this is the first commandment with a promise), 'that it may go well with you and that you may live long in the land.'"*—Ephesians 6:1–3

> *"Children, obey your parents in everything, for this pleases the Lord."*—Colossians 3:20

COMMANDS AND PATTERNS

Many have said to me, "Rob, I agree we have descriptions in the Bible where children were included in corporate worship. But there is a difference between something being described (descriptions) and something being commanded (prescriptions). I can't find a Scripture that says, 'Children must be included in your weekly worship service.' Doesn't that mean we are free to make our own decisions about this?"

My first response is we *do* have commands for parents to include their children in corporate worship in Exodus, Deuteronomy, and Joel. Yes, these commands are in the Old Testament and were specifically for the people of Israel. But is there a compelling theological reason not to apply the principle behind these commandments today? Is the command to include children specific to the Old Testament ceremonial religious law that has now been superseded by Christ? I think that is a difficult case to make.

Second, while we have direct commands and a clear pattern for age-integrated worship, we have no clear examples, and certainly no commands for *segregating* children away from their parents during the corporate worship gathering. All the words God has chosen to give us on this subject line up on one side of the debate. Some hold that Nehemiah 8:2–3 argues for keeping children out of the worship service. But there is no explicit reference to children in this passage, while children are specifically addressed in the many texts we have already considered. We cannot use Nehemiah 8 as the overarching text, while we ignore all the others, for whether or not to include our children in the corporate worship gathering of the local church.

Third, Christians unanimously declare the will of God on issues where there is no explicit biblical command. If we need explicit biblical commands for everything, we cannot say polygamy is wrong. Yes, God forbids the kings of Israel from taking multiple wives (Deuteronomy 17:17), but that is not an explicit command for everyone. So why do we conclude polygamy is forbidden for every Christian? We rightly conclude this from the principles and patterns found throughout the Bible. Even without an explicit command, we can be 100% certain in our conclusion that polygamy is a sin for anyone.

Fourth, God chose to reveal patterns for a reason. Every word of Scripture was inspired by God. There is not one careless word![3] When the Holy Spirit inspired Moses, Joel, Ezra, Joshua, Luke, and Paul, they were led to write down the words "sons and daughters," "children," and "infants." God wanted us to have these words, because He wanted us to know His heart and His mind. God reveals a singular pattern throughout the Bible: children were included in the corporate worship gathering of God's people.

Imagine if I asked my son to mow the lawn, and my son asked me, "Dad, what is the best way to mow the back yard?" "Well son, here is how I have always done it. Your grandpa did it the same way, and your great grandpa did it the same way (without the fancy lawn mower) . . ."

I am not commanding my son to mow the lawn a particular way, but I am revealing my will for him. I am speaking of patterns to tell him what I think is best. I am a human father with a human son. Maybe the way "we have always done it" in our family is not the best way. Maybe he will find a new way of mowing the lawn that yields better results.

But what if this was the answer from our Heavenly Father? Lord, should we include children in our worship service? What if the Lord responded, "In the early church, children worshiped alongside their parents. In the time of Joel, children worshiped alongside their parents. In the time of Ezra, children worshiped alongside their parents. In the time of Moses, children worshiped alongside their parents." If this was God's answer, what would we conclude He was trying to tell us? By revealing a unified ordained pattern in the Bible, God has revealed His will to us.

THINKING THEOLOGICALLY

Before I saw what God had said about this issue in the Bible, my only thoughts on this issue were pragmatic. Can children really get anything out of the sermon? Won't children be distracting for others who are trying to worship?

Before we think pragmatically, we need to think theologically. Practice does not drive theology. Theology drives practice.

Theologically speaking, what *is* the 60-90 minutes of "church" each Sunday? What *is* its nature? How would you describe it? When you think of the church service, do you think of it as an adult education hour? Do you think of it as a Bible study? Or do you think of it as a gathering of the faith community in the presence of God under the authority of His Word? I hope you see it as the latter. If this is what the church service *is,* theologically, then we should ask the question, "Are our children a part of the faith community?" I hope we would all answer, "Yes!" So if church is a gathering of the faith community, and our children are a part of that faith community, they should be included.

I also struggled with the pragmatic question of, "But how will my three year old get anything out of the sermon?" Once again, do we view the church service as a Bible class? If that is what it *is,* then we should get the children out of there. But can a three-year-old worship? Yes! Can a three-year-old be ministered to by the Holy Spirit? Yes!

LET THE LITTLE CHILDREN COME

Here are some "do's and don'ts" to consider for including and welcoming children into your church's corporate worship service.

Don't Have Special "Children/Youth Sundays"

If you have a "Youth Sunday" once a year, the underlying message is, "This is the one Sunday you belong in here, and the other fifty-one weeks you don't." Don't set aside special weeks to welcome and include children. Make it normal. Include children as ushers and greeters. Include children in the worship team. When a child walks into the church service, it should be obvious he or she belongs there.

Do Have Worship Folders for Children

Provide children with a simple outline of the service. Provide them with places to write down the names of the songs which are sung, the text the pastor is preaching from, and important points from the sermon. The worship folder should not be a tool for distraction, but a tool for engagement.

Do Call Everyone to Daily Family Worship in the Home

The most important factor for children, especially little ones, to be able to participate in the corporate worship service is regular family worship in the home. If children do not have family worship at home (Bible reading, prayer, etc.), the worship service is a strange place for them. But children who worship at home develop the skill of sitting still, reading and listening to the Bible, and praying with others.

Do Teach Parents How to Worship with Their Children

For many of us, age-integrated worship is a foreign concept. We have been trained by the world and sometimes by the church that children are a distraction. This is a discipleship issue for the parents as much as it is for the children. Offer ongoing parent seminars on this issue and put good resources into their hands to help them.[4]

Do Intentionally Call Parents to Bring Their Children to Church

Some churches have a "don't ask, don't tell" policy on this subject. If a family chooses to bring their children to church, no one will be at the door telling them to take their children down the hall. (Tragically, some churches actually do this). In the same way, if parents come into the worship service without their children, no one approaches them and asks, "Hey, where are your kids today?" Don't ask. Don't tell. Because many Christian adults have been a part of churches where children were not intentionally included, they may feel awkward or uncomfortable bringing their children to church. This is a message which needs to come from the top!

Pastors need to regularly tell the church, "If you are in church, your children should be with you. When we gather for worship, we want *everyone* here. Perhaps you are here and you don't have children with you, but there are little ones around you, please do everything you can to make them feel welcome. We welcome children in our worship services because that is the model for worship God has given us in the Bible."

Don't Be Distracted If a Parent and Child Need to Step Out

There will be times when younger (and perhaps older!) children need to be taken out of the service by a parent. This may be required for many reasons, ranging from the need for a diaper change to the need to correct a child who is not behaving.

Do Preach to Everyone

The task of the preacher is to teach all of God's Word to all of God's people. We don't want anyone to miss out on anything God has said. If you are preaching through the book of Ephesians, it will require sermons which speak directly to wives. It will require sermons which speak directly to husbands. It will require sermons which speak directly to children.

It is common for a pastor to conclude a sermon with a section of application. He might say, "We have been talking about hope today, and I want to encourage those of you who may be unemployed." Or perhaps, "We have been talking about running the race for God, and I want to encourage those of you who are older this is an important time of your life to continue to be used by God."

Pastors who believe they are called to preach the Bible to everyone sometimes say, "Now I would like to apply this doctrine we have been talking about today to you children." He then proceeds to encourage and admonish the children present in light of the particular text for the day. This is exactly what Paul did in his sermon/letter to the churches in Colossae and Ephesus.

Don't Water Down the Sermon

There is no evidence in Scripture that the inclusion of children led to the watering down of the teaching. In the Scriptures cited above, the children were present for the reading of the entire Torah. Paul preached till midnight. In his sermon/letters to Colossae and Ephesus, the particular message for the children was surrounded by substantive doctrine. Nothing needs to be watered down because children are present. However, skilled preachers can learn to use euphemisms to communicate particular points to those who are older. Instead of using the term "rape," he can say, "the man forced himself on her." Those who are older clearly understand what the pastor is talking about, and he is not using provocative language.

WRAP UP

Imagine a church includes children into the corporate worship services on Christmas and Easter. Children in that family get to see their mother or their father sing praises to God only two times every year! For the first eighteen years of their life, they will see it only thirty-six times.

I am reminded again of Wayne Rice's comments at the D6 2011 Conference. Would a shepherd ever systematically separate the older sheep from the younger sheep? In the same way, why would the shepherds (elders/pastors) in a local church separate the little sheep from the most important gathering?

Following the biblical model accelerates generational faithfulness and generational connection. Visitors are blessed by seeing entire families worshiping together. The atmosphere becomes more and more worshipful because *all* of God's children are there.

Questions for discussion:

1. If you grew up in church, what was the practice of your church regarding children in the worship service?

2. What was your response to the section in this chapter that addressed the issue of commands vs. patterns in the Bible?

3. Have you ever heard a persuasive argument from the Bible for keeping the children out of the corporate worship service?

4. What is one step your church could take to welcome children into worship?

ENDNOTES

[1] See also Exodus 13 for additional instructions from God about the multi-generational focus of the Feast of Unleavened bread.

[2] The Greek word used here indicates a boy between the ages of 7-14.

[3] Proverbs 30:5.

[4] Robbie Castleman, *Parenting in the Pew* (Downers Grove, IL: IVP Books, 2002).

CHAPTER 21:
BUILDING MARRIAGES AND
MULTIPLYING YOUR CHURCH

"And as Isaiah predicted, 'If the Lord of hosts had not left us offspring,
we would have been like Sodom and become like Gomorrah.'"

—ROMANS 9:29

"WE ARE STARTING A MARRIAGE MINISTRY!"

This is what a colleague shared a few years ago at a conference. I asked her, "Why are you doing that?" She was a bit taken aback but said, "Well, we just completed a big survey in our church and we found out the most important concern in our congregation was over their marriages. We realized we needed to do something to help." By this time she had picked up I had asked the question for a particular reason, so I pressed her further saying, "I am so glad you are elevating your attention on marriage, but what will you do in five years if you redo your survey and find out marriage is at the *bottom* of the list of needs. Will you cancel your marriage ministry at that point?" "Of course, not!" she replied. "So there must be a deeper reason than the survey results which have driven you to start a marriage ministry!"

My friend was kind to tolerate my provocations. We then proceeded to have a great conversation about all sorts of wrong reasons why churches launch marriage, parenting, and family ministries. Local churches should *not* be concerned about marriages simply because couples need help, because couples need counseling, or because the divorce rate is high.

Local churches must elevate, nurture, and protect marriage because God created marriage as a Great Commission institution. Marriage is all about disciple making. God calls wives, more than anyone else in the world, to help their husbands become godly men. God call husbands, more than anyone else in the world, to lead their wives to become godly women. God calls couples to partner together in the shared mission of raising godly children. The more a local church commits to "making disciples" the more that church should commit to elevating and nurturing marriage.

THE NUCLEAR WAR OVER MARRIAGE AND BABIES

Satan and his demons are doing all they can to war against the Lord of Hosts. They cannot hurt Him directly, so they focus all of their weapons on those He loves. Satan has "gone nuclear" in his war against marriage and babies. Delay marriage! Avoid marriage! Pervert marriage! Delay babies! Avoid babies! Neglect babies! Abuse babies! Kill babies!

These demonic cries are echoed throughout our culture today. Satan has raised up entire institutions and movements to wage war against God's family. Atheistic evolution is now systematically taught to every child in the Unites States in the government schools. Planned Parenthood is carrying forward the eugenic vision of the 1920s to eliminate as many black and Hispanic children as possible.[1] Communist, socialist, and totalitarian regimes around the world share a common commitment—to prevent children from being born.[2]

My great uncle, Robert Rienow, was a national leader in the population control movement[3] in the 60s and 70s. In a chapter entitled "Too Many People," he talked about the catastrophic results which were sure to come when the population of the United States crossed 300 million around the year 2000. He argued that a small group of intellectual elites must take over functional control of the country and do what was necessary to limit the population. While none of his predictions of disaster have come to pass, his strategic plan for population control is moving forward with great success.

> The first step would be to establish a federal population commission. This would be a propaganda organ, educating the masses as to the connection between rising population and lowering quality of life.

> Secondly, the tax system should be revised as to eliminate any deduction for children; indeed, luxury taxes should be placed on such revered items as diapers and baby bottles.

Third, there should be passed federal laws which not only toss out state laws limiting physician-approved abortions, but provide for mandatory teaching of the need for birth control in all public schools.

Fourth, the shortsighted programs on death control so favored by federal subsidy in biomedicine should give way to the "broader areas" of research in population control.

Should all these fail, scientists tell us, compulsory birth regulation would be the next step.[4]

When my uncle wrote these strategic steps, they were merely proposals. Today, some of them have been implemented. Roe vs. Wade was a federal law that superseded the authority of the states. Birth control has become mandatory teaching in our public schools. Satan is not flailing blindly against the will of God and the people of God. He focuses his greatest firepower against God's foundational institution of the family.

THE WAR INSIDE

If only this battle was outside the local church. Tragically, the demonic anti-marriage, anti-child philosophy of the secular culture has seeped into parts of Christian culture as well. The twisted thinking in the church about marriage and children takes many forms.

If you surveyed a group of forty-year old Christians, and you asked them, "What is the most important thing in your life? A) Your job, B) Your friends, C) Your volunteer work at church or D) Your family?" What do you think people would say? Virtually everyone I know would quickly answer, "D, my family." So adults in the church say their responsibility and ministry to their family is their most important calling (even if they say it out of principle rather than practice). Now, let's consider what young people in the church are called on to prepare for in life. What are the big questions that face Christian youth and young adults? We ask them where they are going to college. We ask them what they want to do for a career. We ask them to consider what kind of ministry God has for them in the world. When was the last time your youth or college ministry had a teaching series entitled, "How to prepare to be a godly spouse and parent?" The world tells us education and career are what really count, and the same message is often echoed in the church.

Consider an eighteen-year-old young woman who is asked, "What do you want to do with your life?" She replies, "My greatest dream is to serve God by being a wife and mother." I expect an answer like that to be hated by secularists, but I have lost track of the number of young women who have told me (1) this is the desire of their hearts and (2) they are ashamed to say it to their *Christian* parents and their *Christian* friends for fear of being looked down upon.

It is common when Christians get married at a young age (for the sake of discussion, let's say in their early twenties), for other believers to express their concern and lack of support. This is the case even when the young people are godly and come from godly families who have given their blessing. Then, if that young couple becomes pregnant on their honeymoon, *Christians* often question their wisdom in not doing more to prevent the pregnancy. When did we start thinking that a person might be mature enough to get married, but not mature enough to raise children? It seems we are far more comfortable following the pattern of the world by extending adolescence into our early thirties.

PREGNANT AND ASHAMED

A few weeks ago, a woman shared a heartbreaking story with me. God had blessed her and her husband with eight children. Every day, they were pouring themselves out with Great Commission intensity to "make disciples" of these immortal souls whom God had entrusted into their care. Then came more blessed news. She was pregnant! Their emotions were completely torn. On one hand, they were rejoicing that God had seen fit to reward them again. On the other hand, they were terrified to share the news. They weren't worried about sharing with their neighbors. They weren't worried about sharing with their co-workers. They were afraid to share with their brothers and sisters in Christ at church. So outside of sharing with two close friends, they chose to rejoice secretly. They could not face the looks, disapproval, and at times outright criticism which they received from their church family.

One of the great concerns in the early church was the infiltration of worldly philosophy into the church. I believe it is happening today in far greater degree than we realize. How could a Christian local church look down upon a couple who was eagerly welcoming children into the world? This happens when the church draws its philosophy from the world, rather than from the Bible alone.

SEPARATING MISSION FROM MARRIAGE

When we think of our "life mission," marriage and raising children are off to the side at best, or ignored at worst. After preaching one morning, I was met by a newlywed couple who had a question for me. They were preparing to head off to a remote part of the world to serve as missionaries. Because of their desire to focus 100% on their ministry, they didn't want to have any children. They proceeded to explain how their vision to reach this particular tribe would require eighty years of ministry. They were praying God would give them the chance to serve for the first forty years! Their number one fear was over who could take over the ministry after they were gone. Who would have the training? Who would know the language? Who could just "step in" and carry the mission forward?

I gently suggested that perhaps it was God's will to bring them a team of people who could train under them for 20 years or so and could then, in the Lord's will, step into leadership. They asked, "But where would this team come from?"

"Perhaps they will be your own children. Have you ever considered the possibility that God is calling you into a multi-generational mission to reach this tribe?" They had never considered that God's call for marriage and children might be connected to their "mission."

Entire nations are falling into the hands of Satan because Christians have separated "the Great Commission" from "be fruitful and multiply." In 2008, our family went on a mission trip to France. I had the opportunity to teach at a missionary training retreat. The missionaries explained to us the dire spiritual condition of France in particular, and Europe in general. Not only do Christians make up a tiny percentage of the population, but Islam is on the rise. How could Islam be spreading like wildfire in a nation so committed to secularism and humanism? How could Muslims be winning so many converts, while Christians who had the truth, be winning so few? Islam was not growing through conversion, they explained. It was growing through birthrate alone. Muslims were moving into France, having as many children as possible and discipling their children in Islam at home. In past centuries, Muslims conquered nations by killing all who would not convert to Islam. Now, they are conquering nations by out-breeding them. If the current trends hold, Muslims in France may soon have a sufficient voting majority to use the democratic apparatus to establish Sharia law and outlaw Christianity.

During these conversations I asked, "What is the church doing to respond to this? Are Christian pastors encouraging young Christians to marry and to eagerly desire many children so the Gospel might be advanced here in France?" Two answers were given. The first, "No, not really." The second, "Even if pastors wanted to do this, there are so few young Christians left."

God wants the earth filled with His worshippers. Satan wants worship too, as long as it is not the worship of the one true God. At the heart of God's plan to fill the earth is the power of multi-generational faithfulness, marriage, family, and babies. Part of Satan's strategy is to destroy those things. Part of his strategy is to *use* those things to fill the earth with lies.

BUT ISN'T MARRIAGE TEMPORARY?

Some might respond to this by saying, "Yes, marriage is important, but there will not be any marriage in Heaven. We should not neglect our spouse, but we don't want to make marriage an idol, or allow marriage to distract us from the Kingdom of God."

Jesus said, "For in the resurrection they neither marry nor are given in marriage, but are like angels in heaven" (Matthew 22:30).

Marriage is, indeed, a temporary institution. But this in no way diminishes its centrality and importance in the Kingdom of God. The necessary questions are, "Why is marriage temporary? How could marriage be at the center of human society, but absent in Heaven?" The answer is simple. There will be no marriage in Heaven because both of God's purposes for marriage will have been accomplished. God's first purpose for marriage is the spiritual transformation of one another. Sanctification will no longer be necessary! He will make good on His promise to make us complete on the day of Christ Jesus! God's second purpose for marriage is the mission of raising godly children. Again, mission complete! Our believing children will have been made perfect along with us, and we will all be "discipled" directly by King Jesus forever. (I can't wait!)[5]

It was His idea to fill the earth with His worship *through* marriage, family, and multi-generational faithfulness. He calls His people to commit themselves to His mission and to His methods. God has told us marriage and family will not be at the center of life in Heaven, but He has ordained them to be at the center of life on earth.

I grieve over the decreasing volume from the evangelical church on the issue of abortion. Have we grown weary in fighting back against those who welcome the murder of children? Have we found more pressing issues which need our attention?

The Christian theology behind the pro-life position is simple and clear:

- We believe God exists.

- We believe God is a loving, personal God who creates each person.

- We believe God has revealed Himself and His will for us in the Bible alone.

- In Psalm 139, God says a baby in a mother's womb is a person.

A person who believes these four things necessarily stands against abortion. No other position is open to them.

Reflecting the character of God in this area requires intentionality at both the personal and societal levels. Personally, there are likely men and women in your church who have participated in the abortion of their own children. Few sins will shred a soul as this one will. Do your pastors proclaim the power of the blood of Christ to completely forgive even the sin of abortion? Do your pastors nurture and care for those who are grieving over the loss of their children?

But this is not only a personal issue. It is a societal issue, one that demands the greatest courage from God's people to do all in their power to save children from being murdered. In my experience, Christian leaders tend to avoid speaking on the macro issue of abortion because they don't want to hurt or alienate individuals who are recovering from it.

As I look back on my life, I see so many areas where my thinking has not been biblical. This issue of abortion was one of them. When I was in my late teens and early 20s, I believed abortion was wrong, but it was one of many important political issues, and it shouldn't be a litmus test for a political candidate. If a candidate held other views I thought were right, I didn't want this one issue to override everything else. The Bible forced me to change my mind. I had been taken captive by the hollow and deceptive philosophy that I could be anti-abortion personally, but pro-choice politically.

Imagine if you agreed with a candidate on every point, except the candidate believed women should have the right to kill their three-year-old child for any reason. Could you *ever* vote for such a person? Of course, not! But what if you agreed with them on every other issue? No way. This *singular* issue would override all the others. Does not the Bible teach that a one month old baby in the womb is equal in value, worth, personhood, and dignity to the three-year-old child out of the womb? In God's eyes there is no difference, and He wants His people to see things as He sees them.

If desperate mothers were bringing their three-year-old children into a clinic down the street to have their children killed, would your local church care? Would you do *anything?* I believe you would. In God's eyes, this is exactly what is happening.

MOVING BEYOND PRO-LIFE

Churches that embrace a biblical vision for marriage and children are not just pro-life, they are pro-child. They not only do all in their power to protect children at risk of being murdered in the womb (pro-life), but they eagerly desire the blessing of many children into their families (pro-child.)

Does your local church *celebrate* the news of a new pregnancy, a new adoption, or a new foster child?

Psalm 127 contains a powerful message, but many people miss it all together. This psalm is a short poem containing only five verses, but it is rarely preached or taught as a single unit. Rather, people take the first two verses and apply them totally out of context with the remainder of the psalm. Here are the first two verses. The words may be familiar to you:

> *"Unless the LORD builds the house, those who build it labor in vain. Unless the LORD watches over the city, the watchman stays awake in vain. It is in vain that you rise up early and go late to rest, eating the bread of anxious toil; for he gives to his beloved sleep."*—Psalm 127:1–2

"Unless the Lord builds the house, those who build it labor in vain." It is a well-known passage from the Bible. Unfortunately, it is often preached as a stand-alone line without paying any attention to the entire subject matter of the psalm. This verse is ripped out of context and Christians are told something along the lines of, "If you plan your life apart from God, you are wasting your time. You need to build your family, your business, and your future on the sure foundation of God." Such teaching is certainly true, but Psalm 127:1 is not a general message about trusting God and including Him in your plans. Remember, this psalm only contains five verses! It is one unit, and was never intended to be separated into disjointed sections. Here are the final three verses:

> "Behold, children are a heritage from the LORD, the fruit of the womb
> a reward. Like arrows in the hand of a warrior are the children of one's
> youth. Blessed is the man who fills his quiver with them! He shall not
> be put to shame when he speaks with his enemies in the gate."—Psalm
> 127:3–5

What is God speaking about in Psalm 127? The blessing, reward, and Kingdom impact of children . . . many children! God says sons are a heritage. God says children are a reward. We pray God's grace will work in the hearts of our six children with such power that when they leave our home they will be like spiritual arrows entering into the battle for Christ and for His Kingdom. God says a man is blessed when the house is filled with kids! The spirit of the world disagrees. Two kids should be enough for everyone. Three at the absolute max!

Let's go back to verse 1. "Unless the LORD builds the house, those who build it labor in vain." What is God saying? The call of this psalm is to allow God to build your family according to His plans, rather than yours. We know God is sovereign over all things in our lives, so second-guessing is not a fruitful exercise. But Amy and I sometimes think about *who* is not a part of our family by intentionally avoiding children for the first three years of our marriage. Each of our six children truly is a blessing from God. We don't want to send any one of them back! To think God had more "blessings" in store for us that we intentionally avoided is more than a little depressing. We didn't realize we were delaying the most challenging, joyous, and important Christian mission of our lives.

Are you concerned about the crises facing the world such as poverty, hunger, and injustice? Do you know what we need more than anything else to address these problems? We need more people who love Jesus Christ and who are willing to lay down their lives for Him. By raising godly children, you can have a greater impact on the world than you can possibly imagine.[6]

God not only grows churches by *spiritual* reproduction but through *physical* reproduction. We are called to make disciples spiritually and literally. Am I saying the Great Commission is all about having, adopting, fostering, and raising godly children? No, it is broader than that. But having, adopting, fostering, and raising godly children is all about the Great Commission!

It is easy to be so focused on our horizontal ministry (ministry to the people who are already here) that we lose our vision for our vertical ministry (our multigenerational ministry even to those yet to be born).

Does your church boldly proclaim that having and raising godly children is missional, externally-focused, Great Commission ministry? Does your church celebrate the godly mother who is laying her life down over and over again through pregnancy, delivery, and sleepless nights so the world might be increasingly filled with the worship of God?

The point here is not that all good Christians have lots of kids, or if you don't have children or have a small family you are unspiritual. We have friends who have lost many children due to miscarriages (praise God those babies are safe with their Heavenly Father). Others are called to the ministry of adoption and foster care. You may be in a season where your primary investment in the next generation will be in the lives of your nieces and nephews, or in the lives of children at church. Perhaps you have never been able to have children. This is a deep grief that can only be understood by those who have experienced it. God is the One who opens and closes the womb. If this is your situation, continue to trust God. Trust His sovereignty. Bring Him glory every day through your faithfulness.

EVERY MINISTRY A MARRIAGE MINISTRY

You may not need a "marriage ministry" department in your church. You might have an elder/pastor who gives particular attention to this area, but marriage ministry can't fit into a compartment because discipleship and marriage can't be separated. Every discipleship ministry of the church must take responsibility to care for, nurture, and equip marriages (and marriages-to-be).

Train all your ministry leaders to continually disciple through the spheres. First, we lead people to God through repentance and faith. Second, we call them to minister to, in, and with their families. For those who are married, we give our greatest discipleship efforts to helping husbands and wives embrace their biblical roles, spiritually transform one another, and engage together in their most important divine calling to do all in their power to raise godly children.

When we nurture marriages, we advance the gospel to the next generation. When we help couples move toward spiritual oneness, we advance the gospel to the next generation. When we help young people find godly spouses we advance the gospel to the next generation.

> "And as Isaiah predicted, 'If the Lord of hosts had not left us offspring, we would have been like Sodom and become like Gomorrah.'"— Romans 9:29

Questions for discussion:

1. What impact did your parents' marriage, or lack thereof, have on your life?

2. Is your church engaging in helping men and women facing unwanted pregnancies? Is your church engaging in fighting the battle in the larger culture to protect children from being murdered?

3. How would you describe the culture of your church regarding children?

4. What practical steps could your church take to keep discipleship and marriage together?

ENDNOTES

[1] http://www.blackgenocide.org/sanger.html.

[2] http://www.demographicwinter.com/index.html.

[3] Not only does the myth of overpopulation come from the radical left, but it is totally unsupported by the numbers. Did you know the entire population of the earth could fit into the state of Texas, and every person would have 1,090 square feet all to themselves? This figure is reached by (square mileage of Texas) * (5280*5280) / World population.

[4] Robert and Leona Train Rienow, *Man Against His Environment*, (Sierra Club: San Francisco, 1970), 22–23.

[5] I also believe I will be closer with Amy in Heaven than we have ever been on earth. We will not be married in Heaven, but we will still be in relationship as brother and sister in Christ. My sinful nature will be gone. Her sinful nature will be gone. We will be able to enjoy fellowship with one another, and Lord-willing with our children, forever!

[6] Rienow, *Visionary Marriage*, 136–138.

CHAPTER 22:
ELEVATING SINGLES MINISTRY

God settles the solitary in a home...

—Psalm 68:6a

I f a local church catches the biblical vision for family ministry, what impact does that have on those who are single? Won't unmarried men and women feel increasingly marginalized if we emphasize the importance of marriage, family, and children?

Some of the confusion and difficulty in "singles ministry" comes from the diversity of people who are in the category of "single." I appreciate the thoughts of Carolyn McCulley:

> This is one of the potential pastoral challenges to ministering to single adults. We are often The Singles, one monolithic block of unmarried people. But there are as many stages and seasons to single adult life as there are for married adults. A single woman in her 50s with a demanding career caring for elderly parents is not equivalent to a recent college grad who is still living at home. Both are unmarried, yes, but chances are, the older single woman and the parents of the college grad may have more in common.[1]

I confess it makes me angry, perhaps unrighteously so, to see how single people are often treated within local churches. In my judgment, it borders on abusive.

I am convinced the primary reason that so many singles are feeling disenfranchised in our local churches is we are not applying the doctrine of the sufficiency of Scripture to *how* we do single's ministry. Many of the *methods* we use to minister to singles are found nowhere in Scripture, and those methods God *has* revealed to us in His Word are largely ignored. We must take captive every thought into obedience to Christ, including our thoughts about how the local church should minister to those who are not married. My objective in this chapter (which should come as no surprise to you), is to examine the Bible to see what God has said about how to minister to, care for, and disciple those who are single.

When we do this, three overarching principles emerge:

- God calls the local church to teach about the gift of singleness.
- God calls the local church to care for singles in need.
- God calls Christian families to welcome and include singles into their family life.

TEACHING ON THE GIFT OF SINGLENESS

We must teach and preach a clear biblical theology of singleness. As we discussed earlier, God does not pit marriage and singleness against one another. He spoke through Paul in 1 Corinthians 7 to chastise the Corinthian Christians who were elevating the call to singleness above the call to marriage. Later in that chapter, Paul describes the call to singleness as a gift God gives to some people and not to others (1 Corinthians 7:7).

If we are silent about what God has said about the gift of singleness, those who are single in the church will be vulnerable to deceptive philosophies of the world. Consider these two examples of how singles are hurt by a lack of teaching and biblical discipleship in the area of singleness.

I had a conversation with a single, twenty-five-year-old man. He was a serious Christian and was making preparations to leave for the mission field. He did not have an overwhelming desire to be married, to have sex, or to have children.[2] He believed God had given him the gift and calling to be single. He was involved in the singles ministry at church, but after a while became fed up and left. What got him so upset? People continued to say things to him such as, "So, are you dating anyone?" "You know, I met a really nice girl the other day. I think you would like her." Obviously, these were well-meaning Christian friends. No offense was intended. This particular singles group offered little teaching on the gift of singleness. Even though that should have been a fundamental discipleship issue for that context, it was rarely discussed. What was the end result? A man who believed he had the gift and call to singleness was regularly being pressured toward marriage! I don't blame him for leaving.

On the other hand, I once spoke with a thirty-year-old woman who greatly desired to be married, have sex, and have children. God had not yet blessed her with a husband. She continued to pray for God to prepare her to be a godly wife and mother and to hurry up and bring Mr. Right onto the scene! Yet, do you know what her friends and pastors were telling her at church? They were telling her to "embrace and celebrate her singleness!" They were not just counseling her to "be content and to trust God with your desire for marriage," but telling her to *accept* and *embrace* her singleness. I think this is unconscionable. This woman has a desire for marriage, sex, and babies. Yes, her current state of being single was something to accept from the sovereign hand of God, but not to be *embraced*. She left hurt and confused.

One of the top priorities in our ministry to youth and young adults must be to help them discern whether God has called them to serve Him through marriage or to serve Him through singleness. This can be difficult to discern, and for some they may sense a particular leading in one direction only to have God redirect them later. Thousands of vital life decisions are affected by the two potential callings of marriage and singleness. It should be an ongoing part of our discipleship conversations with youth and young adults.

In the same way, if your church does not have a clearly explained doctrinal position on divorce and remarriage many in the church can experience shame, confusion, and may even be led into sin.

CELEBRATING THE GIFT OF SINGLENESS

Based on 1 Corinthians 7, the early church not only taught on the gift of singleness, they honored those who were called to singleness and sought to release them into ministry. Jesus honored those who had accepted the call to singleness "for the sake of the kingdom of heaven" (Matthew 19:12).

I have been to many wedding ceremonies where the pastor says something like, "This man and this women have come together to glorify God and serve Him through His gift of marriage." How beautiful and true! But when was the last time a pastor said of a single person in the congregation, "This man has chosen to glorify God and serve Him through His gift of singleness." Those are rare words indeed. If we only celebrate marriage, but not singleness, those called to singleness cannot help but feel excluded.

This is another reason why clear teaching, discipleship, and discernment related to the calling and gift of singleness is so important. We should not celebrate a young man or woman who "one day wants to have a family" but is putting that off to "enjoy their twenties." That is not embracing the gift of singleness for the sake of the gospel. That is extending adolescence.[3] When a local church shepherds the congregation in this essential area of discipleship, those who are called to singleness are in an environment which encourages them to be obedient, and looks for opportunities for them to serve in accordance with their calling.[4]

CARING FOR WIDOWS

Not only did the early church seek to teach a proper theology of singleness and marriage, but they had a highly organized ministry to widows. We cannot claim to have a *biblical* ministry to singles if we do not have a formal ministry to widows. Once again we must ask ourselves if the instructions God gave to the early church should be applied to our local churches today. God gave the necessary principles and practical instructions for how the local church should care for widows. If it was established that a widow had no children or family members who would care for her, the elders/pastors of the local church used church funds to support her completely if necessary.

> *"Let a widow be enrolled if she is not less than sixty years of age, having been the wife of one husband, and having a reputation for good works: if she has brought up children, has shown hospitality, has washed the feet of the saints, has cared for the afflicted, and has devoted herself to every good work."*—1 Timothy 5:9–10

This was a big budget operation, as noted in Acts 6 it required extensive organization and leadership.

Many churches apply the principles of "widow care" found in 1 Timothy 5 more broadly in an effort to support and care for single parents and those in the church with ongoing needs (such as an adult with developmental disabilities).

Reformation Church[5] in Castle Rock, CO has made it a top priority to care for single parents, particularly single mothers. They knew that the needs of the single moms in the congregation would never be met by starting a singles group or special Sunday school class. The discipleship and support needs are extreme and therefore their ministry is as well.

Deacons take the lead in making daily contact with these mothers. The purpose of this contact is to encourage them, pray with them, and keep them accountable. Keep them accountable to what? In some of these situations, the church has generously given them needed finances. The deacons trained the moms in financial stewardship, and helped to keep them accountable to being responsible with their money. Over the course of five years, the church has given nearly $100,000 to a few single mothers who were in crisis. The financial support was not on a monthly basis, but was project or crisis related, toward the goal of helping these women become financially stable and independent.

Also toward that end, Christian men in the church worked with the women to build and develop home-based businesses. The elders/pastors viewed it as a high priority to help these mothers develop a home-based business so their children could remain at home with them. The men also took an active role in providing discipleship by being godly male role models for the sons. As early as possible, the sons were encouraged to work so they could help support the family.

This kind of ministry is messy, filled with challenges and heartbreak. One mother who was a part of this ministry ended up leaving the church because she didn't want the accountability. However, the majority have been richly blessed.

BEYOND CRISIS RESPONSE

Many churches are responsive when they become aware a widow is in crisis. Few have an intentional, organized plan for ongoing care. New Commandment Men's Ministries[6] has helped many churches move past crisis response to proactive care.

Through the NCMM model, men divide into teams and are assigned to serve a widow on an ongoing basis. The ministry team plans monthly visits to take care of things around the house needing to be done (fix leaky faucets, clean windows, haul trash, etc.). At the end of the service time, the ministry team prays with their care receiver. The same team returns month after month to build trust and a long-term relationship. The men also ask the widow if she has neighbors who are also in need. The team prays for those neighbors and looks for the Lord to open opportunities to serve them as well.

Another way churches move from crisis response to proactive ministry is by offering short-term pastoral care classes for those recovering from divorce (such as DivorceCare[7]), or those facing the challenge of single parenting (to meet this need, we developed a Bible-driven DVD resource entitled *Visionary Parenting: Encouragement for Single Parents*[8]). These are valuable first steps in supporting a widow or widower who is grieving, or a single parent in need of encouragement and discipleship.

DEVELOPING AUTHENTIC COMMUNITY

When a church decides, "We need to start a singles ministry," what is usually meant is some sort of regular gathering where singles meet together for discipleship. A great singles ministry means having a great "singles group," right?

But is there any precedent in Scripture for this *method* of ministering to unmarried adults? Is there any example or command in the New Testament for God's local church to segregate singles into their own homogenous community? Churches often adopt this segregated approach in response to the "felt need" of some of the singles in the church. A group of singles "ask" for the church to start a singles group; of course we don't want to be uncaring, so the pastors/elders start a singles group.

Segregating singles into a homogenous ministry robs them of care and connections God desires for them in the whole body of Christ.

A female friend recently sent me this email:

> At my previous church I was active in the young singles group (which made a certain amount of sense as I was in my 20s and hoping to marry). I did, however, miss the friendship and fellowship of older women and so one Sunday I asked the person at the information desk at church about getting involved in the women's Bible study. He told me that the church had a singles Bible study and that's where I belonged and that the women's Bible study was for women. For some reason, I thought I was a "woman."

In the same way, seniors, married men and women, and children are robbed of the fellowship God wants them to have with those who are not married. I appreciate McCulley's call for singles to be treated like "people," not like "singles:"

It's important that unmarried men and women are discipled as men and women and not a generic lump of singleness. From my perspective, Scripture's emphasis is on being made a man or a woman in the image of God, with a secondary emphasis on how that looks in the various roles and seasons of life. Unmarried men and women are no less masculine or feminine because of being single.[9]

God speaks clearly in Romans 12 and 1 Corinthians 12: we need the body. The arms don't need to connect with all the other arms. The ears don't need to be segregated with all the other ears. God has brought *all* of us together in our local church. We preach the need for diversity and authentic community, but then we split up in church classrooms with people just like us!

Here is a common pattern experienced by churches that launch segregated singles ministries:

- A Friday night singles group is started with energy and excitement.

- A few months in, the honeymoon is over.

- Those who are in the twenties and eager to be married express some discomfort being with the fifty-year-old divorcees.

- The fifty-year-old divorcees are on one hand grieving and needing support, and on the other hand, start to see the ministry more like a youth group for grown-ups.

- Those who are eager to be married and have more social skills are on the lookout for prospective dates and want the pastor to plan more socials.

- Those who have the gift of singleness think the whole thing is just a "meat market."

How can all of these life-stages, needs, perspectives, callings, and opinions be brought together? Some churches respond by creating multiple singles groups. Young singles. Middle-aged singles. Old singles. Divorced singles. Grieving singles. Social singles. Bible study singles.

Again, I would ask, is there any biblical command or pattern that would encourage us to adopt this ministry methodology? I don't believe there is, and when we use methods God has not given to us, we see less than the best fruit from our labors. This is not to say that segregated singles ministries see no spiritual impact. My conviction is we are missing out on far greater blessing and impact! So what is God's plan for unmarried men and women to experience community? In Psalm 68 God gives us a powerful principle for singles ministry.

> "God settles the solitary in a home . . ." (ESV)
> "God sets the lonely in families . . ." (NIV)
> —Psalm 68:6a

What is God's plan to meet the relational needs of singles in the local church? This ministry has been entrusted to families. Creating Christian fellowship with unmarried men and women should not be the responsibility of a "singles pastor" but a responsibility of the Christians and Christian families in the church.

Pastor Jonathan Ziman from Wheaton Bible Church[10] shared with me some of the challenges he was facing in singles ministry. The group had gone through a number of iterations under different leaders. As expected, there was a wide range of perspectives about what the group should be, and in what direction it should head. But there was one thing everyone agreed on. They all remembered when the singles ministry was "at its best."

For a few years, the "singles ministry" was driven by a couple of families who regularly opened up their home to all who wanted to come. They ate together. They played games together. They prayed together. They watched football together. There was no band. There was no special speaker. They just met together in a Christian home. Why was this "working?" It was in line with the biblical methodology of family hospitality.

What would happen if you took some of the energies you are currently putting toward running a singles program and sought out ten godly families who would embrace this ministry of hospitality?

What would happen if you moved away from a homogenous "life-stage" small group ministry, and, as we talked about in the chapter on youth ministry, invited people to participate in age-and-stage-integrated groups?

One of the most difficult situations I faced as a pastor was dealing with a situation where a friend of mine was caught in his secret life of homosexuality. Years of lies to his wife and to the church came to the surface. He feigned repentance but continued doing what he wanted to do. In the end, he left the church and they divorced. Suzanne and her children moved in next door to our family. For the next couple of years we "did life together." The kids played. We shared meals. We talked, prayed, and counseled. Other families did the same for Suzanne and her children. They had extreme ongoing needs, and they needed extreme and ongoing care. A once a week class or support group at church could never give all of the care this family needed. This single mom and her children needed *families* to welcome them into their homes, lives, and hearts. Not only did our family have a chance to bless this single mom and her children, but our lives were enriched, blessed, and encouraged through our mutual friendship in Christ.

A number of years later, when one of Suzanne's boys was applying to go to a Christian school, he was asked if there was someone who had been an example of a godly man in his life. To my surprise, he mentioned me. What made such a difference in this young man's life? We simply welcomed him, his siblings, and his mother into our lives.

LOVING SINGLES INTO FELLOWSHIP

Be prepared for both rejoicing and resistance if your church chooses to embrace this fuller and more diverse view of community. Some will rejoice to no longer be treated only as "single" and quarantined off with others who share the label. However, you may also face resistance from men and women who want to form the singles ministry into their image, to meet their particular needs. It will require loving leadership and difficult conversations. "I know you want to be with people who are going through the same things you are going through, and I want that for you too. But because there are no examples or commands in the Bible for us to systematically separate single people, we have chosen not to do that. We don't want all the men, women, and children to miss out on being in fellowship with you. We don't want you to miss out on being in fellowship with them. It may be harder at times, but it will be better. At the end of the day, when it comes to how the church works, we have to try and follow what God has said."

As you have read this chapter, perhaps you don't agree with my conclusions. I am convinced God has given us the following instructions in the Bible related to singles ministry:

- Teach about the gift of singleness.
- Care for singles in need.
- Welcome and include singles into the homes and lives of families.
- Encourage singles to use their homes for Christian fellowship as well.

When I lock myself in a room with the Bible and search for what God has said specifically on the issue of ministering to those who are single, this is what I find.

Your conclusions may be different. I am not "dying on the hill" that my conclusions about singles ministry are correct. I am, however, "dying on the hill" that in the Bible God has given us divine commands, principles, and patterns which speak *directly* to the issue of singles ministry, and the Lord wants His people to do *what* He wants; the *way* He wants it done.

If you have reached different conclusions about singles ministry, have those conclusions come from specific Scriptures where God speaks about ministry to those who are single? God's Word can thoroughly equip us for every good work.

Questions for discussion:

1. What blessings and difficulties have you seen in ministering to unmarried men and women in your church?

2. Does your church clearly teach a theology of singleness? Does the congregation know where the pastors/elders stand on the issues of divorce and remarriage?

3. What would it take to lead a culture change in your church so Christian families would see it as their responsibility to minister through hospitality to the singles around them?

ENDNOTES

[1] Carolyn McCulley, *How to Serve the Singles: Ministry to Unmarried Adults In Your Church*, http://www.desiringgod.org/blog/posts/how-to-serve-the-singles-ministry-to-unmarried-adults-in-your-local-church.

[2] Grudem and Piper, *Recovering Biblical Manhood and Womanhood*, 18.

[3] For more on this read Albert Mohler's article, *Looking Back at the Mystery of Marriage*, http://www.crosswalk.com/news/al-mohler/looking-back-at-the-mystery-of-marriage-part-one-1280013.html.

[4] For instance, a local church may develop a missions initiative in a particular part of the world that is dangerous or otherwise not conducive to raising a family. The pastors/elders in that church could rightly begin praying for God to turn the hearts of those in the church who have the gift of singleness to engage in this ministry.

[5] http://reformationchurch.com/.

[6] http://www.newcommandment.org/.

[7] http://www.divorcecare.org/.

[8] http://visionaryfam.com/dvds-2/.

[9] McCulley, *How to Serve the Singles: Ministry to Unmarried Adults in Your Church*.

[10] Personal interview in October 2011.

CHAPTER 23:
DISCIPLING MEN AND WOMEN

"Teach me, O LORD, the way of your statutes; and I will keep it to the end. Give me understanding, that I may keep your law and observe it with my whole heart."

—Psalm 119:33–34

In this chapter, we will discuss men's and women's ministry through the doctrinal lenses of sufficiency and jurisdiction. The first question we must consider when thinking about any ministry of the local church is, "Has God, through His commands and ordained patterns in the Bible, authorized the local church to function in this particular way?" Specifically, "Has God given His local church jurisdictional responsibility for men to disciple men, and women to disciple women?" If God has not told His church to do something, through command or pattern, we shouldn't do it.

So, has God given His local church the responsibility for men's and women's ministry? The answer is, "Yes." In Titus 1–2, God provides specific instructions for the unique discipleship of men and women. For a local church to thrive it must be increasingly filled with godly masculine men and godly feminine women.

MEN'S MINISTRY

The book of Titus, as a "pastoral epistle," gives specific instructions from God for how pastors/elders are to lead, minister, and organize the local church. In portions of the first two chapters of Titus, God gives us the description of a godly man. The end goal of men's ministry is simple: to disciple men into the godly masculinity which is given by God in Titus 1–2.

> *"If anyone is above reproach, the husband of one wife, and his children are believers and not open to the charge of debauchery or insubordination. For an overseer, as God's steward, must be above reproach. He must not*

*be arrogant or quick-tempered or a drunkard or violent or greedy for
gain, but hospitable, a lover of good, self-controlled, upright, holy, and
disciplined. He must hold firm to the trustworthy word as taught, so
that he may be able to give instruction in sound doctrine and also to
rebuke those who contradict it."*—Titus 1:6–9

*"Older men are to be sober-minded, dignified, self-controlled, sound
in faith, in love, and in steadfastness."*—Titus 2:2

Through these Scriptures, God provides the local church with a *methodology*
and discipleship plan for men's ministry. God doesn't command how often men
are to meet to disciple one another. He doesn't command how those meetings are
to be structured. He does, however, provide us with the "core curriculum" and a
clear picture of a godly man.

FOR ELDERS ONLY?

It is a fair to ask, "But isn't Titus 1 only speaking about the qualifications for
pastors/elders?" Yes, it is. But what qualified a man to serve as a pastor/elder in
the early church was not that he was a *super-Christian* man. He simply needed to
be a *mature* Christian man.[1]

Would we not want all men in the church to be *qualified* to serve as an elder/
pastor or deacon? Go back and read through the list of qualifications again. Is
there anything on that list you would not want for your father, husband, brother,
or son?

The picture of godly manhood in Titus 1 is specifically applied to the
qualifications for elders/pastors, but it also serves as a picture of masculine,
godly, spiritual maturity to which all Christian men should aspire. A few verses
later, God speaks to the issue of men's discipleship in broader terms.

*"Older men are to be sober-minded, dignified, self-controlled, sound
in faith, in love, and in steadfastness."*—Titus 2:2

All men in the local church, as they mature in Christ, are to exhibit these
characteristics. Therefore, these should be central to the discipleship goals and
strategy in every men's ministry. When was the last time the leaders of your men's
ministry sat down to develop a long-term focus on leading the young men of the

church to be sober-minded? To be dignified? Ministering to men is a necessary good work, and God has promised His Word will thoroughly equip us for success.

SPHERES OF DISCIPLESHIP

God affirms the spheres of discipleship in His picture of the mature, godly man. A godly man is a family man, a church man, and spiritually engages in his community and the world.

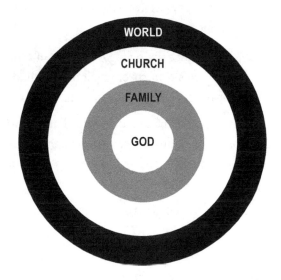

What is the first mark of a godly man? He must be "the husband of one wife, and his children are believers, and not open to the charge of debauchery or insubordination." A godly man is first and foremost a family man. He shows honor to his parents and seeks to care for them as they age. If he is married, his loving-servant leadership and ministry to His wife is to be his top priority. It is God's most important mission for him, and so it should not surprise us it is the first thing on the list. His ministry to his wife flows into his ministry to his children. A mature, godly man, if he is a father, understands his most important Great Commission is the evangelization and discipleship of his children, grandchildren, and beyond. The most important "organization" of which he is a part is his family. He may be a janitor at his workplace, but he is the divinely appointed CEO of his home. It is not a call to simply manage the home by paying bills and mowing the lawn, but rather a call to be the spiritual shepherd, trainer, protector, and leader. A man's spiritual health is first demonstrated through his relationship with his parents, siblings, wife, and children. He is a family man first, a church man second, and from those spiritual foundations, he engages *with* his family and brothers and sisters in Christ in ministering to the world.

PERSUADING MEN TO LEAD THEIR FAMILIES

During the Reformation, as many reclaimed the doctrine of the sufficiency of Scripture, pastors increasingly called men to lead their homes as their first Christian priority. The 17th century pastor Richard Baxter wrote the following ten challenges to men so they might live for God, beginning in their homes:

Challenge #1: Consider that the holy government of families is a considerable part of God's own government of the world, and the contrary is a great part of the Devil's government.

Challenge #2: Consider also than an ungoverned, ungodly family is a powerful means to the damnation of all the members of it; it is the common boat or ship that hurries souls to hell and is bound for the devouring gulf.

Challenge #3: A holy and well-governed family tends not only to the safety of the members but also to the ease and pleasure of their lives.

Challenge #4: A holy and well-governed family tends to make a holy posterity and to propagate the fear of God from generation to generation.

Challenge #5: A holy, well-governed family prepares for a holy and well-governed church.

Challenge #6: Well-governed families tend to make a happy state and commonwealth.

Challenge #7: If governors of families faithfully performed their duties, that would be a great supply as to any defects on the pastor's part and a means to propagate and reserve religion in times of public negligence or persecution.

Challenge #8: The duties of your families are such as you may perform with the greatest peace and least exception or opposition from others.

Challenge #9: Well-governed families are honorable and exemplary to others. Even the worldly and ungodly bear a certain reverence to them; for holiness and order have some witness that commends them in the consciences of many who never practiced them.

Challenge #10: Lastly, consider that holy, well-governed families are blessed with the presence and favor of God.[2]

Do the men in your church receive challenges such as these? There is a tendency to emphasize the outer two spheres. We call men to engage in ministry at church and we call men to live for Christ in their workplace. Amen and amen! But I am convinced the primary reason why so many church leaders complain of the men in their church "not taking their faith seriously" or "being passive" is because we are calling them to outer ministry (local church and world), while their inner ministry (personal walk with Christ and family discipleship) is non-existent.

Are you eager to see men rise up to lead your church with humility, godliness, and sound doctrine? Are you eager to see men rise up to impact their community and world for Christ? Then call them, train them, equip them, and hold them accountable to private prayer and Scripture study and to the leadership of family worship in their homes. If we want to maximize a man's impact on the world, we must first maximize his impact at home.

Here are a general series of principles that should flow through our ministry to men: As the man goes, so goes the marriage. As the marriage goes, so goes the family. As the family goes, so goes the local church. As the local church goes, so goes the nation and the Great Commission.

WOMEN'S MINISTRY

Imagine you are in a church leadership meeting and the question on the table is, "What should be our strategy in our women's ministry next year?" Ideas start flying. Programs are proposed. Particular Bible studies are suggested. Retreats and special events are envisioned.

Suddenly, the lights go out, the room shakes, everyone falls out of their seats, and everyone hears the loudest, most majestic voice say:

"Older women likewise are to be reverent in behavior, not slanderers or slaves to much wine. They are to teach what is good, and so train

the young women to love their husbands and children, to be self-controlled, pure, working at home, kind, and submissive to their own husbands, that the word of God may not be reviled."—Titus 2:3–5

The earthquake stops. The lights come back on. You stumble back to your seats.

Here is the question. Would this event change the course of your conversation about your strategy for your women's ministry? I have no doubt it would!

Well, *it has happened!* This is exactly how we should read and receive the words of Almighty God given to us in Titus 2:3–5. He has thundered His instructions, for all people, in all places, and in all times for how the women He loves are to be discipled.

What is God's plan to fill His local church with godly women? The women who are more spiritually mature are to "train the younger women." But God takes His instructions a step further. This is not a generic call to women to help one another grow in the vast and various areas of the Christian faith. Instead, God provides an explicit "curriculum" of discipleship for the young women in the church.[3]

The women who are more spiritually mature are to train the younger women to:

- Love their husbands
- Love their children
- Be self-controlled
- Be pure
- Work at home[4]
- Be kind
- Be submissive to their own husbands

These are essential practices and character traits of a woman who pleases God.[5] A women's ministry built on the sufficiency of Scripture plans and strategizes year after year to be increasingly effective at nurturing *these particular* character traits and skills in the lives of women. Has God spoken to *how* we should do women's ministry in the local church? Yes. Are His words *enough* for us, or do we need to add our own good ideas into the mix? Everything hinges on how we answer this question.

THE PRIORITY OF THE HOME

God calls men to begin their Christian life and ministry at home, and He gives the same call to women. The older women were instructed to train the younger women first to love their husbands and to love their children. A married woman's most important calling from God is to help her husband become a more godly man. Next to Christ, her husband is to be her first love. Then in partnership with her husband, she is called to embrace the Great Commission by doing all in her power to make disciples of her children.

In fact, four out of the seven curriculum points given by God in Titus 2 focus a woman's faith and character on who she is at home. How this flies in the face of our godless culture that tells women marriage, child-bearing, and child-raising are somewhere between annoyances to be endured and prisons to be fled.

Terrible things begin to happen when we distort God's spheres of discipleship. I have witnessed situations in which a woman was made to feel guilty because she was not able to be part of the weekly women's Bible study at church. Why wasn't she there? Because almost all of her time was being given to care for her aging mother.

I wish these words of Charles Spurgeon would be heard from every pulpit today:

> O dear mothers, you have a very sacred trust reposed in you by God! He hath in effect said to you, "Take this child and nurse it for Me, and I will give thee thy wages." You are called to equip the future man of God, that he may be thoroughly furnished unto every good work. If God spares you, you may live to hear that pretty boy speak to thousands, and you will have the sweet reflection in your heart that the quiet teachings of the nursery led the man to love his God and serve Him. Those who think that a woman detained at home by her little family is doing nothing, think the reverse of what is true. Scarcely can the godly mother quit her home for a place of worship, but dream not that she is lost to the work of the church; far from it, she is doing the best possible service for her Lord. Mothers, the godly training of your offspring is your first and most pressing duty. Christian women, by teaching children the Holy Scriptures, are as much fulfilling their part for the Lord, as Moses in judging Israel, or Solomon in building the temple.[6]

Older women are to "train" the younger women. Think of all the things young women are trained to do. If they play sports while growing up, they spend countless hours in practice, training to play well during the game. Young women are trained in proper study habits so they can be accepted into a good college. Young women are trained in career skills. The list goes on.

But how many Christian girls have been trained by their Christian mothers to love their future husbands and children, to manage a home, and to submit to their future husbands? In your local church, how many older, mature Christian women are actively engaged in *training* younger women to be successful in these, the most important callings in their lives? Men do not naturally succeed at their greatest life mission of being the spiritual leader of their family, neither do women naturally succeed in their God-given roles in the family. Training is required, and God has given this responsibility both to parents with their children, and to the local church in the context of men's and women's ministry.

WHAT IS AT STAKE?

Is it really that important for a women's ministry to organize around the principles and discipleship areas from Titus 2? Certainly, these are good thoughts and valuable things for women to talk about as opportunities arise, but isn't it going over the top to say that these character traits and skills should be the drivers behind our entire strategy?

As if to ensure we would understand how serious God is about doing women's ministry *His way,* the Lord declares what is at stake if we depart from His will in this area:

> ". . . train the young women to love their husbands and children, to be self-controlled, pure, working at home, kind, and submissive to their own husbands, *that the word of God may not be reviled.*"[7]— Titus 2:4–5

What is at stake if we decide to do women's ministry our way instead of God's way? What is at stake if the women in a local church do not increasingly grow in these particular areas of Christian character and ministry? God says His Word is on the line. God says if women do not disciple one another in these areas, and if women do not live out these areas of the Christian life, it will encourage people to hate the Bible. Godly women are essential to the functioning and spiritual success of God's local church.

God has not entrusted the functioning of His local church to our creativity and innovation. He has given us explicit instructions for what the local church is to do, and how it is to do it. This is once again demonstrated as we consider men's and women's ministry. God is not silent about the nature, purposes, and discipleship goals of these ministries.

Not only does the Lord give us divine methodology for the discipleship of men and women in the church, He frames that discipleship in light of particular jurisdictions, beginning with the family.

Perhaps you disagree with my conclusions about the discipleship goals the local church should have for men and women. You may well be right. I have no corner on the truth. But I would ask you, "What specific texts in Scripture, *which speak directly to men's and women's ministry in the local church,* have shaped your thoughts?" While Jesus' spiritual training of his disciples is rich and valuable, it is one step removed from the explicit instructions Jesus has given us in Titus 1–2 for men's discipleship.[8] Studying the great (and the wicked) women of the Bible is powerful, but those narratives do not speak directly to the issue of *how* women are to disciple one another within the local church.

In Titus 1–2, God speaks directly as to how His local church is to engage in men's and women's ministry. How will we respond?

Questions for Discussion:

1. Have you experienced an older believer systematically discipling you in the four spheres of discipleship (God, family, church, world)?

2. In what ways does the men's ministry in your church call, equip, and keep men accountable to their most important ministry at home?

3. In your church, what role has Titus 2 played in the strategic planning for the women's ministry?

ENDNOTES

[1] As noted earlier, the core difference between the qualifications for elder/pastor and the qualifications for deacon is the gifting and ability to preach.

[2] Richard Baxter, Randall J. Pedersen, ed., *The Godly Home* (Wheaton, IL: Crossway, 2010), 105–113.

[3] The terms "younger women" and "younger men" refer to older adults ministering to younger adults. In some cases, it may be a younger person is "older" or more mature spiritually, and may actually be helping to disciple a person who is physically older. While Titus 1–2 provide fathers and mothers with essential areas of discipleship for their children, these chapters do not provide warrant for church leaders to systematically segregate children away from their parents for discipleship.

[4] This does not forbid a woman from having any type of work outside the home. The Proverbs 31 woman engaged in economic work for the good of her family. This is a simple instruction for the Christian woman to be faithful and dedicated to her work and ministry in the home.

[5] If a woman has the gift of singleness, she, of course, does not need to be trained in loving her husband. However, many younger women are single and desirous of marriage, and it is the responsibility of the mature women to play a key role in training her for her future role as a wife and, Lord willing, a mother.

[6] Charles Spurgeon, *Spiritual Parenting* (New Kensington, PA: Whitaker House, 2003).

[7] Italics mine.

[8] As noted many times earlier, it is right and proper to refer to the entire Bible as the words of Jesus.

"You are the light of the world. A city set on a hill cannot be hidden."
—Matthew 5:14

The central passion of this book is the advance of the Gospel of Jesus Christ to the ends of the earth. Here in our last formal chapter, we will turn our attention to the specific issue of personal evangelism.

LET THE PROS HANDLE THIS

It is easy for the responsibility of personal evangelism to be delegated to the "professionals" in our local church. Have you ever had someone say to you, "Pastor, when is the next big outreach event at church? I really want to invite my neighbor to come and hear the Gospel."

Ten years ago, my eyes would have lit up and I would have energetically shared the details of all the dynamic, non-threatening, gospel-presenting opportunities we were planning. But what if the conversation went a different direction?

> "Pastor, when is the next big outreach event at church? I really want to invite my neighbor to come and hear the Gospel."

> "We have some big things coming up, but can I ask you a question?"

> "Sure."

> "When was the last time you invited your neighbor over to your house and looked for an opportunity to share the Gospel?"

> "Well, uh, I really wouldn't know what to say. I just think it will work best to see if they would come to church."

"I understand how hard it is to confidently share our faith with others. How about meeting with me a few times over the next few weeks so I can teach you how to do it?"

In the same way some Christian parents simply drop their children off at Sunday school and call that biblical discipleship, some Christians simply bring their friends to outreach events and call that biblical evangelism.

Evangelism and discipleship are in serious crisis in the United States.[1] The percentage of Bible-believing Christians has been in decline for decades. Much of this decline can be attributed to our failure to follow the biblical and jurisdictional plan for parents to disciple their children at home. But have we also lost sight of the biblical model and jurisdictional thinking regarding evangelism?

HOW TO SHARE OUR FAITH

As we have seen throughout this journey, not only is the Bible sufficient for knowing *what* God wants us to do (His mission), but it is also sufficient for knowing *how* God wants us to do it (His methods). My prayer is you have joined me in becoming thoroughly convinced of the doctrine of the sufficiency of Scripture for every matter of faith and life.

If God's primary method of sharing the gospel with the lost was (1) the pastors/elders in the local church put together welcoming, non-threatening, Gospel-preaching events at church and (2) the Christians within that church were called to bring their friends to those events *then we would see this method either commanded or patterned in Scripture.* But it can't be found!

As with every area of ministry, we must think jurisdictionally about the mission of personal evangelism. Which jurisdictions are explicitly charged in the Bible with the task of evangelism?

- Christian individuals
- Christian families
- Local churches
- Governments

We can quickly cross "governments" off the list. While God desires civic leaders govern "Christianly," there is no Scriptural support to suggest that governmental role has been established by God for personal evangelism. This is not to say a Christian mayor should not share his faith. Rather, when he shares His faith, He does so out of his individual Christian responsibility, not his mayoral responsibilities.

Not that long ago I would have thought what I am about to write was absolutely crazy. Here goes. I cannot see any Scriptural support to suggest the institution of the local church is responsible for personal evangelism. The Christians *within* that local church are called to personal evangelism. The Christian families *within* that local church are called to family evangelism. When we speak of the "mission of the local church" we must not confuse that with the mission God has given to the individuals and families with the church.

The burden and call to personal evangelism rests squarely on the two jurisdictions of the Christian individual and the Christian family. Evangelism is not for the pros, it is for every believer.

PREDICTABLE JURISDICTIONAL RESULTS

You remember the basic principle of jurisdictional violation:

> When institutions act outside their God-given authority (1) the crisis will not be solved and (2) the institution that is responsible for responding properly to the crisis will be robbed of motivation, time, and resources, making it more difficult for that institution to respond in the future.

So what happens when the local church takes over the mission of personal evangelism? First, the crisis is not solved. How effective are all those outreach events? Yes, many times the seats are filled and a good time is had by all. But are souls saved? How many of the "I trusted Christ tonight" check marks are evidence of true conversions? Where are all those who "checked the box," next Sunday?

There is no denying people come to Christ through outreach events in church buildings. God graciously works His will through our imperfect ministries. But after running evangelistic events in a large church for almost two decades, I am thoroughly persuaded the true conversions that result from these methods are precious few.

When there is jurisdictional violation not only will the crisis not be solved, but the institutions responsible will increasingly disengage. The more pastors in the local church take the lead in running outreach events in the church building, the more the Christians and Christian families are robbed of motivation, time, and resources to take responsibility for sharing Christ with their friends and neighbors. I don't need to learn to share the gospel; I can just bring them to church. I don't need to do the work to open my home; the pastor will do the work to open the church.

How easy it is to sit back and be proud of all the great outreaches in the local church the pastors and their recruits are doing . . . while we sit on the sidelines. Pastors are always struggling with how to get the congregation to engage in ministry. How do we energize and activate the believers in our church for ministry? (As a side note, "ministry" often is synonymous with "volunteering to help with church programs.")

How many sermons have been given calling the congregation to get out of the stands and get out on the field! Don't be spectators, be participants! But what do the spectators see when they look out on the field? They see a great game being played. Pastors, leaders, and overworked volunteers are playing with frenetic energy. They see a myriad of ministries being done and they think, "Why do I need to get on the field?"

If pastors want the congregation to "get on the field" when it comes to evangelism, then the pastors need to get "off the field." The pastors need to do what God has commanded them to do: "to equip the saints for the work of ministry" (Ephesians 4:12). Far too often the congregation *pays and watches* the pastors "play the game," rather than the biblical model of the pastors *coaching* the congregation to play the game. When pastors are driven by the sufficiency of Scripture they choose to stop doing certain things, so the men and women in the church will engage in ministry.

Rob, are you saying that pastors/elders don't need to share their faith? Of course not! Remember, pastors are Christians too. A pastor is not just a pastor. He is first a Christian man, and is called by God to function as a Christian man. Secondly, he is a family man. He is called to love and lead his family.[2]

Here are some key Scriptures that speak to the issue of personal evangelism. As you read each text, consider carefully the jurisdictional context of the command or example.

"Go therefore and make disciples of all nations, baptizing them in the name of the Father and of the Son and of the Holy Spirit, teaching them to observe all that I have commanded you. And behold, I am with you always, to the end of the age."—Matthew 28:19–20

"But you will receive power when the Holy Spirit has come upon you, and you will be my witnesses in Jerusalem and in all Judea and Samaria, and to the end of the earth."—Acts 1:8

"Now those who were scattered went about preaching the word." —Acts 8:4

"To the weak I became weak, that I might win the weak. I have become all things to all people, that by all means I might save some."—1 Corinthians 9:22

"But in your hearts honor Christ the Lord as holy, always being prepared to make a defense to anyone who asks you for a reason for the hope that is in you; yet do it with gentleness and respect."—1 Peter 3:15

It is Philip, as an individual Christian, following the prompting of the Holy Spirit to share the gospel with the Ethiopian eunuch (Acts 8). It is Peter, as an individual Christian, who led Cornelius and his household to repentance and faith in Jesus (Acts 10). Paul and Timothy led Lydia and her household to the Lord (Acts 16). Paul and Silas, not as pastors/elders, but as Christian men, shared their faith with the Philippian jailer, and he and his household were saved (Acts 16).

The jurisdictional responsibility for personal evangelism rests on every Christian individual.[3] This is not to say evangelism must be *done* individually. Paul and Timothy shared their faith together. A large group of believers may work together to share the Gospel with their entire community. The point here is to recognize God does not give the commands and examples related to personal evangelism to the institution of the local church. The commands are given to the individuals and families *within* the local church.

Just as there are spheres of discipleship, God gives us spheres of evangelism. The early church launched with these spheres clearly in view:

> *"And Peter said to them, 'Repent and be baptized every one of you in the name of Jesus Christ for the forgiveness of your sins, and you will receive the gift of the Holy Spirit. For the promise is for you and for your children and for all who are far off, everyone whom the Lord our God calls to himself.'"*—Acts 2:38–39

Where does the gospel begin? It begins with us. *"For the promise is for you."* Before we can be used by God to bless others and point them toward Christ, we must first be converted by the grace of God which leads us to repentance and faith.

After we are converted, our Great Commission begins with the souls of our children—the second sphere of evangelism. "For the promise is for you *and for your children."* Peter is echoing the Great Commandment from Deuteronomy 6.

> *"You shall love the LORD your God with all your heart and with all your soul and with all your might. And these words that I command you today shall be on your heart.[4] You shall teach them diligently to your children . . ."*—Deuteronomy 6:5–7

God's first call, and first priority is our love relationship with Him through His Son Jesus Christ. Once we are saved, justified, and being sanctified, God calls us to minister to others. But this call to ministry is not random. God's first missional priority for those who are saved is embracing the Great Commission at home with their family.

CHARACTER EVANGELISM

Perhaps the most common charge against Christianity in our culture today is, "You are just a bunch of hypocrites!" One of the dangers I see in our evangelical culture is an elevation of the call to personal evangelism over the call to godly character. Personal evangelism is an overflow of godly character. If a person is not growing in godliness, their witness and testimony is dramatically hindered. This is not a call to sinless perfection, but rather a process of discipleship where we refuse to elevate ministry to others above holiness before God.

The following Scripture is probably familiar to you:

> *"Religion that is pure and undefiled before God, the Father, is this: to visit orphans and widows in their affliction. . . ."*—James 1:27a

But this is not the end of the verse. When we quote only this portion we miss God's essential second point. Here is the whole verse.

> *"Religion that is pure and undefiled before God, the Father, is this: to visit orphans and widows in their affliction,* and to keep oneself unstained from the world."[5]—James 1:27

There is a dramatic call to personal ministry (in this case to orphans and widows) *and* a dramatic call to personal holiness. They must be held together. Throughout the Scriptures, God calls His people to "come out" and "separate yourselves" from the world (2 Corinthians 6:14–18). It is only when God's people are separate and distinct that we have something to offer to a lost and dying world.

Jesus spoke to this issue in His Sermon on the Mount.

> *"You are the salt of the earth, but if salt has lost its taste, how shall its saltiness be restored? It is no longer good for anything except to be thrown out and trampled under people's feet. You are the light of the world. A city set on a hill cannot be hidden. Nor do people light a lamp and put it under a basket, but on a stand, and it gives light to all in the house. In the same way, let your light shine before others, so that they may see your good works and give glory to your Father who is in heaven."*—Matthew 5:13–16

Jesus, in speaking privately to His disciples, did not say, "Go be salty! Go share the light!" Rather He said, "You *are* the salt of the earth . . . You *are* the light of the world." A believer, living in obedience, *is salty*. A believer, living in obedience, *is a light.*

What was Jesus calling them to do? His concern was they not *lose* their saltiness. His concern was their light would be *hidden*. Jesus fully understood their Gospel mission was inextricably linked to their personal holiness. As saved men, they were already salt and light! Jesus concern was they not lose that saltiness or cover up that light.

I had an incredible experience a couple years ago. My family and I were having cake in the café at Nordstrom's. We enjoyed our time, paid our bill, and left. As we were walking in the mall, we were approached by an elderly couple. They introduced themselves as Frank and Maria, and they proceeded to say, "We were eating in the café at the same time you were there. We loved watching your family! Your kids were so well behaved. It was obvious you really love each other and it was special for us to be able to see that."

Frank then asked me, "What do you do?" I told him I was a pastor and he said, "Really? I read the Bible every day. Every day I write down questions I have. These are real serious questions. I have a couple friends who are ministers, but I don't want to ask them, because I know them, and frankly I don't know how they keep their jobs."

I'll never forget what he said next, "I want to ask my questions to a man who lives like you. Here is my card."

Amy and I were stunned. How could eating cake at Nordstrom's become a short-term family mission trip? Jesus says, "You *are* the salt of the earth . . . You *are* the light of the world . . . Let your light shine before others, so that they may see your good works and give glory to your Father who is in Heaven." Jesus then speaks through Paul saying, "So, whether you eat or drink, or whatever you do, do all for the glory of God" (1 Corinthians 10:31). The more Christians become heavenly-minded, the more they become earthly-good.

HOSPITALITY EVANGELISM

The early Christians saw their homes as a primary place of ministry. Not only did they prioritize their marriages and seek to disciple their children, but Christian fellowship was centered in homes as well.

> *"Contribute to the needs of the saints and seek to show hospitality."*— Romans 12:13

> *"Show hospitality to one another without grumbling."*—1 Peter 4:9

If a man desired to serve as a pastor/elder, one of the qualifying marks was he used his home as a place of ministry.[6] In fact, Jesus taught that loving Christian fellowship was a *prerequisite* to sharing the gospel with the world.

> *"By this all people will know that you are my disciples, if you have love for one another."*—John 13:35

But families are not only called to love and fellowship with believers in their homes, but with unbelievers and strangers as well.

"Do not neglect to show hospitality to strangers, for thereby some have entertained angels unawares."—Hebrews 13:2

Consider the dramatic difference between church-building evangelism and hospitality evangelism. Inviting non-Christians to the church building for *anything* can be awkward.

> Christian: "Hey, some of my friends and I are getting together for a giant barbeque! Would you like to come?"
>
> Neighbor: "Sounds great! I wouldn't miss it! Where is it?"
>
> Christian: "It's at my church this Saturday."
>
> Neighbor: "Oh, yeah . . . I forgot, um . . . that isn't really a great day for me. Maybe next time."

No matter how hard we try, the local church cannot become a place where unsaved people feel *comfortable*. While we want to welcome our unsaved friends at our worship services, it is impossible for darkness to feel at home in the light. There is no way to invite an unsaved person to the church building without making them uncomfortable. Imagine if the conversation went like this:

> Christian: "Hey, some of my friends and I are getting together for a giant barbeque! Would you like to come?"
>
> Neighbor: "Sounds great! I wouldn't miss it! Where is it?"
>
> Christian: "It's at my house this Saturday."
>
> Neighbor: "Just tell me the time, and what to bring! Thanks for letting me know. Is it OK if I invite some other people too?"

Pastors and church leaders rack their brains to come up with "non-threatening" outreach events at the church. The problem is, they don't exist. Inviting unsaved people to the church is uncomfortable for them, and as much as we tell ourselves the events are not "bait-and-switch," they usually are. "Come to the barbeque! (Oh yeah, a guy is going to share his testimony, read the Bible, and invite you to repent of your sins)."

Hospitality evangelism, which is at the heart of the New Testament model, isn't a bait and switch. A family of believers simply invites those around them into their lives. They act how they always act. When the lost come into a Christian home, they taste the salt and see the light.

Imagine how your church would be transformed if your pastor announced instead of a quarterly outreach event at the church, he was calling every family to have a quarterly "outreach event" in their homes![7]

Don't be thrown off by the word "event." The call is not to host a massive block party. Simply invite a neighbor into your home for dinner, dessert, coffee, or even just conversation. Then, in the context of a natural relationship, pray for God to give you the boldness and courage to talk directly with your friend about the gospel.

Hospitality evangelism also transforms "volunteerism" in the church. In the church-based evangelism model, the pastors come up with the idea for the outreach program, and then call on the congregation members to volunteer to make it happen. I have been on both sides of that call, as a pastor pleading and pleading with people to help, and sitting in the pew feeling overwhelmed with all I am being asked to do.

But what would your response be if your Christian neighbor came to you with a desire to put on an event in the neighborhood and asked you to be a part of it?

One of the reasons why hospitality evangelism is so rare is because of the natural results of jurisdictional violation. When "outreach" is done by the professionals at the church building (assisted by the army of volunteers), the proper jurisdictions (individuals and families) are robbed of time, resources, and motivation to do the job.

Some Christian families have little or no time to invite their unsaved neighbors over for dinner, because they are volunteering at church four nights a week. In the same way, a Christian family may be making additional financial contributions to a special outreach event at church, which reduces their ability to afford being able to invite friends for dinner. And as we discussed above, when a local church is filled with dynamic, church-building based outreach events, there is little motivation for Christians and Christian families to take personal responsibility for evangelism and open their homes to the lost.

Your church does not need to establish satellite ministry centers in the community. You already have them. They are called Christian homes. The responsibility of the local church is to engage, equip, and release those homes for the glory of God.

THE ROLE OF THE LOCAL CHURCH

If God has given the responsibility of personal evangelism to individuals and Christians, what role, if any, does the institution of the local church have?

Most importantly, the local church is responsible to *equip* believers for the mission of evangelism. Pastors/elders are called to teach sound doctrine to everyone, disciple everyone toward holy living, and train them how to share their faith and to "always [be] prepared to make a defense to anyone who asks." Pastors practice this when they offer discipleship environments that help believers fully understand the gospel and give them apologetic tools to defend it. Pastors practice this during prayer in the corporate worship service when they pray for the lost, pray for unreached people groups, and pray for the Lord of the Harvest to send out workers.

EQUIPPING FAMILIES

Many years ago, the children's ministry team at Wheaton Bible Church made a big shift regarding their summer outreach ministry. Rather than invite unsaved children to come to the church building for a week of Vacation Bible School, they equip and encourage Christian families in the church to host week-long Neighborhood Bible Clubs. Families volunteer to host a five day "club" at their home, and they take responsibility for asking friends to help, and inviting the neighborhood to come. The church provides training, resources, and supplies to help the families be successful. Families build evangelistic relationships with other families in the context of neighborhood life. Children and their parents repent and trust Christ! The responsibility for "follow-up" does not rest on the pastor, but on the Christians who are already in that neighborhood.

EVERY SUNDAY

The pastors/elders in the local church also play an important role in evangelism when they preach the gospel message. While the corporate worship service is a gathering of believers in the worship of God, we recognize there are unsaved people who are present. Those who are unconverted may have been attending the church for years, or they may be there for the first time. Here are three reasons why the gospel message, along with the opportunity to respond in repentance and faith, should be a regular part of the corporate worship service.

- Unsaved people (even if they "look saved") are likely present. "It [the gospel] is the power of God for salvation . . ." (Romans 1:16).

- Those who are converted continue to need the message of the Gospel, not for renewed salvation, but for their sanctification and obedience.

- Those who are converted, in hearing the repetition of the gospel message, are increasingly equipped to share it with others.

ACCELERATING GLOBAL MISSIONS

The local church also plays an essential role in accelerating global missions. In the New Testament, Christians within local churches freely gave their money to the elders who then supported those going to the mission field. Christians also gave their money directly to missionaries in need (2 Corinthians 8–9).

While the call to missions comes to individuals and to families, God has ordained much of the funding for missions should come through the local church.

CONCLUSION

God has been moving in the hearts of thousands of pastors in the last few years, calling them away from the modern "attractional model" of evangelism (big events at church) toward a more relational model. Exciting things are happening. But my fear is the driver behind this positive change is, once again, the spirit of pragmatism. We had to face the reality the attractional model was not winning large numbers of people to evident conversion. It wasn't *working.* The relational model will *work better.*

We should not return to personal and hospitality evangelism because we think it will work better, but because we are committed to the doctrine of the sufficiency of Scripture; and when we use the Bible alone, we see the mission of personal evangelism entrusted to individuals and families. If we don't base the change on doctrine, we will be vulnerable to the next "new method" of reaching those apart from Christ.

From the beginning, God set out to fill the earth with His worship. He has invited His children into that eternal mission. The mission is too important to do it our own way. He has given us His Word so we might clearly see His mission and completely embrace His methods.

Questions for discussion:

1. Who did God use to lead you to repent of your sins and trust Christ alone for salvation?

2. In your opinion, what percentage of believers in your local church use their homes for Christian fellowship? For evangelism?

3. Is the gospel shared more inside or outside your church building?

4. When was the last time someone from your church stepped out in faith as a missionary? To what degree did you and your church support them financially?

ENDNOTES

[1] As discussed in the introduction.

[2] A pastor who is single is called to honor his parents, love his siblings, and care for extended family members who are in need.

[3] The individual responsibility for evangelism can also be seen in Isaiah 6:8, "And I heard the voice of the Lord saying, 'Whom shall I send, and who will go for us?' Then I said, 'Here am I! Send me.'" See also Matthew 9:37–38, "Then he said to his disciples, 'The harvest is plentiful, but the laborers are few; therefore pray earnestly to the Lord of the harvest to send out laborers into his harvest.'"

[4] Italics mine.

[5] Italics mine.

[6] Titus 1:8.

[7] Some churches host weekly "seeker" events such as Alpha. What would happen if instead of one Alpha meeting in the church building each week, there were 10 Alpha meetings every week in homes throughout the community?

CHAPTER 25:
EVERY THOUGHT FOR THE GOSPEL

"And as for me, this is my covenant with them," says the LORD: "My Spirit that is upon you, and my words that I have put in your mouth, shall not depart out of your mouth, or out of the mouth of your offspring, or out of the mouth of your children's offspring," says the LORD, "from this time forth and forevermore."

—ISAIAH 59:21

In this book we have discussed the Bible, individuals, families, local churches, governments, worship, preaching, discipleship, fellowship, equipping, church discipline, leadership, caring for the poor, youth and children's ministry, singles ministry, men's ministry, women's ministry, and evangelism . . . among other things.

Do we believe God, in the Bible, has spoken directly to all of these important issues? Do we believe in the Bible alone He has given us everything we *need* to know about His plan for the world, His purpose for the family, and His purpose for the local church?

When we understand and embrace the doctrine of the sufficiency of Scripture, we have the key that unlocks every door. We have all we need to worship God rightly, please Him completely, and fully engage in the mission He has given us.

WHERE THERE IS NO VISION

As a pastor (and I hate to admit this), I sometimes cringe when I look back at sermons I have preached. I am particularly burdened if I ripped a text of Scripture out of its context and used it to preach my thoughts, rather than God's thoughts. Here is a text which I misused many times.

"Where there is no vision, the people perish."—Proverbs 29:18a (KJV)[1]

I would often use this text in the context of leadership meetings. Vision! As leaders, we need to have a plan. We have to know where we are going. We can't lead people toward nothing. If there is no vision, if our church doesn't have a mission statement, if your corporation doesn't have a vision statement, all the people on your team, in your company, at your church, and in your small group—they are in trouble! My eloquent challenge would then catapult us into the vision-casting portion of our meeting. My guess is you have walked through a similar process.

So what's the problem? I interpreted the Word of God with 21st century business principles, rather than allowing Scripture to interpret Scripture. I had a message *I* wanted to give and I used the Bible to suit my purposes.

The text hinges on the word "vision." The Proverbs are given to us in the larger context of the Old Testament. Put this particular verse aside for a moment. If someone were to ask you, "I have been reading the Old Testament, and I keep finding this word "vision." It says this person had a vision. That person had a vision. What does that mean?"

I expect you would say, "Well, in these situations God was revealing truth to people, through a vision or a dream. He spoke to many of the Old Testament prophets in this way." Let's apply this basic understanding of "vision" to the text in Proverbs 29.

> *"Where there is no vision, the people perish."*—Proverbs 29:18a (KJV)

This verse has nothing to do with leading a team, company, or church! This verse is all about God's Word. It is all about the truth He has revealed. Ironically, I was misusing a Bible verse about the Bible. In addition, if I had bothered to read the entire verse, the other half of the Proverb, I might have avoided abusing God's Word.

> *"Where there is no vision, the people perish: but he that keepeth the law, happy is he."*—Proverbs 19:18 (KJV)

The NIV translates the Hebrew to that end:

> *"Where there is no revelation, the people cast off restraint; but blessed is he who keeps the law."*—Proverbs 29:18 (NIV, 1984)

The ESV does the same:

> *"Where there is no prophetic vision the people cast off restraint, but blessed is he who keeps the law."*—Proverbs 29:18 (ESV)

What is God saying in this famously quoted Scripture? He declares without the truth He has revealed to the prophets (what we now have as the Bible), the people cast off restraint. They perish! Without the Bible we are in trouble! Without the Bible, we do what *we want* rather than what *God wants*. But blessed is he who keeps the law. Blessed is the person who seeks to do all of God's revealed will in all of God's revealed ways.

Obeying every word of the Bible is at the heart of Christian discipleship. Jesus reiterated this to His disciples when He spoke the words of the Great Commission.

> *"Go therefore and make disciples of all nations, baptizing them in the name of the Father and of the Son and of the Holy Spirit, teaching them to observe all that I have commanded you. And behold, I am with you always, to the end of the age."*—Matthew 28:19–20

What is the end result of discipleship? A person who, by the grace of God, is fully committed to obeying everything God has said in His Word.

EVERY GOOD WORK

Many times throughout the book we have returned to 2 Timothy 3:16–17.

> *"All Scripture is breathed out by God and profitable for teaching, for reproof, for correction, and for training in righteousness, that the man of God may be complete, equipped for every good work."*—2 Timothy 3:16–17

God claims the whole Bible speaks to every important matter of faith and life, and it is enough to complete us in Christ, and to equip us for *every* good work. God has given us the full mission, and all the details we need to carry out the mission.

No army general stands before his troops and simply says, "Men, I want you to go out there and win this war!" If those were the only instructions chaos would ensue and the war most certainly would be lost. Each man would do what was right in his own eyes. Small groups of men would band together for their own private strategies. It would be a disaster. Instead, a general proceeds to give the most detailed and particular plans. Specific units are given precise missions on exact time tables. Certain weapons are to be used in particular situations. The men are trained to follow the general's orders, to the letter, without question.

We are not engaged in a war, we are engaged in *the war*. We don't follow a general, we follow God Almighty. He has not left this war to chance. He has not left His people to fend for themselves. He spoke through the prophets and apostles and inspired them to write down *everything* we need to know about the mission and *everything* we need to do to live it out.

The fundamental battle today has not changed from the battle in the Garden of Eden. Satan still comes at us with the words, "Did God really say?"[2]

WHAT NOW?

In light of all the important things we have explored in this book, what is the next step? Where do we go from here? At the end of the day, my greatest prayer is God will use this book to deepen your love for His Book. Are you willing to shine the light of the Bible on every area of your personal, family, professional, and church life? Whenever I do this I find sin. I find my personal sins of thought, commission, and omission.

Where do we go from here? The first step is always the same. We must repent. We agree with God we have done what was right in our eyes, rather than doing what was right in His eyes. I had to repent of not being a spiritual leader for my wife and children. I had to repent of not paying attention to what God had said in His Word about how youth ministry should function in the local church. My list keeps on going, and the Holy Spirit continues to reveal areas of my life that need to be reformed back to Scripture alone.

If the elders/pastors in a local church embrace the doctrine of the sufficiency of Scripture they begin a long, blessed, difficult, God-honoring journey of reformation. They must turn their hearts to their wives, and make their marriages their top priority. They must turn their hearts to their children and begin their Great Commission calling by doing all in their power to impress the hearts of their children with a love for God. They must set the example for the church by blessing both the saved and the lost through hospitality in their homes.

As they make the important decisions faced in their local church, they must always first ask, "What has God said about this issue in the Bible?" Then as they come to doctrinal unity about what God has said, they must patiently, loving, and firmly lead the congregation to that end.

Let us join with the prophet Isaiah and call everyone back to everything God has said in His Word.

And when they say to you, "Inquire of the mediums and the necromancers who chirp and mutter," should not a people inquire of their God? Should they inquire of the dead on behalf of the living? To the teaching and to the testimony! If they will not speak according to this word, it is because they have no dawn."—Isaiah 8:19–20

Everything is at stake. If we want to be faithful in advancing the Kingdom of God, we must not meddle, using our human innovation, with God's family and God's local church. If your family or your local church has slipped in the doctrine of the sufficiency of Scripture and the doctrines of jurisdiction, let nothing deter you from reforming on Scripture alone. Consider Calvin's plea for believers on this issue:

> When we repair the ruins of the Church, we give our labours to the Lord, in obedience to his laws and injunctions, and yet the restoration of the Church is His own work. Nor is it without good reason that this is taught in every part of Scripture, and that it is so earnestly enforced by the prophet Isaiah. Remembering this doctrine, therefore, and relying on the assistance of God, let us not hesitate to undertake a work which is far beyond our own strength, and let no obstacle turn aside or discourage us, so as to abandon our undertaking.[3]

EVERY THOUGHT CAPTIVE

When it comes to the Gospel, the Kingdom of God, and Lord's war against sin, death, and the devil, there is no such thing as a free thought. Every thought about our lives, families, churches, and nations *will be taken captive.* We will either *be taken captive* by philosophy and empty deceit, according to human tradition, and according to the elemental spirits of the world (Colossians 2:8), or we will destroy arguments and every lofty opinion raised against the knowledge of God, and *take every thought captive* to obey Christ (2 Corinthians 10:5).

There is no neutral. There is no middle ground. Light is light. Dark is dark. This is the hill our King calls us to live on, and if necessary, to die on.

> *"Therefore, having this ministry by the mercy of God, we do not lose heart. But we have renounced disgraceful, underhanded ways. We refuse to practice cunning or to tamper with God's word, but*

by the open statement of the truth we would commend ourselves to everyone's conscience in the sight of God. And even if our gospel is veiled, it is veiled to those who are perishing. In their case the god of this world has blinded the minds of the unbelievers, to keep them from seeing the light of the gospel of the glory of Christ, who is the image of God. For what we proclaim is not ourselves, but Jesus Christ as Lord, with ourselves as your servants for Jesus' sake. For God, who said, "Let light shine out of darkness," has shone in our hearts to give the light of the knowledge of the glory of God in the face of Jesus Christ."—2 Corinthians 4:1–6[4]

In the Bible alone, we find the truth we need about God, ourselves, and the world in which we live.

In the Bible alone, we discover the mission God has for us as individuals, families, and local churches.

In the Bible alone, we are thoroughly equipped for every good work, so we might do God's will, God's way.

"I bow down toward your holy temple and give thanks to your name for your steadfast love and your faithfulness, for you have exalted above all things your name and your word."—Psalm 138:2

Join me in praying that in our lives, in our families, in our churches, in our nations, and in our world—God would exalt above all things His name and His Word!

Questions for discussion:

1. Have you ever made the mistake of misusing Proverbs 29:18?

2. Do you agree there are no "free thoughts" when it comes to the Kingdom of God?

3. Is there an area of your personal, family, or church life in which you need to repent?

4. If you had to pick one doctrinal issue from this book to do more research in, what would it be?

5. Is there an area of your personal, family, or church life in which you need to take a courageous stand on God's Word, regardless of the consequences?

ENDNOTES

[1] I chose to use the KJV in this case because the KJV translated the verse in a way that made it easier for me to use the verse to preach my message.

[2] Genesis 3:1.

[3] Calvin's Commentaries—Volume VII, *Commentary on the Book of the Prophet Isaiah* (1–32), 23.

[4] Italics mine.

Here are additional books and resources from Rob Rienow, and Visionary Family Ministries, which can equip your family and your church to advance the Gospel.

- *Visionary Parenting* (book and DVD series) seeks to equip and and inspire parents to pass faith and character to their children.

- *Visionary Marriage* (book and DVD series) helps married and engaged couples embrace a shared, Bible-driven vision for their life together.

- *When They Turn Away* (book and DVD series) encourages empty-nest parents who have prodigal children, that it is never too late for God to use them to draw their adult child back to Christ.

- *Encouragement for Single Parents* (DVD series) is designed to bless and strengthen single parents in their mission to raise their children for the glory of God.

Learn more at www.visionaryfam.com.

What is **D6**?

BASED ON DEUTERONOMY 6:4-7

A **conference** for your entire **team**

A **curriculum** for every age at **church**

An **experience** for every person in your **home**

Connecting
CHURCH & HOME
These must work together!

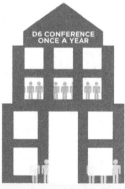

D6 CONFERENCE
ONCE A YEAR

DEFINE & REFINE Your Discipleship Plan

www.d6family.com

ONE HOUR
A WEEK

POWER OF
PARENTAL INFLUENCE

CPSIA information can be obtained
at www.ICGtesting.com
Printed in the USA
LVHW052057080819
626989LV00002B/4